THE
WHITE
SHIP

Also by Charles Spencer

Althorp: The Story of an English House
The Spencer Family
Blenheim: Battle for Europe
Prince Rupert: The Last Cavalier
Killers of the King: The Men Who Dared to Execute Charles I
To Catch a King: Charles II's Great Escape

THE WHITE SHIP

Conquest, Anarchy and the
Wrecking of Henry I's Dream

Charles Spencer

WILLIAM
COLLINS

William Collins
An imprint of HarperCollins*Publishers*
1 London Bridge Street
London SE1 9GF

WilliamCollinsBooks.com

HarperCollins*Publishers*
1st Floor, Watermarque Building, Ringsend Road
Dublin 4, Ireland

First published in Great Britain in 2020 by William Collins

7

Copyright © 2020 Charles Spencer

Maps by Martin Brown

Typeset in Adobe Garamond Pro by Palimpsest Book Production Ltd, Falkirk, Stirlingshire
Printed and bound in Great Britain by CPI Group (UK) Ltd, Croydon CR0 4YY

*For Christopher Dixon, who taught me forty years ago,
and who inspired me to write.*

Contents

PART THREE: CHAOS

List of Illustrations

The hanging of thieves, from MS M.736, f.19v, *Miscellany on the Life of Saint Edward* (*The Morgan Library and Museum*)

The four kings, from Royal 14 C. VII, f.8v, *Historia Anglorum* (*Alamy*)

The Battle of Brémule, from BnF, MS. Fr.2813, f.201v, *Grandes Chroniques de France* (*Bibliothèque Nationale de France*)

William Clito

Louis VI of France (*Alamy / Chronicle*)

The *White Ship* sinking, from Cotton Claudius D. II, f.45v (© *British Library Board. All Rights Reserved / Bridgeman Images*)

The *Blanche Nef* (*Royal Collection Trust / © Her Majesty Queen Elizabeth II 2020*)

Henry I in mourning, illustration from Royal 20 A. II, f.6v, *Chronicle of England* (*Bridgeman Images*)

Adeliza of Louvain, illustration from Lansdowne 383 f.14, *Shaftesbury Psalter* (© *British Library Board. All Rights Reserved / Bridgeman Images*)

The wedding banquet of Henry V and Matilda, from MS 373, f.95v, *Chronicle of Ekkehard of Aura* (*The Parker Library, Corpus Christi College, Cambridge*)

Henry I during a stormy Channel crossing, from MS 157 p.383, *Worcester Chronicle* (*Bridgeman Images*)

Queen Matilda holding a charter, from Cotton Nero D. VII, *Golden Book of St Albans* (© *British Library Board. All Rights Reserved / Bridgeman Images*)

The remains of Reading Abbey (*Charles Spencer*)

King Stephen at the Battle of Lincoln, illustration from Arundel 48, f.168v (© *British Library Board. All Rights Reserved / Bridgeman Images*)

Hangings at Bedford Castle, from MS 16, f.64r, *Chronica Majora* (*The Parker Library, Corpus Christi College, Cambridge*)

King Henry II arguing with Thomas Becket, illustration from Royal 20 A. II, f.7v, *Chronicle of England* (© *British Library Board. All Rights Reserved / Bridgeman Images*)

NORMAN ENGLAND
*c.*1100

0   *miles*   50

CARLISLE

BATTLE OF THE
STANDARD

BATTLE OF
STAMFORD BRIDGE

*Irish
Sea*

North Sea

SELBY

E

N

G

Trent

LINCOLN

CHESTER

L

A

N

NORWICH

W

A

Severn

ELY

L

E

NORTHAMPTON

S

OXFORD

D

Thames

WALLINGFORD

LONDON

BRISTOL

READING

ROCHESTER

DEVIZES
CASTLE

ALTON

DOVER

WINCHESTER

New Forest

SOUTHAMPTON

ARUNDEL
CASTLE

BATTLE OF
HASTINGS

English Channel

BARFLEUR

ROUEN

N O R M A N D Y

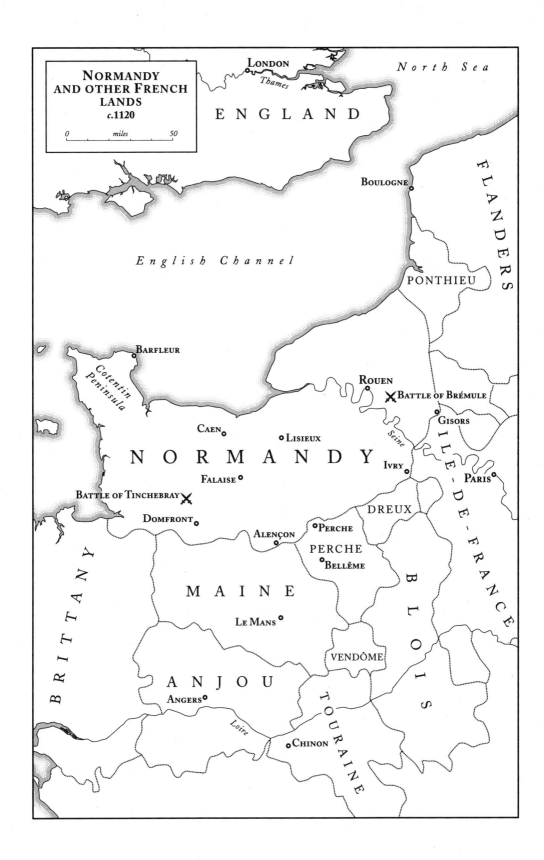

NORMANDY
AND OTHER FRENCH
LANDS
c.1120

0   *miles*   50

North Sea

LONDON
Thames

E N G L A N D

FLANDERS

BOULOGNE

English Channel

PONTHIEU

BARFLEUR

Cotentin
Peninsula

ROUEN

✕ BATTLE OF BRÉMULE

GISORS

CAEN

LISIEUX

Seine

N O R M A N D Y

IVRY

PARIS

FALAISE

ILE - DE - FRANCE

BATTLE OF TINCHEBRAY ✕

DREUX

DOMFRONT

ALENÇON

PERCHE

PERCHE

BELLÊME

B L O I S

M A I N E

LE MANS

VENDÔME

B R I T T A N Y

A N J O U

ANGERS

Loire

TOURAINE

CHINON

PROLOGUE

A Cry in the Dark

Looking back on this, a night whose repercussions would change Europe's history for ever, some claimed to remember nothing more than a distant noise. It had skimmed across the surface of the icy sea, the sound waves amplified by the stillness of the water, their notes hammered taut by the frost of a late November night.

It caught in the northerly wind, and perhaps reached the ears of those awake on King Henry I's ship, a dozen nautical miles ahead in the voyage across the Channel. Those who claimed to have heard it in the dark would admit that they had no idea what it was. It was shrill and short-lived, like the distant squawk of a passing gull.

The same noise had made it back to shore – only a mile away – in a clearer form. Some in the Norman harbour of Barfleur heard it. They were near the point where they had earlier watched the port's finest vessel, the *White Ship*, cast off into the night. Her departure had attracted a crowd – some present were related to those on board, and had come to say their farewells, while others were intrigued by the glamour and power of those putting out to sea.

These passengers included Henry I's sole legitimate son,

William, the seventeen-year-old heir to the kingdom of England and to the duchy of Normandy. Two of the king's many illegitimate children, who were openly acknowledged and loved by him, were also aboard the *White Ship*. With the trio of royal children sailed much of the flower of the Anglo-Norman aristocracy, as well as leading bureaucrats who made Henry's realm run smoothly and celebrated knights who kept the peace while protecting its borders.

The distinguished passengers had spent much of the afternoon and evening in the harbour, drinking hard and encouraging the crew to join in the revelry. Those in Barfleur who heard the noise assumed the merriment was reaching a crescendo on the *White Ship*, out at sea, and headed for the warmth of home, unsurprised and unconcerned by the cry in the dark.

In fact, what these witnesses to history had heard, at sea and on land, was a collective scream for help. The passengers of the *White Ship* had gone from wild festivity to dire panic in an instant, when they realised the crunch that had brought the vessel to a grinding halt was a rock – a rock that had pierced the timbers, leaving a gaping hole and allowing water to pour in. This caused the *White Ship* to heave to one side, making her spill her human cargo into the shockingly cold sea.

Perhaps the lowliest of those on board was Berold, a butcher from Rouen who had pursued his social superiors onto the ship, determined to get outstanding bills settled. Berold clung to part of the *White Ship*'s mast. Then, despite the weight of his saturated goatskin tunic, he hauled himself from the freezing waves onto this lifesaving perch. Next to him clambered Geoffrey de L'Aigle, a nobleman who was one of the king's illustrious knights. The unlikely pair had rescued themselves from drowning, but now they lay vulnerable to the extreme cold. They shivered uncontrollably.

In the moonlight they watched as their companions cried out

and thrashed in the water, desperate for life. Berold would later note William, the prince, getting safely away, in the *White Ship*'s small boat. The quick-thinking royal bodyguards had bundled him into it and were rowing hard for land, aware that their sole duty in this unfurling disaster was to preserve the life of the king-to-be. They had even left the royal treasure chest behind, in the *White Ship*'s hold.

As William headed quickly to safety, Berold and de L'Aigle watched with mounting horror as the tragedy around them played out.

PART ONE

TRIUMPH

ONE

Conquest

In the year of grace 1066, the Lord, the ruler, brought to fulfil-
ment what He had long planned for the English people. He
delivered them up to be destroyed by the violent and cunning
Norman race.

Henry of Huntingdon, English historian and
archdeacon (c.1088–c.1157)

The youth in the boat embodied the dynastic hopes of his
royal father. King Henry I was in his fifties at the time that
the *White Ship* was pinned on the rocks outside Barfleur. Unlike
his son, who had been born as the undisputed heir to the throne,
Henry had started life as a junior member of the royal family,
seemingly destined for well-bred obscurity. But he had seized his
chances to become one of the most powerful men in Europe.

Two decades earlier Henry had pounced on the English throne
when it unexpectedly fell vacant. This he had done after leaving
his elder brother on a forest floor to stiffen in death, rather than
lose time tending to him. On that summer's afternoon in 1100,
Henry kicked his horse on into a gallop, his ruthlessness and

speed enabling him to seize the royal treasury before any rival even knew the crown was in play.

Six years later he had stolen the dukedom of Normandy from his eldest brother. Henry crushed him in battle before casting him into prison, where he would remain, without hope of freedom, for the rest of his exceptionally long life.

Henry, English king and Norman duke, established strong rule over his lands by overcoming dangerously powerful enemies among the Anglo-Norman nobility. He was focused and uncompromising, clear in how he wanted to rule and determined that his way would prevail. Contemporaries noted that Henry had a face that looked friendly and open to humour, but people knew he could be harsh, and they heeded the steely intensity of his gaze. This was not a man to be trifled with, and his various rivals for power knew as much.

Apart from a hard-nosed drive, Henry also possessed subtlety. He was canny enough to deprive his enemies of diplomatic advantages. He ruled at a time when tensions over religious investiture were at their peak. Since the 1070s a succession of reforming popes had attacked the customary right of lay rulers to appoint bishops and abbots, key officers in the Church hierarchy. So closely fought was the contest that rival popes ('anti-popes') were set up and supported, while emperors and kings risked excommunication, or even being deposed.

In what became, for Christian leaders, one of the great questions of the age, Henry had insisted on maintaining his crown's ancient rights, in the face of papal stubbornness that matched his own. But he was realistic and pragmatic enough to find compromise, long before the question would eventually be settled between pope and emperor. By doing so, he headed off the dangerous possibility of his many enemies harnessing papal power to their cause, which could in turn fatally undermine his position.

Contests for territory and power were a standard part of medieval statecraft. Many of Henry's neighbouring rulers were also his relatives, through marriage or common ancestry: three of his wife's brothers would, in turn, become kings of Scotland, and he maintained peace with each of them; while his bloodline sprang from the competing forces that lay off England's southern flank.

Henry's father, William the Conqueror, was the most celebrated Norman of them all. Henry's mother, Matilda, was the daughter of the count of Flanders, a powerful figure from a land made wealthy by commerce: the fine reputation of its woollen cloth had been established in Roman times, and Flanders's busy seaports traded with England and Scandinavia, before dispersing goods to France and Germany along inland arteries, principally the Rhine.

Henry's mother was also, on her maternal side, a niece and a granddaughter of French kings. He was, therefore, a second cousin of the monarch who would prove to be his most persistent enemy, Louis VI of France: at the time of the wrecking of the *White Ship* Henry and Louis had spent much of the previous twelve years at war.

The France of the early twelfth century formed a different outline to the republic of today: it included what is now Belgium, while the Roman Empire controlled Burgundy in the south-east and Lorraine in the east.* The area that Louis truly dominated was more modest again, comprising as its core the Île-de-France. This royal heartland was surrounded by a constellation of other territories that enjoyed various levels of independence from its nominal overlord: the king of France

---

* The term 'Holy' Roman Empire (or Emperor) was only used from 1157, when Frederick Barbarossa set his cap at controlling all of Italy, including the papal territories.

claimed feudal superiority to his neighbours, but his scope for enforcing it was limited.

To the far west lay Brittany, a Celtic land that had seized its freedom in the ninth century and had remained self-governing ever since. To the east of Brittany sat the county of Maine, which had Anjou to its south. Maine and Anjou both extended eastwards to abut the county of Blois. Blois, in turn, bumped up against the western border of Louis VI's axis of power. Meanwhile, when Louis looked to his north-west, he saw the imposing duchy of Normandy, whose capital, Rouen, covered a greater land area than his principal city of Paris.

Several generations of French kings had viewed Normandy as something of a pirate state. But in 1066 it transformed itself from the status of troublesome, subordinate neighbour to that of deadly rival. This was thanks to the gamble of one man, of Viking stock and persuasion, who had built a fleet to transport his army across the Channel and capture the kingdom he claimed by right.

———

In 799, speedy, shallow-draughted longships arrived on the French coast from Scandinavia, carrying marauders who had come to attack and plunder. These invaders were known as 'Normanni' – Northmen. The persistence and the savagery of their assaults succeeded eventually, in 911, in peeling off what became known as Normandy as a formal concession from Charles the Simple of France. In return for this tract of land that lay between the River Epte and the sea, the Norman leader, Rollo, swore three things: loyalty to the French king, protection against other raiders, and a willingness for he and his men to convert to Christianity.

He did well with the first two and gave his third commitment a good go. But on his deathbed Rollo's true pagan leanings emerged for a farewell flurry. He had his Christian servants sacrificed to his ancestral deities: to Odin, the one-eyed god of wisdom, poetry and death, and to Thor, the fierce, hammer-wielding god of thunder.

This uncompromising warrior trait remained strong in the Norman genes. Henry of Huntingdon, a twelfth-century arch-deacon who wrote the history of England from its earliest Anglo-Saxon roots up until his own time, recorded that the Normans 'surpassed all other people in their unparalleled savagery'.[1] Abbot Suger, a French statesman and chronicler also writing in the twelfth century, said: 'Being warlike descendants of the Danes, the Normans are ignorant of the ways of peace and serve it unwillingly.'[2]

Rollo's successors certainly shared his instinct for warfare and ruthlessness. Rollo was followed by William Longsword, a son by one of his Christian lovers, who subscribed to his mother's religion while aggressively adding new territory to his inheritance. Longsword's marriage to the daughter of a powerful count cemented his place in the senior aristocracy of France. His bloody career was ended just before the Christmas of 942: while attending a peace conference on an island in the River Somme, he was ambushed and assassinated by order of the count of Flanders, a diehard enemy of the Norsemen.

Longsword's son, Richard the Fearless, succeeded his father at the age of ten. The boy was taken into custody by Louis IV, the French king, as a first step towards retrieving Normandy for France. But the Normans were having none of it, capturing Louis and forcing him to give back their young duke. Richard would rule Normandy for more than half a century, during which time he opposed the Carolingian dynasty that was clinging to the French throne and helped his brother-in-law Hugh Capet to supplant it. He also reversed some of the devastation caused by his Viking forebears, restoring ravaged abbeys, resurrecting the archbishopric of Coutances and establishing a monastery at Mont Saint-Michel.

The house of Normandy's influence extended further during Richard the Fearless's lifetime. Two of his daughters became, respectively, duchess of Brittany and countess of Blois; while, in 1002, his eldest daughter, Emma, married Æthelred the Unready, King of England. For Æthelred, the match was a way of ending damaging Viking raids on his south coast, which emanated from Normandy.

Emma had three children with Æthelred, including the future king, Edward the Confessor. After Æthelred's death she married Cnut, the man who eventually conquered her husband's kingdom. She continued as queen of England, while also gaining the crowns of Denmark and Norway. The tide of Viking influence had now risen so high around Europe that its waves were washing back to Scandinavian shores.

Richard II succeeded to his father's dukedom in 996 and held it for thirty years. Again, his prime duties were military: ruthlessly crushing a revolt by the Norman peasantry, seeing off an invasion from England and supporting his overlord – the French king – in campaigns against powerful Burgundy. Richard II's rule saw Normandy become wealthy and stable, and he pushed ahead with reform of the Church. In return the grateful bishops and abbots gave strong support to the duke's authority.

But Richard II left discord in his wake by splitting the Norman inheritance. While he consigned the bulk of his territory to his eldest son, another Richard, he left a county to his younger son, Robert. Dissatisfied with the size of his bequest, Robert rebelled and captured the castle of Falaise, the duke's main power base in central Normandy, before being defeated. But Richard's sudden and unexpected death soon after victory convinced many that he had been poisoned at his brother's command.

Robert 'the Magnificent' – so-called because of his generosity – became duke of Normandy in 1027, aged twenty-seven. Soon afterwards he was said to have spied Herleva, an eye-catching resident of Falaise, as she bathed in a river. The daughter of a tanner, Herleva became the duke's lover, bearing him two children out of wedlock. The elder of these, born perhaps in 1028, was called William.

In 1035 Robert announced that he was going on pilgrimage to Jerusalem, in penance for having seized Church properties when younger. Norman nobles insisted their ruler could not undertake such a dangerous expedition while without an heir. Robert countered by presenting them with the illegitimate William as his successor. He left his son in the guardianship of a handful of trusted aristocrats and courtiers, the most important of whom was Alan III, Duke of Brittany.

Robert reached Jerusalem successfully, but he died on the return journey. William, perhaps aged eight, was recognised as duke by many of his people and by his overlord, Henry I of France. Despite this, his life was in constant danger from those relatives of his late father who felt their claims, as members of the wider ducal family, born in wedlock, outshone that of the boy they called 'William the Bastard'. One by one, his powerful guardians were murdered by cliques eager to control or replace the boy-ruler. William even awoke one morning to find his chamberlain in the bed next to him, his throat slashed open in silent assassination.

One of the young duke's more powerful enemies was Guy of Burgundy, a cousin and former friend of William's, whose rebel faction attempted to assassinate the teenaged duke during a hunting expedition in 1046. William escaped to safety alone, on horseback, before riding on to Henry of France, to demand the help the king owed him as Normandy's feudal overlord.

The following year, the duke's small force and the troops of the French king defeated the vastly superior numbers of Guy of Burgundy at Val-ès-Dunes, south-east of Caen. A freewheeling succession of cavalry skirmishes ended in utter defeat for the rebels, and many thousands of Guy's men were cut down as they fled, while a great number of others were corralled into the Orne river. In an age when very few knew how to swim, they drowned. It took a further two years of siege warfare before William captured Guy of Burgundy and the castles that had underpinned his power.

In the struggle to impose his authority William acquired a ruthless streak. When the town of Alençon, on Normandy's southern frontier, declared its support for the rival count of Anjou, William laid siege to it. Some of Alençon's inhabitants, confident that their defences were impregnable, draped animal hides from the tops of the town walls in mocking reference to William's mother's humble roots as the daughter of a tanner. This was a mistake. When William eventually took Alençon, he ordered the hands and feet of those who had insulted Herleva to be cut off.

It took William more than twenty years to establish himself securely as ruler of Normandy. In 1053 he put down a revolt led by William of Arques, an uncle who had long challenged his illegitimate nephew's right to rule. William of Arques had his Norman lands confiscated and was sent into exile.

Duke William gradually asserted control over his neighbours. Maine proved to be a hard-won prize, William only receiving its count's submission in 1062 after laying waste to much of the land. He brought Normandy's old rival Brittany to heel in 1065, after the surrender of its duke, Conan II. When Conan died suddenly, late the following year, it was accepted that he had been assassinated at William's command. The fatal weapons were believed to be his own gloves, which had been laced with poison: when Conan took them off and wiped his mouth with his hand, death soon followed.

A devout Christian, William saw to it that Normandy embraced the key reforms that the papacy was starting to encourage: he outlawed the buying and selling of clerical offices, and barred priests from marrying. His changes were supported by a younger half-brother, Odo, who he made bishop of Bayeux when Odo was a teenager: in an era when the power of Church and state was intermingled, it was common for men of high birth to commit relatives to influential positions at court and on the battlefield, while others were sent to scale the peaks of ecclesiastical high office. The crossover between the various branches was fluid: Bishop Odo remained a counsellor and a warrior for the rest of his life (the Bayeux Tapestry shows him wielding a mace in battle), while continuing in his churchly duties.

From his earliest days, William would have been aware of the figure of Edward the Confessor at court. Edward was William's first cousin once removed. He and his siblings had been exiled from England after Cnut overran half of England. The children had been welcomed in Normandy by their maternal uncle, Duke Richard II. In 1035 Cnut died, and his son Harold Harefoot claimed the throne while Cnut's true heir, Harold's half-brother Harthacnut, was distracted by rebels in Scandinavia.

Hoping the moment was right to reclaim his family's crown, Edward the Confessor's brother Alfred landed in southern England with an army of Norman mercenaries. Outside Guildford, thirty miles south-west of London, he was greeted by the powerful Earl Godwine, who declared his backing for Alfred. But it was a ploy. Godwine suddenly turned, taking Alfred prisoner and massacring his troops. The earl had Alfred's eyes put out during the hundred-mile journey north-east to the monastery of Ely, where the royal prisoner was committed to the care of the monks. But Alfred never recovered from the brutality of his blinding, his life ending after months of agony in early 1036.

After five years' rule, Harold Harefoot died in 1040, aged twenty-four, just as Harthacnut was poised to invade England from Denmark. Harthacnut desecrated Harold's tomb and had his corpse decapitated before consigning the mutilated remains to an anonymous marshland grave. Yet the new king's rule was briefer still: the last Scandinavian to rule England dropped dead at a wedding, in June 1042, while toasting the bride. This could have been the result of a stroke, caused by Harthacnut's excessive drinking, or perhaps by poison, presumably authorised by Edward the Confessor.

Edward now sailed to England with a retinue of Norman aides to take the throne. He owed his elevation to the support of three powerful noblemen, the most significant of them Earl Godwine.

Edward cemented a pragmatic alliance with this kingmaker by marrying his daughter, Edith of Wessex. But by 1051 there was no child of the marriage, and Godwine and his formidable sons had fled abroad after a failed rebellion against the king. William of Normandy visited England during this interlude, when Edward was free from the overbearing Godwines. The Confessor appears to have invited William to become his successor at this time.

A year later the Godwines returned to England in force, but Earl Godwine died soon afterwards. His most able son, Harold, slowly took on his mantle as indispensable royal supporter, and by 1057 he and his brothers controlled the earldoms of Wessex, East Anglia and Northumbria. Harold twice led armies to crush uprisings in Wales. Edward, who had no instinct for battle, devoted himself increasingly to his twin passions, prayer and hunting, while occasionally displaying flashes of decisiveness in matters of foreign policy.

In 1064 or 1065, Harold set off on a mysterious voyage from Bosham, near Chichester. It ended in shipwreck on the coastline of Ponthieu. Guy I, Ponthieu's count, was known to enslave, imprison and torture those washed up on his shores. But William went in person to demand that Harold be handed over to him, the count's feudal superior. Harold was shown the respect due a great lord from a neighbouring land, and he repaid the compliment by fighting for William against Brittany: he is shown in the Bayeux Tapestry saving two Norman knights from drowning in quicksand on the flats near Mont Saint-Michel. William would always claim that Harold swore to acknowledge him as rightful heir to the English throne at this time.

After a series of strokes, the childless Edward the Confessor died on 5 January 1066. Harold lost no time. He declared that on his deathbed Edward had selected him as his successor. The next day he both buried the king and had himself crowned in the recently built Westminster Abbey. News of the coronation provoked William into preparing for an attack, his men felling the woods around the Norman coast for timber that could be shaped into warships. The great lords and bishops of Normandy found themselves urged to pay for as many vessels as they could, their subscriptions underwriting their duke's aggressive intent.

William's wife, Matilda of Flanders, ordered a magnificent ship to be built for her husband secretly, in the port of Barfleur. It needed to be a vessel worthy of William's dynastic dreams and ambitions, as he prepared to risk all in the gamble of a lifetime. Matilda called her the *Mora*. The meaning of this name is unknown, but it may well be nothing more than an anagram of '*Amor*', the Latin word for love, for the Flemish princess and the Norman duke's dynastic marriage had blossomed into a romantic triumph. 'The wife of my bosom', William called Matilda, 'whom I love as my own soul.'[3] She was the mother of all the duke's children – there would be at least nine of these, including four sons. Unusually for the time, the duke appears to have had no mistresses and to have fathered no illegitimate offspring.

The *Mora* served as William's flagship, sailing at the head of the huge invasion fleet that, with support vessels, numbered several hundred strong. This he led across the Channel in late September that year. The *Mora* was skippered by Stephen FitzAirard, the natural son of a nobleman. Also with William on his ship were his right-hand men – his commanders, advisers and key household officers – and the knights who had been handpicked by the duke to land beside him on the English soil that he claimed as his own.

The *Mora* had been built to advertise the importance of the leader she carried, as well as the military imperative of his cause. The royal lion carved onto her rear, its tongue rippling out from open jaws, roared defiance. The flagship had a mainsail of red and gold, and atop the mast fluttered the square papal banner: white with a blue border and emblazoned with the golden cross of St Peter. It had been sent by Pope Alexander II from Rome as confirmation that he – and therefore God – supported William's cause. Also high on the mast hung a lantern to guide the following fleet in night-time. The ship's figurehead, according to the twelfth-century monk and chronicler Orderic Vitalis, was 'the image of a child, gilt, pointing with its right hand toward England, and having in its mouth a trumpet of ivory'.

The Bayeux Tapestry shows FitzAirard's ship longer, stronger and built to be faster than the rest of the fleet: she had nineteen oars on each side, while many of her escorts had twelve, and others extended to sixteen. The Latin words on this panel of the tapestry, when translated, read: HERE DUKE WILLIAM CROSSED THE SEA IN A GREAT SHIP AND CAME TO PEVENSEY, immortalising the *Mora*, and the place in southern England where the invading army landed.

At first the winds were against William's invasion fleet, and it seemed possible the expedition would disintegrate before it could set out. William's father, Robert the Magnificent, had suffered similarly a generation before, his ships unable to cross the Channel, so he had turned his soldiers around and attacked Brittany instead. But there was good fortune for William in the bad weather. Commanders of the Anglo-Saxon fleet on the south coast felt it marked the end of the fighting season and sent their ships into hibernation. Then, while the Normans were forced to bide their time on their side of the Channel, Harold and his army were called away to fight elsewhere.

Harold's younger brother, Tostig, had disgraced himself through his cruelty when serving as the earl of Northumbria, and had been declared an outlaw. Having failed to secure the aid of his brother-in-law, the count of Flanders, or of William of Normandy, Tostig had eventually persuaded the warrior Norwegian king, Harald Hardrada, to join him in an invasion of England. Ten thousand Norsemen sailed up the Humber in three hundred ships, defeating an Anglo-Saxon army at Fulford before occupying York.

Harold marched north at once, surprising the invaders at Stamford Bridge with a bold attack early on 25 September 1066. The Anglo-Saxon army won the hard-fought contest, with Hardrada and Tostig in the mounds of enemy dead: fewer than a thousand of the invaders managed to get away, although Hardrada's son Olaf was among them, spared by Harold. The euphoria of crushing victory soon evaporated. News arrived that William and his Norman army had landed at Pevensey. The Anglo-Saxons wheeled round to meet the invaders, and marched 260 miles south as quickly as possible, gathering what-ever reinforcements they could as they went.

The Battle of Hastings was fought on 14 October 1066, just nineteen days after Stamford Bridge. For much of the day it proved an even struggle. The two armies matched one another for bravery and military skill, and their infantry units locked together with discipline and grit, neither side able to gain the advantage. However, when some of the Normans appeared to flee the battlefield, the Anglo-Saxons broke ranks in pursuit. They then found themselves exposed to William's waiting cavalry, which cut them down.

There were very few prisoners taken that day, Harold and his men choosing to fight to the death in defeat, as was the Anglo-Saxon custom. William of Jumièges, a Norman monk writing very soon after the battle, recorded Harold falling in the final clash of the day, 'covered in deadly wounds'. *The Song of the Battle of Hastings*, a Norman celebration of the victory that was also written at the time, reported Harold being dispatched by four knights, including Duke William, who deliberately rode at the point where Harold's banner flew.*

Some of the English wanted Edgar Ætheling† to be their king. The fifteen-year-old was a great-nephew of Edward the Confessor and a grandson of Edmund Ironside – a celebrated king whose staunch resistance to Danish invaders explains his nickname. But many of the fighting men who might have supported Edgar's claim lay dead on the battlefield at Hastings. While he was proclaimed king by the Witan – the gathering of the most powerful nobles and churchmen in England – Edgar would never be crowned.

The victorious Normans pushed north, claiming London after some resistance around Southwark, before Anglo-Saxon leaders

---

* The popular notion that Harold was killed by an arrow through the eye stems from thirty-five years after the event, and originates from the interpretation of an image on the Bayeux Tapestry, where the Anglo-Saxon king is seen with an arrow descending from a height towards his head.

† Ætheling was the Old English word for a male from the main line of the royal family who possessed a direct and legitimate claim to the throne.

submitted to William in Wallingford and Berkhamsted. On Christmas Day 1066 Westminster Abbey witnessed its third momentous royal ceremony of the year. William was crowned king of England by Ealdred, Archbishop of York, the English Church endorsing the validity of his claim as the pope had done beforehand.

At the height of the ceremony the congregation was asked by Archbishop Ealdred (in English), and by Geoffrey, Bishop of Coutances (in French), if it accepted William on the throne. The Anglo-Saxon leaders present bellowed their loud approval, as was their tradition. But Norman soldiers standing guard outside the abbey mistook the clamour for the launch of an uprising. They started to torch the surrounding buildings. The congregation and most of the priests fled in terror, leaving William to complete the service with 'only the bishops and a few monks and clergy' on hand. It was noted how, with all the drama unfurling around him outside, the new warrior-king shook with fear.

Fear was an emotion that William was more used to provoking in others than experiencing himself. He began establishing his rule in the wake of Hastings by culling what remained of the Anglo-Saxon aristocracy. In its place came his own lords, knights and prelates, whom he rewarded with captured territories that they could control and grow rich from. Even Stephen FitzAirard, the captain of the *Mora*, received his share: he was granted lands in Berkshire.

Castles sprouted up across the kingdom, tightening William's hold on England and helping to guard the borders with Wales and Scotland. The Anglo-Saxons had some strongholds, erected on the sites of Roman ruins, but these were basic when compared with the Norman motte and bailey castles,* which were easy to erect and hard to overcome.

By the end of the Conqueror's reign, in 1087, there were thirty-six major castles (including first-rate ones, partially made of stone), as far afield as Rochester in the south-east, Corfe in the south and Bamburgh in the north-east, as well as a thick thread of lesser fortresses draped across the land. At their fulcrum stood the Tower of London, constructed on the site of a Roman fort. Together these garrisons placed a chokehold on Anglo-Saxon resistance to Norman rule so successful that, Henry of Huntingdon recorded, 'there was scarcely a noble of English descent in England, but all had been reduced to servitude and lamentation, and it was even disgraceful to be called English'.[4]

Anxious that Scandinavian forces might cross the North Sea again, seeking to overthrow his rule, William decided to deprive any future invaders of food and supplies, other than those they could stow in their warships. So, in the winter of 1069–70, he took his armies to lay waste to the north. The entire population of England at this time was perhaps 1.5 million to 2 million, and of these roughly 100,000 now perished, as the Normans destroyed villages and farms in a scorched-earth policy.

So thorough was the destruction that it was still clearly evident in 1086, the year when royal officials finished Domesday Book – a record of ownership, resources and wealth in William's England, laid out parish by parish. Its pages show that the north remained devastated, sixteen years on from the Conqueror's shattering aggression. The greatest chronicler of this age, William of Malmesbury, writing half a century after 'the harrying of the north', found evidence of its prior desolation. The continued

---

* The motte was an earth mound surrounded by a defensive ditch. The bailey was thrown up either as an extra line of defence, around the motte, or to one side of it, as a protective enclosure.

scarcity of resources in the region so long afterwards is testimony to the ruthlessness of the Conqueror: nothing would be allowed to threaten his dynasty. He wanted his descendants to remain the undisputed rulers of England and Normandy for generations to come.

TWO

Youngest Son

The Normans are an untamed race and, unless they are held in
check by a firm ruler, they are all too ready to do wrong.
Orderic Vitalis, Anglo-Norman monk
and chronicler (1075–c.1142)

Henry I of England's life story starts with unanswerable
questions. He is generally believed to have been the
youngest child of the Conqueror (there were four sons and five
or six daughters), and he was probably born in northern England.
Tradition suggests Henry's birthplace was Selby, in Yorkshire,
but there is no written record to support this. We do not know
the day (or even the year) of his birth but, from references to
a birthday tribute four decades later, it is likely it was in the
last few weeks of the year. It seems probable, through a process
of elimination and an understanding of key moments in his
later life, that the year was 1068, but 1069 is possible too.

We do know for certain that Henry was much the youngest
of the Conqueror's four sons: although these royal children's
birth dates are similarly unrecorded, with Robert being born in

1052 or 1054, Richard in 1054 or 1056, and William Rufus at some point between 1056 and 1060.

As the only son of the Conqueror to appear after his triumph at Hastings, Henry was alone in being born 'in the purple' – that is, after his father began to rule as a king. Henry was as mindful of this differentiation as his brothers were dismissive of it. He felt it set him apart in importance from the older children, calling on a tradition with roots that extend back to the ninth century at least.

The Conqueror's eldest son, Robert, was, according to William of Malmesbury, considered 'a youth of proven valour', by the year 1066. We know the names of three of his childhood tutors: Raturius, who served as 'an adviser on children'; Tetbold, 'a teacher of literature'; and, later, Hilgerius, 'a master of boys'.

While being groomed to rule, Robert was teased at home. He received the nickname 'Curthose' from his father, on account of his short legs. We know, from examination of the single thigh bone that survived a sixteenth-century desecration of his grave, that William the Conqueror stood probably five foot ten inches tall. Robert may have inherited his more truncated form from his mother: Matilda of Flanders was five foot, which was two or three inches shorter than was average for a woman at the time. Robert Wace, a reliable chronicler from the Channel Islands, writing in the second half of the twelfth century, recorded of Curthose that: 'He was a small man, but burly, with short legs and big bones.'[1] Others picked up on these features, calling him 'Gambaron', or 'Fat Legs'.

The second son, Richard of Normandy, was good looking and popular. His father planned to give him the Norman title of count of the Cotentin when he came of age but, 'to the great grief of many', it was recorded, he died 'when a youth who had not yet received the belt of knighthood'.[2]

Richard met his premature end while hunting in the New

Forest, crushed between the branch of a hazel tree and the pommel of his saddle. He died a week later. While his brothers' exploits are well known, Richard's brief life remains an indistinct footnote to history. Born ten or twelve years before the Conquest, he died at some point in his late teens and he was buried in Winchester – a Norman princeling, committed to the soil of the ancient capital of Wessex.

William, the third-born son, was known as 'Rufus', probably on account of his ruddy complexion, or because, as a child, he had inherited the red hair of his father. William Rufus's turned blond as he grew older, and he wore it with a centre parting, framing his forehead in an inverted 'V' above flecked eyes. Rufus was also of a robust build, which would extend to a protruding belly as he grew older and began to run to fat. Daring, energetic, loyal and fun-loving, Rufus would be his father's favourite son.

All the boys inherited the bull-like physique of William the Conqueror, whose strength was such it was said that, in archery, he could fully draw back bows that others simply could not bend. With this muscularity went Christianity: William ensured that all his children were raised from their earliest years with piety at the centre of their existence. Daily Mass became a feature of the royal court from the Conqueror's time onwards, and he liked to conclude his day with the evening service of Vespers.

Despite their rigidly Christian code, the men in the royal family formed a dysfunctional unit. We see an example of the Conqueror's three surviving sons falling out in the Norman town of L'Aigle, in the autumn of 1077. The teenaged William Rufus and the child Henry were up in a gallery, rolling dice with soldiers, when they saw the adult Robert with some of his friends below. As a prank they tipped a chamberpot full of urine over them, and Robert stormed upstairs to sort out his infuriating younger brothers.

The ensuing rough and tumble was broken up only when the

Conqueror appeared and tried to calm things down. But Curthose felt far from appeased. The following night he left his father and rode to Rouen, intent on taking control of the ducal castle there. In this he failed, but it was the start of open hostility between the Conqueror and Curthose, after years of simmering resentment.

William had long had a difficult relationship with his eldest son. Robert Curthose attracted an entourage of 'factious young knights, who incited him to rash undertakings',[3] according to Orderic Vitalis, and who expected to profit from his generous handouts: these 'jongleurs and parasites and courtesans'[4] had already consumed what resources Curthose had, and were living off a diet of promises from their highborn benefactor.

Eager to satisfy his followers' greed, Curthose demanded his father give him control of Normandy. He had long been recognised as the duke-in-waiting, a charter of 1063 declaring him his father's heir there, and he had been appointed co-regent of the dukedom – alongside his mother – in 1067.

But with that official status had come no increase in authority or wealth. William was outraged by Curthose's cheek. 'My son,' Orderic Vitalis reports him as having said, 'your demands are premature. Do not try to snatch recklessly from your father the power which you ought to receive from him in due time, with the acclamation of the people and the blessing of God, if you continue to deserve it.'[5]

Curthose stormed out. His Norman hangers-on began to be joined by powerful supporters from abroad, who were only too happy to sow some discord in overmighty Normandy. Disaffected members of the nobility from Anjou, Brittany and Maine came to him first. Robert then approached his uncle, Robert I, Count of Flanders, who was known to contemporaries as 'an active man and a very daring knight'.[6]

Crucially Curthose also persuaded his mother's cousin, Philip I of France, to take his side against his father. In 1078 the French king gave Curthose the important castle of Gerberoy as a base for his military operations. This impregnable fort, thirty-five miles east of Rouen, stood menacingly on the frontier between France and Normandy. Curthose garrisoned Gerberoy with unruly knights who used it as a platform from which to launch wild forays into his father's lands.

During the winter of 1078–9 William arrived at Gerberoy to deal with the son whose men were damaging his interests and undermining his authority. In the ensuing siege the Conqueror found it impossible to force a victory. A battle followed. William received a wound in an arm and was toppled from his dying warhorse by Curthose who, on recognising his father's distinctive guttural voice from behind the helmet, gave him a fresh mount on which to ride away. William of Malmesbury would later rank Gerberoy as the worst humiliation of the duke's military career.

The conflict between father and son became a serious contest for control of Normandy. The Conqueror was understandably appalled and infuriated to learn that his wife, Matilda of Flanders, had been sending large sums of money to Curthose secretly, as her son battled the continuing poverty caused by his financial incontinence. In vengeance William ordered one of his wife's messengers, a man from Brittany called Samson, to suffer blinding – the same fate that had befallen his biblical namesake. Warned of the duke's intentions, Samson escaped the Conqueror's reach by becoming a monk, a move that gave him immunity.

Matilda of Flanders had not aimed to meddle in politics and warfare, but to establish peace in her family. She helped to engineer a partial reconciliation between her husband and eldest son in 1080. But three years later Matilda died, leaving nobody in her place capable of patching up the differences between the generations. The Conqueror and Curthose remained bitterly at odds, despite the Norman barons' attempts to appease the pair.

The *Anglo-Saxon Chronicle* and Orderic Vitalis record that Henry was knighted at Westminster at Whitsun (which fell on 24 May) in 1086. He was perhaps seventeen years old. In a society that needed military excellence as its cornerstone, knighthood took on grave importance, and its exponents were glamorised.

Orderic Vitalis noted the accoutrements handed over during the ceremony: 'The future King Henry I of England received investiture with hauberk,* helmet and sword-belt on coming of age from Lanfranc, archbishop of Canterbury.'[7] He will have had a fine horse as well: in the *Similitudo Militis*, written in the early twelfth century, the author records the horse as the knight's 'most faithful friend'. It was also one of his more valuable possessions.

Despite his official entry into the adult world of knighthood, Henry's status remained humble when compared to that of his older brothers: they were referred to as 'counts' during the Conqueror's life, while he was not. It seems possible that Henry was being prepared for high office in the Church rather than in the lay world: his education appears to have been overseen by Osmund who, in the easy medieval crossover between state and Church power, had been the Conqueror's chancellor before, in 1078, becoming bishop of Salisbury. Henry is recorded as being in Osmund's company on many occasions between 1080 (when the extremely wealthy Osmund built Devizes Castle) and 1086. There are other hints of religious intent in Henry's upbringing. In 1084, while the Conqueror took Robert Curthose and William Rufus on campaign with him, Henry was ordered to spend time at the ancient Benedictine monastery of St Mary's in Abingdon.

It may well have been during these years with the bishop of

---

* Armour which, at this time, was made for the knight's protection, from the neck down to the mid-thigh.

Salisbury that Henry received an education in the classics, which gave him the ability to read. This level of literacy, being a rarity among his family – or the upper reaches of the aristocracy as a whole at that time – contributed to his being regarded as something of an intellectual. There was some truth in this verdict: certainly, during his later life, Henry showed enthusiasm for mixing with learned men, challenging and enjoying their new ideas. Nicknamed 'clerc' by some during his lifetime, three centuries after his death Henry was being referred to as 'Beauclerc'. His reputation for scholarliness had grown through the Middle Ages, but it should be kept in perspective: while he was able to read, there is no evidence that Henry could write.

Henry found his father's rugged, soldierly illiteracy embarrassing. He once said, within the Conqueror's hearing, that an illiterate king was no better than a crowned ass. William remained uncompromisingly Norman till his dying day. He tried to learn Old English, but his efforts fell away when confronted by its endless intricacies and irregularities, as well as by the other demands on his time. Henry, meanwhile, understood the language of the country of his birth, even if Franco-Norman was his first tongue.

In 1087 William – by now unrecognisable from the vigorous figure of his youth, after gaining significant weight throughout middle age – crossed the Channel for the seventeenth time in his twenty-one-year rule and prepared to fight once more. The Vexin was a strategically important county on the eastern flank of Normandy, which lay between Rouen and Paris. It was in dispute, Philip of France having swooped on it a decade before when its ruler retired to a monastery. Philip had declared half of it to be naturally French territory. From this 'French Vexin' he had launched raids into Normandy. The Conqueror led his army in a revenge expedition, defying his obesity to ride into action during an assault on Mantes, thirty miles west of Paris.

But in the turmoil of sacking the town his horse faltered and William was struck hard in his stomach by the pommel of its saddle, causing a serious internal wound.

Clearly gravely injured, William was taken to be treated in the priory of St Gervais, on the outskirts of Rouen, the city that was the administrative, legal and trade fulcrum of Normandy. There was no hope of recovery. It was obvious that the man who had won a kingdom overseas was going to die in this, the hub of his Anglo-Norman realm. Less easy to discern was how his great inheritance would be divided.

Orderic Vitalis noted how, in contrast to their elder brother, 'William Rufus and Henry . . . were obedient to their father [and so] earned his blessing, and for many years enjoyed the highest power in the kingdom and duchy.'[8] Henry may well have had expectations of a sizeable inheritance, as a result of his father's favour and his mother's legacy: it was common for the property of a royal or aristocratic mother to be passed on her death to younger sons. Matilda of Flanders had owned estates in Buckinghamshire and Gloucestershire, which would have provided Henry with a substantial income of around £300 per year.*

Robert Curthose was still at war with his father as William lay dying. The Conqueror wanted to disinherit him, but he was persuaded by his lords to leave Normandy to his eldest son, in common with the dynasty's custom since the death of William Longsword. Besides, in happier times, the Conqueror had twice insisted that his leading men swear to acknowledge Curthose as the legitimate heir to the dukedom.

Primogeniture would not be recognised in England until the end of the twelfth century, though, and the Conqueror felt free

---

* Domesday Book recorded that in 1086 the entire annual landed receipts of the kingdom of England totalled £72,000.

to leave his English throne to William Rufus. This was reward for his favourite son's unfailing loyalty, but the Conqueror appreciated too that Rufus was a brave and charismatic soldier, capable of keeping control of this hard-won prize that attracted covetous looks from across its various seas, and which had Scottish and Welsh enemies on its northern and west fronts.

'And what, Father, do you give to me?' Orderic Vitalis quoted Henry as asking William on his deathbed: 'The king answered to him, "I give you five thousand pounds of silver from my treasure." To which Henry said, "What shall I do with treasure, if I have no place to make my home?"'[9]

After encouraging Henry to accept his two elder brothers' seniority to him in the line of succession, the Conqueror said: 'You in your own time will have all the dominions that I have acquired, and be greater than your brothers in wealth and power.'[10] Ever practical, and aware that the limited inheritance left him by his father was vulnerable to his brothers' whims, Henry had his silver carefully weighed to see it was all there, then took it away for safe storage.

Henry was by his father's side on his final day, 9 September 1087. As soon as the Conqueror died and the grandees had left the room, his attendants fell upon his belongings in an orgy of self-enrichment. Even his robes were despoiled, and his hulking carcass was left all but naked on its deathbed. His remains were taken by boat to Caen. But the stately progress of the dead ruler, designed to give all a chance to bid farewell to their great duke, was undone when a fire broke out in the city, prompting onlookers to flee for safety.

Of the three surviving sons only Henry attended the Conqueror's funeral, at the Abbey of Saint-Étienne, in Caen. With the service underway a man in the congregation stood up and launched into an astonishing tirade, claiming the church had been built illegally on land that rightly belonged to him.

An even greater commotion blew up when the time came to lay William to rest in his stone sarcophagus. It had been carved when the duke was younger and slimmer, and it proved too small for his immense body. After much effort by the monks to squeeze him into the tomb, his guts burst open in a putrid cascade. The stench surged through the abbey, assaulting the nostrils of the congregation, causing widespread nausea. The abbey was quickly vacated, and the burial of one of the greatest men of the eleventh century was attended only by those clergy prepared to brave the foul smell of his rotten flesh.

This was the start, for Henry, of more than a decade of insecurity that would often tip over into real personal danger. During this time, he would be seen as an accoutrement of the royal and ducal family, but not as a central figure in it. His status stemmed from his royal parentage, but he had neither the title nor the lands required for real power and wealth.

On his deathbed the Conqueror had committed his English crown, sword and sceptre to Rufus, together with a letter to Archbishop Lanfranc confirming his wish that his second son succeed him in England. The coronation was performed by the archbishop of Canterbury in Westminster, on 26 September – 'Michaelmas Day' – 1087, just seventeen days after the Conqueror's death. 'William Rufus crossed the sea, was crowned and reigned for thirteen years,' recorded Robert Wace succinctly.[11]

But Wace's description fails to point out what a difficult time Rufus often had during those thirteen years. His succession was contested, despite his father's unambiguous directions. Within months of being crowned, Rufus faced a serious rebellion in England in favour of Robert Curthose. It was led by two of the Conqueror's half-brothers, Odo, Bishop of Bayeux, and

Robert, Count de Mortain, and supported by a clutch of leading bishops and noblemen.

After decisive military action Rufus pulled out the roots of the revolt by promising to be a strong and fair ruler, uphold the laws of his predecessors as kings of England, stamp out unjust taxation and respect the people's rights in the forests. But Curthose remained determined to displace his younger brother from the English throne that he was convinced was his by right.

Curthose's hopes of military gain were compromised by his extravagance. He heaped gifts on his supporters, and was so bad with money that he was said to pay whatever outrageous sum was requested, whether for a horse or for a hound. Within six months of inheriting Normandy, he had gone through all the treasure left to him by the Conqueror. By contrast Rufus's English wealth seemed infinite.

Curthose became so financially hobbled that, in 1088, he accepted a payment from Henry of £3,000 in return for the rights to the land of the Cotentin. This was the peninsula in the north-west of Normandy that included Barfleur, a favoured crossing point for ships heading to the southern coast of England. Henry became count of the Cotentin, in practice and probably in name, taking the rank that had been planned for his brother Richard during his brief life. He was around twenty years of age at this stage, and starting to establish himself as a man of importance.

Henry must surely have sworn homage to Curthose on assuming his duties. While the revenues and the castles of the Cotentin were now his, so was the responsibility of serving his eldest brother as peacekeeper there. Henry expanded his control, and his new power base included the monastery-fortress of Mont Saint-Michel and the counties of Avranches and Coutances. He remained on the south side of the Channel for nearly all of the next seven years. The one trip to England that we know of during this period of his life took place in the second half of 1088. It was a failure, for he was unable to persuade William Rufus to hand over those properties that, Henry remained adamant, their mother had left to him. More disappointment and frustration followed: when Henry returned to Normandy Curthose imprisoned him in Bayeux. So toxic was the relationship between the two older brothers that Curthose was convinced Henry had been sent by Rufus to undermine him. Henry remained a prisoner for six months, being released only after paying for his freedom.

Shorn of much of his wealth, Henry seemed to face a modest future. He appears to have inhabited a desolate no man's land while his brothers fought one another across a broad front. Because of his rootlessness and limited resources, Henry remained at the mercy of whichever one of them temporarily showed him favour, as and when they required his help. On his release from Curthose's prison in Bayeux Henry sought a place in Rufus's court, but was rebuffed. Feeling he had nowhere else to go, Henry felt compelled to swallow his pride and offer his services to Curthose, despite having so recently been his captive.

It was humiliating, but Henry bided his time, waiting for an opportunity to step forward into a role suited to his drive and ambition. Soon enough his chance seemed to come along.

———

In 1090 William Rufus secretly sent money to leading citizens of the Norman capital of Rouen who were unhappy with Curthose's rule. When this disaffected group plotted a riot on Rufus's behalf, Henry rode to Rouen Castle to help Curthose deal with the uprising.

Open fighting broke out on 3 November, Curthose and Henry leading their men out of the castle to meet the rioters. What followed was brutal, and in the bloody mayhem Curthose was persuaded by courtiers to slip away to safety rather than risk his life in a street fight. He lay low in a church in Rouen's suburbs while Henry led his soldiers into the heat of the action. Henry was eventually joined by the troops of Gilbert de L'Aigle, a nobleman from the south-east of Normandy, who had penetrated Rouen from the south. Their forces fought through to unite, and began to put the rebels to the sword with gusto. The survivors faltered, then scattered, pursued by Henry's men who were eager for bloodshed and plunder, as well as ransom from the richer prisoners.

They quickly captured the leader of the rebellion, who Curthose ordered to be taken away in chains. But Henry insisted the prisoner be brought to him at once. The man turned out not to be a powerful aristocrat, but a rich merchant by the name of Conan. Henry found the lowly status of the rebel particularly maddening: by breaking the homage he had sworn to Curthose, Conan had shattered the social conventions of the time. Such oaths formed the glue of feudal society, and their infringement was seen as being beyond the pale.

Wace explained the gravity of such treachery: 'No one could do worse [than he] who betrays his liege lord. No man, for any reason, should fail his earthly lord; he should protect his life and limb and uphold his earthly honour.'[12] Henry decided Conan should pay for his unforgivable transgression immediately.

He ordered the prisoner to accompany him and his men as they went up the stairway of Rouen Castle's great tower. While Conan followed, no doubt becoming increasingly terrified, Henry is said to have given a goading commentary of the sights opening up to them as they ascended the steps: 'Admire, Conan, the beauty of the country you tried to conquer. Away to the south there is a delightful hunting region, wooded and well stocked with beasts of the chase. See how the River Seine, full of fishes, laps the wall of Rouen and daily brings in ships laden with merchandise of many kinds. On the other side see the fair and popular city, with its ramparts and churches and town buildings, which has rightly been the capital of Normandy from the earliest days.'

Panicked by the barely controlled fury of his captor, Conan misread his man. He hoped for some way out of his predicament and he trusted that it might lie in bribery on a colossal scale. 'My Lord,' he conceded, 'I deserve condemnation for my own guilt, but now I ask mercy for the sake of God who created all things. For my ransom I will give my Lord all the gold and silver that I can find in my own and kinsmen's treasure-stores, and in compensation for my treachery I will give you faithful service until I die.'

'By my mother's soul!' Henry countered with contempt. 'There shall be no ransom for a traitor, only swift infliction of the death he deserves.'[13]

Conan, realising that his life was over, begged for time to confess his sins, believing he could purify his soul before meeting judgement in the afterlife. But Henry's patience was shot. He was said to be 'trembling with anger' when he seized the merchant and hurled him from a high window. Conan plunged to his death, and his broken corpse was tied to the tail of a horse, which dragged it through Rouen's streets in a grisly circuit of shame.

Contemporaries and chroniclers applauded Henry's delivery of such instant and fitting justice. William of Malmesbury wrote of this episode: 'The punishment of a man who turned traitor after swearing loyalty and doing homage ought never to be deferred.'[14] Conan had broken the sacred bond that tied him to Robert Curthose, his duke, and he had paid for his treachery with his life.

The contrast between Henry's bold conduct that day and that

of his eldest brother could hardly have been more vivid. Henry, fighting hard, then dispatching the defeated rebel leader with apt ruthlessness, was considered to have behaved admirably. Meanwhile Curthose's decision to quit bloody hand-to-hand combat for the sanctuary of a church was viewed as humiliating. As a result, even though Henry had put down the dangerous rebellion he received no gratitude from Curthose. Instead, soon afterwards, his brother forced Henry to leave Rouen, his status yet again that of a wandering knight without a cause.

The tit for tat between Curthose and Rufus continued. Having failed to remove Rufus from the English throne, Curthose found himself attacked from across the Channel. But in a move as sudden as it was unexpected, in 1091 Rufus and Curthose agreed a peace treaty, witnessed by twelve barons on either side. They recognised each other as one another's heir, in the event that either should die before fathering a legitimate son. At the same time Rufus was fed various slivers of Normandy: Cherbourg, the county of Eu, the abbeys of Fécamp and Mont Saint-Michel, and those castles that had repudiated their loyalty to Curthose and already come over to him. Henry had no role in their plans, except as victim: the two had also agreed to turn on their younger brother, and to deprive him of his lands.

Henry looked to one of his father's most faithful supporters, Hugh, Earl of Chester, to help him defend against the imminent attack. But Hugh had weighed his affection for Henry against the combined strength of Curthose and Rufus, as well as the loyalty he owed to his anointed king. The earl was among those who, in the words of Orderic Vitalis, 'deserted the noble prince [Henry] in his military need, and handed over their castles to the king'.[15]

Although Hugh of Chester felt compelled to surrender rather than face the inevitable consequences, he remained quietly supportive of Henry. He advised Henry to assemble his forces and take a stand at his most promising defensive position. This was Mont Saint-Michel, the monastery that stands in a bay joining Normandy to Brittany, which Rufus was now claiming as his own. Mont Saint-Michel has significant natural protection: a craggy rock, it becomes an island at high tide. Hugh suggested that Henry should add to this some man-made fortifications of his own.

Wace wrote of Henry: 'He did not leave [for Mont Saint-Michel] without companions, taking a large number of men with him; he took with him the brothers and sons of the most noble and high born and they all served with him very willingly, for they put great hope in him.'[16] Bolstering this force of enthusiastic adventurers, who chose to believe in Henry's potential, came a body of mercenaries from Brittany who were confident that Henry would find the money to pay for their services. Further help arrived from an unlikely quarter: Mont Saint-Michel's religious foundation. John of Worcester, writing in the late 1090s till 1118, noted how some of the monks assisted Henry as he dug in, preparing to fight.[17]

After Henry fell back to Mont Saint-Michel, William Rufus and Robert Curthose soon followed, besieging him there from March 1091. Frequent skirmishes took place on the same sand flats in front of the monastery where the man who would briefly rule England, Harold, had fought in support of Henry's father, William, a quarter of a century beforehand. These small engagements cost Rufus and Curthose many casualties, of which Rufus was nearly one. According to William of Malmesbury, Rufus launched a singlehanded attack against some of Henry's knights, during which his horse was mortally wounded. It galloped on, with Rufus's ankle wedged in a stirrup, until slowing up, collapsing in death and leaving him sprawled out on the sand.

One of Henry's knights stepped forward, raised his sword

and was about to smite the life out of the helmeted figure lying defenceless before him when a distinctive voice bellowed up from the ground: 'Hold, wretch! I am the king of England!' Recognising Rufus for who he claimed to be, Henry's men shrank back, shocked that they had been about to dispatch a man who (in common with the beliefs of the time) they took to have been transformed by holy anointment at coronation from mere mortality to the status of God's regent on earth. They put aside their weapons and offered Rufus one of their mounts.

As the king swung his leg up over the saddle, he asked the soldiers which of them had unhorsed him. The man responsible stepped forward, admitting that it was him. Fearing punishment, he nervously explained that he had mistaken the king for one of his knights. Rufus, who loved courage in another as much as he enjoyed magnanimity in himself, voiced his favourite oath, 'By the face of Lucca!', then promised: 'From now on you shall be my man and, being placed on my muster list, you shall be well rewarded for your gallant deed.'[18] It was a typical gesture by Rufus, who was a soldier's soldier. Robert Wace recorded that the king 'was brave, and very generous. He did not hear of any knight whose prowess he heard praised and then fail to mention him in his register and give him some . . . reward.'[19]

As the siege dragged on through Lent, Rufus departed, leaving operations under the complete command of Curthose. William of Malmesbury recorded how Henry sent a messenger to his eldest brother at this point, saying that he and his men were dying of thirst. While Mont Saint-Michel's main strength lay in the protection of the surrounding sea, its weakness was an inability to access fresh water. Henry challenged his brother to allow him and his men something to drink, so that any victory gained could be fairly and gloriously won, and not come about through something as banal as the defenders' lack of supplies.

Curthose sent what was requested – and is reported to have thrown in some good wine too, for his brother to enjoy.

When he found out what Curthose had allowed in his absence, Rufus was furious: 'This is a fine way indeed to run a war, allowing the enemy all the water they need! How shall we ever conquer them if we indulge them with food and drink?' Curthose is said to have replied: 'Indeed, should I condemn my own brother to die of thirst? And if we lose him, where shall we find another?'[20]

Exasperated by Curthose's softness, Rufus refused to continue the fight in Normandy, and the two older brothers went their separate ways. But Henry failed to profit from the falling out: after a six-week siege, he was still obliged to surrender Mont Saint-Michel, on terms that guaranteed his liberty. He had now lost all the land that he had purchased from Curthose with the money left to him in their father's will. Henry of Huntingdon recorded: 'When Robert had sold Henry part of Normandy in return for this treasure, he took the land away from him. This was very displeasing to God, but He deferred vengeance for a time.'[21]

Allowed safe conduct from Mont Saint-Michel, Henry paid off his mercenaries with his remaining money. Banished from Normandy by his brother, he set off for Brittany before arriving in France. So began the start of a reduced life, when Henry was forced to learn 'to endure poverty in exile'.[22] The next year, from 1091–2, is a mystery; this man, who was to become a titan of medieval history, simply disappears from view, a dispossessed younger son, deceived and degraded by his brothers, seemingly condemned to a life of obscurity and dependence.

With him went a retinue of five men – a chaplain, a knight and three servants. Wace has Henry spending some of this time serving the king of France. In his account Henry was eventually spotted in Paris by a supporter called Haschier, who was travelling through France in a disguise that seems to have comprised nothing more than a plaster placed over an eye. Haschier is credited by Wace with persuading Henry to leave his life of Parisian poverty for hope of greater things in Normandy.

Wace's version, written decades after the events, is hard to verify. It remains part of Henry's myth in a period when he is otherwise unaccounted for. One thing the chroniclers agree on, though, is that this time of want instilled in Henry an eagerness to help the poor and an understanding of the need to account for resources in a thoughtful manner. Both would be notable traits during his later years of power.

THREE

Out of the Shadows

Robert, Duke of the Normans, told his brother King William the Younger through envoys that he would no longer keep the peace which they had both agreed. Furthermore, he called him faithless and deceitful unless he discharged fully the terms of the agreement they had made in Normandy.

John of Worcester, English monk and chronicler (*d.* 1140)

When Henry reappears for sure, it is in mid-1092, at the invitation of Domfront, a fortified Norman town fifty miles south of Caen, which sat at a point where Normandy met Maine and Brittany. The inhabitants of Domfront could take no more of the vicious rule of their lord, and invited Henry to come to their assistance by taking his place.

Their tormentor was Robert de Bellême, a powerful aristocrat who had been knighted by the Conqueror as a youth. At the time of Domfront's rebellion de Bellême was in his mid-thirties. The tall and strongly built de Bellême came from impressive stock. A distant cousin of Henry's, he was the eldest surviving son of Roger de Montgomery, one of the Conqueror's closest advisers. Roger

seems to have helped govern Normandy at the time of the invasion of 1066 before crossing the Channel to assist in the
administration of the captured kingdom. William gave him land
in eleven English counties, including nearly all of Shropshire and
a large section of what is now West Sussex. In making Roger de
Montgomery one of the half-dozen greatest landowners in
England, William was relying on him in turn to counter the
Welsh, and to protect a key stretch of the south coast.

At the time that Domfront turned to Henry for salvation,
Robert de Bellême had yet to receive any lands from his father.
But he had already become a major Norman aristocrat thanks
to his inheritance from his mother, Mabel, a significant force
in her own right. On her death she passed to Robert the lordship of Bellême, which was vitally important to the dukes of
Normandy as a protective buffer against Maine: Bellême lay
thirty-five miles north-west of Maine's capital, Le Mans. Robert
de Bellême was also the lord of Sées and of Alençon, and owned
a scattering of other significant castles, of which Domfront was
one of the more important.

The diminutive Mabel was judged to have passed on to her
eldest son not just her portfolio of power, but much of her
daunting character. Orderic Vitalis (whose monastery suffered
from some of the de Bellême family's excesses) described her as
'small, very talkative, ready enough to do evil, shrewd and jocular,
extremely cruel and daring'. Mabel tried to poison a member
of the eminent Giroie family, with whom the de Bellêmes were
locked in a feud, but her own brother-in-law, parched after a
long ride, downed the lethal goblet of wine before he could be
stopped, and died in place of her intended victim. Yet Mabel
persevered, and got her man next time, after bribing one of his
servants to administer the fatal brew.

Mabel had little respect for religion. She once brought her
large retinue to a monastery that she knew was obliged to provide

all who came to its doors with food and lodging. She did this in the knowledge that it would impose financial strains on her hosts that they would find crippling. When admonished by the abbot for her thoughtlessness, she replied that next time she would descend on him with even more mouths to feed.

Mabel focused on further enriching her family at the cost of its rivals. This she did once too often, seizing the stronghold of Peray, twenty miles south-east of Alençon, which was the inheritance of a nobleman called Hugh Bunel. It provoked Hugh, who was reported to be 'frenzied with grief',[1] into gathering together some of his male relatives for vengeance. Breaking into Mabel de Bellême's home one December night in 1077, they found her relaxing on her bed, having just emerged from her bath. Before she could escape, Hugh decapitated her with his sword.

Mabel's epitaph acknowledged that she was:

> To some neighbours dear,
> To others terrible; she died by the sword,
> By night, by stealth, for we are mortals all.[2]

Robert de Bellême perpetuated the consternation that his mother had sown among her neighbours, using his maternal inheritance – of castles and cruelty – to cast a largely malevolent shadow throughout his decades of influence. Orderic Vitalis called him 'proud and evil in every way', and said de Bellême 'committed innumerable crimes'.[3]

De Bellême had been one of the young and unruly supporters of Robert Curthose during the latter's years of armed opposition to the Conqueror. Captured in 1079, de Bellême was spared punishment by William, but never again trusted by him. The Conqueror saw to it that de Bellême's potential for troublemaking was negated by billeting his household troops on the young man's garrisons.

De Bellême was on his way to pay his respects to the duke in 1087 when he heard that the old warrior had died. His first reaction was to order all of William's troops to quit his castles. He quickly imposed some of his own men on the garrisons of his weaker neighbours in an opportunistic appropriation of power. The neighbours either agreed or had their fort destroyed.

De Bellême soon became a leading participant in Curthose and Rufus's contest for power. In 1088 he arrived in Rochester, thirty miles south-east of London, to bolster Odo of Bayeux's revolt against Rufus's reign. But it quickly became clear that Rochester would fall to Rufus, and when de Bellême and his accomplices started negotiating for their lives and freedom in return for their surrender, the king insisted the rebels be hanged. It was thanks to Roger de Montgomery, and other powerful fathers whose sons had fought for Curthose, that the men holding Rochester were eventually allowed to lay down their arms without also forfeiting their lives.

Before long, de Bellême patched up his differences with Rufus, and he fostered a friendship with Henry. He accompanied Henry back to Normandy, but was arrested alongside him, thanks to Curthose's suspicion that they had come to cause him trouble.

Bishop Odo encouraged Curthose to strike against de Bellême's power base, while he was imprisoned. Curthose made good progress, capturing de Bellême's castle of St Cénéry, east of Sées, mutilating some of the garrison and blinding its commander. But, typically, Curthose failed to push home his advantage by making further inroads. He followed the example of his father and of Rufus, releasing the dangerous de Bellême to continue on his path of self-interest and destruction.

In a cruel age, he became a byword for particular viciousness. At a time when the fear of God persuaded many to respect (or at least bear in mind) the concept of mercy, and divine retribution, de Bellême seems to have been devoid of religious belief or conscience. He chose not to ransom his prisoners – then normal practice, since it was lucrative – because he preferred to keep victims on hand for torture and mutilation.

The chroniclers are unanimous in their condemnation of this curiously sadistic aristocrat. Orderic Vitalis told of how those who fell into his clutches 'groaned and wailed as they were torn by his iron talons'.[4] The historian-monk recorded how, one Lent, rather than repent of his sins, de Bellême chose to let three hundred prisoners starve and freeze to death while chained in his dungeons.

Henry of Huntingdon noted that de Bellême enjoyed thinking of excruciating ways to inflict pain on captives of both sexes: 'He impaled men and also women on stakes. To him the most horrible butchering of men was pleasant nourishment for the soul.'[5] William of Malmesbury recalled de Bellême's rage when upset by the father of a boy he was holding hostage. Even though de Bellême was the child's godfather, he tore out the boy's eyes with his fingernails. We read too of de Bellême carrying off the son of a defeated rival and, contemporaries were sure, poisoning him.

Wace called him 'a baron whom people considered very treacherous, but who was on very good terms with the king. Robert de Bellême was a traitor and knew many forms of treachery and evil; he was an expert in treacherous games and feared on account of the harm he did.'[6]

Despite his outrages de Bellême remained a favourite of William Rufus, who approved an advantageous marriage that had been arranged for him in the final year of the Conqueror's life: de Bellême's wife, Agnes, was heiress to the powerful count of Ponthieu, whose brother had distinguished himself at Hastings, being in at the kill when Harold was dispatched. But being married to de Bellême was far from easy: Agnes was kept locked up in one of his castles until she succeeded in escaping and found refuge with the Conqueror's youngest daughter, Adela, Countess of Blois.

When the inhabitants of Domfront rebelled in 1092, anyone must have seemed a better choice to be their lord than the depraved Robert de Bellême. But the loss of Domfront infuriated de Bellême. It would be the starting point of a personal hostility between him and Henry that, apart from one brief rapprochement, proved impossible to overcome. Domfront's powerful fortress provided Henry with a base from which to build his reputation and grow his influence. He swore to respect and uphold the laws and customs that the townspeople had in place, and he gave his word that only he would be their lord, for as long as he lived. Henry offered security, in place of de Bellême's savagery.

As Henry began his ascent to prominence and power, his two brothers' animosity towards one another rekindled. By late 1093 Curthose was threatening to end the peace between them, because he was tired of Rufus's relentless untrustworthiness. Meanwhile Rufus prepared for renewed aggression by bribing some leading Normans to join his cause.

But when hostilities resumed Curthose was able to rely on the support of Philip I of France. Philip laid siege to the key frontier castle of Argentan, thirty-five miles south-east of Caen. He took it in a day, and in the process captured 700 royal knights and 1,400 squires.[7] At the same time Rufus found himself fighting a bitter war from England with the Welsh. He needed Henry's support now more than ever. Henry of Huntingdon noted how Rufus 'sent his brother Henry to Normandy with a great deal of money, to attack it on his behalf with daily raids'.[8]

From 1095 Henry and Rufus were as one against Curthose, and in the process Henry's star rose. From political and territorial irrelevance four years earlier, he had now achieved a firmer grip than ever on the Cotentin: Rufus had been forced to confirm him in his authority there as part of the price of his crucial support. In return Henry brought his military ability and energy to bear against Curthose. While leaving the fighting in Normandy to Henry, Rufus tackled his enemies in Britain. After much ravaging of the western counties of England, he led an expedition into Wales at the end of 1094.

Curthose also found himself under considerable pressure, since his inheritance lay in total disarray: 'For at that time there was exceptional unrest among the magnates of Normandy and a great stirring of evil throughout the land,' remembered Orderic Vitalis. 'The law of the strong was to rob and ravage. The whole country was devastated by fire and plunder, which drove many of the inhabitants into exile and left whole parishes destroyed and churches abandoned as the priests fled.'⁹

Given the pitiful state of the Church in Normandy at the time, it was ironically the papacy that seemed suddenly to offer Curthose an exit from the chaos.

———

At the Council of Clermont, held in November 1095, Pope Urban II summoned an impressive gathering of prelates and aristocrats. He had recently received urgent requests from the emperor of Byzantium, the head of the Christian faith in the East, for mercenaries to help fight the Turks. Urban took the opportunity to ramp things up to an altogether greater level. He announced a great Christian undertaking, to retake Palestine and drive out Islamic people from the Holy Land.

Fulcher of Chartres is considered the most accurate of the chroniclers present at Clermont. He recorded Urban as saying: 'I, or rather the Lord, beseech you as Christ's heralds to publish this everywhere, and to persuade all people of whatever rank – foot-soldiers and knights, poor and rich – to carry aid promptly to the Christians [in the East] and to destroy that vile race from the lands of our friends. I say this to those who are present, and to those who are absent. Moreover, Christ commands it.'[10]

One of Pope Urban's many reasons for calling Christians to arms, against an enemy whose threat he hugely exaggerated, was a wish to bring about greater peace in western Europe. He had already tried to initiate the concept of the 'Peace of God', to protect non-combatants from the rolling bloodshed of endless wars, and he had brought in the 'Truce of God', marking out fixed days in the year when no fighting was allowed.

Pope Urban insisted that private wars cease during the life of the Crusade, exhorting 'Let those who have been fighting against their brothers and relatives now fight in a proper way against the barbarians.'[11] This looked attractive to the hard-pressed Curthose, who was buckling under the pressure of fighting against his brothers and their supporters in Normandy.

The pope also guaranteed that all those pilgrims who answered his call would not only be assured of a place in heaven, they would have their possessions protected while they were serving God far away from home. Curthose could remove himself from the disgrace brought about by his being 'a weak duke . . . sunk in sloth and voluptuousness . . . who feared the vassals in his own duchy more than they feared him',[12] and garner some much-needed prestige as one of the leaders of an enterprise that was divinely blessed, and hugely popular.

Curthose arrived in England in the spring of 1096 to make peace with Rufus and to ask the king to fund his role in the Crusade. The brothers agreed that, in return for three years' control of the dukedom of Normandy, Curthose would be paid ten thousand marks of silver. Rufus raised some of the enormous sum needed for this most Christian of endeavours by plundering his churches of many of the gold, silver and bejewelled treasures given them by previous generations of kings and aristocrats. That September the king accompanied the money raised in this way to Normandy, and Curthose set off on the Crusade soon afterwards.

Having gained control of his family's ancestral lands at such expense, Rufus set about making good his investment. He realised he could best achieve this by placing strong and loyal lieutenants throughout Normandy to bring it back under control. The king had pressing requirements in Britain and, according to John of Worcester, after Easter 1097 he 'set out a second time for Wales with an army of horse and foot with the intention of killing all the male population'.[13] Unable to direct operations in Normandy, Rufus gave the military governorships of Coutances and Bayeux to Henry. These lay, respectively, at the western and eastern bases of the Cotentin which Henry already controlled, and so considerably increased his hold over the western part of the dukedom.

In the campaigns of 1097 and 1098, Henry proved one of his brother Rufus's leading commanders in Normandy, fighting to gain control of the French Vexin and to regain control of Maine, which had been occupied by Fulk IV, Count of Anjou. The retrieval of Maine held great importance for Rufus because of the county's long associations with his family. It had been given to his ancestor Rollo, Duke of Normandy, in 924, by the king of France. Normandy, to the north, and Anjou, to the south, had played a game of tug-of-war with it ever since. William the Conqueror's brutal invasion of 1063 had succeeded in quietening down Maine for a while, reassuring him of safety on that troublesome flank when he set off for England. But the Normans had been overthrown in a rebellion in 1070, and Maine remained unsettled for the rest of the Conqueror's reign.

With Curthose absent on Crusade, it was Rufus's turn to fight for Maine. This he did vigorously, forcing Fulk IV to hand back

Le Mans and all the castles that had belonged to Normandy during the Conqueror's pomp. But Le Mans flared up again the following year, provoking the king to cross the Channel at astonishing speed and once again drive out the rebels from the city.

These were times of widespread and brutal warfare for Rufus across many fronts, Orderic Vitalis noting how, in the autumn of 1098, his forces 'advanced rapidly into France as far as Pontoise [twenty miles north-west of Paris], burning, plundering, taking captives, and so destroyed all the wealth of that fair province'.[14]

Meanwhile Rufus had to cope with other dangers back in England, including the continuing possibility of invasion from across the North Sea. His father, William, had had to contend with various Viking threats, including a planned invasion by Cnut the Holy of Denmark, in 1085. The Scandinavian menace remained in Rufus's reign, even if the protagonists had changed. After becoming king of all Norway in 1095, the aggressive Magnus Barefoot took control of a string of islands around the north and west of Scotland, moving on to the Isle of Man, then the Welsh coast, before landing on the island of Anglesey.

However, the chroniclers of England recorded how, for many of Rufus's subjects, the great fear was not of invasion, but of a visit from the lawless royal household. The king let his men do as they wished, without punishment or restraint. Once it was known that they were approaching, people would flee with their families into the woods, abandoning homes and possessions rather than risk their personal safety. 'When they could not consume all the provisions that they found in the homes that they had invaded,' the contemporary historian and churchman Eadmer of Canterbury wrote, 'many of them, intoxicated by their own wickedness, made the inhabitants take the remaining provisions to market and sell them for the benefit of the invaders; or else they set fire to the goods and burned them up; or if it was drink, they washed their horses' feet with it and poured the rest on the ground . . . It is shocking to contemplate the cruelties they inflicted on the fathers of families, the indecencies on their wives and daughters.'[15] Henry of Huntingdon also wrote of how 'the King's friends robbed and subverted everything, even going unpunished when they committed rape'.[16] They were, he concluded, guilty of 'unspeakable debauchery'.[17]

Orderic Vitalis portrays Rufus as the debaucher-in-chief: 'He was generous to knights and foreigners, but greatly oppressed the poor inhabitants of his kingdom and took from them by force the wealth that he lavished on strangers.[18] Orderic was appalled by the identity of some of these royal hangers-on, calling them 'effeminati' – homosexual men who flaunted their ostentatious clothing and what the monk saw as their blatant immorality. 'He never had a lawful wife,' Orderic noted of Rufus, 'but gave himself up insatiably to obscene fornications and repeated adulteries. Stained with sins, he set a culpable example of shameful debauchery to his subjects.'[19] It has never been established for sure if Rufus was homosexual. He had no wife, and there are no records of mistresses or illegitimate children. The consensus among his modern biographers seems to be that he was probably bisexual, and that he enjoyed frequent sex with an ever-changing cast of lovers of both genders.

It is unsurprising that so many of the chroniclers of the time wrote so scathingly of Rufus, for they were churchmen, and the Church suffered terribly during his reign. The income from the estates of the archbishoprics, bishoprics and abbeys of England was vast – Domesday Book had estimated that churches and monasteries held a quarter of the land value of the kingdom, in 1086 – and Rufus found it irresistible. He chose to leave senior ecclesiastical offices vacant so the revenue would fall to him. He even left the see of Canterbury unfilled, after the death of the Conqueror's last archbishop, Lanfranc, in May 1089. At

Christmas 1092 Rufus announced his intention to keep the see empty for the rest of his life.

Three months later, while staying at a royal hunting lodge in Alveston, in Gloucestershire, Rufus was struck by a life-threatening bowel condition. He was rushed to Gloucester, twenty-five miles away, so he could be treated by the monks there. Attending the king's sickbed in Gloucester Castle, they persuaded Rufus that his affliction was divine punishment for his sins. 'Thinking that he would die soon,' wrote John of Worcester, 'he vowed before God, following his barons' counsel, to reform his way of life, never again to sell or tax churches, but to guard them with royal power, to annul unjust laws, and establish just ones.'[20]

But still Rufus remained critically unwell. His confession was taken by Anselm of Bec, a sixty-year-old Italian who was one of the most respected churchmen in Europe. When the sickness reached its most dangerous point Anselm administered the last rites to the king. Contemplating how to appease the God who he feared he was about to encounter, Rufus told Anselm he wanted him to become the new archbishop of Canterbury.

Problems quickly arose when William Rufus began to get better. Anselm seemed reluctant to take the position, citing his age and his poor health as barriers. Perhaps he was concerned about the demands of high ecclesiastical office, for Anselm was at heart a man of contemplation. Coming from the quiet of the Aosta Valley, in the modern-day Italian Alps, he had seriously considered life as a hermit, and a yearning for tranquillity was in his soul. His Christianity was earnest, but without personal ambition. It centred around a belief that he had answered God's calling to serve Him. In turn it was his duty to persuade others to live as good Christians, so they could earn the reward of joy in the next life. He said he was keener to remain in Bec than to move to England.

Anselm eventually yielded to Rufus's wishes, and agreed to become archbishop provided the king honour three stipulations. First, Rufus was required to recognise Urban II as the true pope, rather than contemplate supporting his rival, Antipope Clement III. Next, Rufus had to commit to returning all Church lands that he had wrongly taken for himself. The third point was more personal: the king must agree to receive his spiritual counselling from Anselm. The king reluctantly agreed, and Archbishop Anselm was enthroned at Canterbury in September 1093.

It was a relationship forged in a moment of panic. As Henry of Huntingdon wrote, Rufus had 'promised to amend evil laws and to establish peace in the house of the Lord', when in fear of his life. 'But as soon as he recovered, he went back on this, and behaved worse than ever.'[21]

In 1094, with Rufus preparing to cross the Channel to fight Curthose once more, Anselm offered to bless the English fleet. The archbishop's chronicler, Eadmer, recorded Rufus's thoughts on the matter: 'As to his blessings and prayers, I utterly abominate them and spew them from me!'[22] When Rufus's campaign that year went less well than its predecessors, Eadmer was unsurprised.

After further arguments – over Anselm's wish to travel to Rome to receive the symbol of his office from the pope, over doctrine, over the archbishop supposedly sending too few knights when the king raised an army against the Welsh – the relationship between Anselm and William Rufus disintegrated.

The king insisted the elderly archbishop submit to his authority, and not to the pope's, or receive perpetual banishment. In 1097, Anselm chose exile. William Rufus allowed him to go but, in a fit of petulance, forbade him from making any part of his journey through Normandy, even subjecting Anselm to a final indignity before he sailed: the king's men unpacked his bags on Dover beach, searching for supposed secret correspondence. There was none. Anselm set sail for Boulogne, and travelled on to Rome, remaining in exile for the remainder of Rufus's reign.

Henry of Huntingdon summed up all that was wrong in the land, when Anselm departed: 'Then Archbishop Anselm left England because the evil king would permit nothing right to be done in his kingdom. He harassed the shires through taxes which never ceased: for the building of the wall round the Tower of London, for the building of the royal hall at Westminster, and to satisfy the rapacious and aggressive habits of his household wherever they went.'[23]

William Rufus bequeathed to his successors a building that was, most likely, the largest in Europe. 'He began and completed one very noble edifice,' William of Malmesbury noted, 'sparing no expense to manifest the greatness of his liberality.'[24] Westminster Hall was constructed a mile and a half to the west of London's city walls, between 1097 and 1099. The king wanted to impress his subjects with the scope and majesty of this architectural masterpiece, and placed at the palace's core his marble throne. When he summoned the first royal court to attend him there, in May 1099, his brother Henry was among those present.

Henry was viewed by many of the grander courtiers there as something of an eccentric adjunct to the earthy, irrepressible king. Few can have imagined how the following year would conclude for the Conqueror's overlooked and underestimated youngest son.

FOUR

Opportunity

They went into the New Forest, intending to hunt stags and hinds; they set up their watch throughout the forest, but departed in great sadness. For the king, the knights and those who were his archers took up their positions and stretched their bows just as they saw the hinds coming.

Robert Wace, Jersey-born poet and historian (*c.*1110–*c.*1174)

William the Conqueror's passion for hunting knew no bounds, the *Anglo-Saxon Chronicle* noting that he:

> . . . preserved the harts and boars
> And loved the stags as much
> As if he were their father.[1]

This obsession led to ruthless punishment for poachers who dared to interfere with his royal prey: 'If anyone caught a stag or a boar, [William] put out his eyes, and no one murmured,' recalled Henry of Huntingdon.

Not content with all the land available to him, which had

produced ample hunting country for previous monarchs, William took advantage of his conquest of a new land to expand the territory devoted to his gratification. He eventually treated a fifth of England as park and forest where he and his companions could enjoy their sport. There was no law in these lands: they fell under the king's pleasure, and so did their regulation.

The Conqueror carved out a huge, fresh area in the south for quarry to breed in without interference. 'He loved the beasts of the chase,' wrote Henry of Huntingdon. 'On account of this, in the woodlands reserved for hunting, which are called the "New Forest", he had villages rooted out and people removed, and made it a habitation for wild beasts.'[2] Two thousand inhabitants of thirty villages were turfed out of their homes so as not to infringe on the king's hunting habitat, and the forest was expanded by twenty thousand acres. Some suggested the sacrilegious removal of so many religious sites, at the heart of the cleared communities, would surely result in divine retribution against the king.

William passed on his infatuation for hunting to his sons. This was to be at huge cost to them. We have seen how the Conqueror's second son, Richard, died of injuries sustained while out in the New Forest, crushed between a branch and the pommel on his saddle.

In early May 1100 Richard, one of Robert Curthose's illegitimate sons, also died in an accident in the field. A knight in the hunting party missed a deer with his arrow but struck the youth, killing him outright. His shocking loss caused consternation because, as Orderic Vitalis wrote, 'Many had prophesied a lofty destiny for him.'[3] The guilty knight fled to the Priory of St Pancras, in Lewes, Sussex. He showed penance for causing the death, and in becoming a monk he avoided any penalty for his wayward shot.

A few weeks later the royal pursuit claimed its most celebrated victim.

On 1 August Fulchred, abbot of Shrewsbury, gave a fiery sermon condemning the disarray that had beset England under Rufus's rule. The abbot referred to 'the leprosy of villainy', 'unrestrained lust' and 'the sickness of evil' that stalked the land. But, he told his congregation, he believed deliverance to be imminent.

'Not much longer will effeminates govern,' he was said to have warned. 'Behold, the bow of divine anger is bent against the wicked, and the arrow swift to wound is taken from the quiver. It will strike suddenly; let every wise man avoid the blow by amending his life.'[4]

That same night, William of Malmesbury wrote, Rufus had a nightmare. In it he allowed his surgeon to let his blood, but the procedure took on a terrifying tone when the king began to see the blood form a steam that 'clouded the light, and intercepted the day'.[5] Rufus awoke with a start and called out to the Virgin Mary for protection. He ordered servants to stay with him in his room for the remainder of the night.

The next day – a Thursday – the royal hunting party started out later than usual, reports soon afterwards claiming the hard-living William Rufus was suffering not only from the fright of the nightmare, but also from a hangover that had slowed the start of his day. The king was eating with his companions, which included his brother Henry, when a blacksmith came forward with six arrows for the day's sport. Rufus is said to have kept four of these for himself while passing the other two to a French knight, Walter Tirel, with the words: 'It is only right that the sharpest arrows should be given to the man who knows how to shoot the deadliest shots.'[6]

Before setting out Rufus was allegedly handed a letter from Abbot Serlo of Gloucester, in which he warned the king about dreams that had been troubling his monks at night. Their message seemed clear: the king was soon to be punished by God for his constant abuse of the Church. Rufus laughed off Serlo's letter, then mounted his horse and steered it into the New Forest with huntsmen and companions falling in around him.

The details of what happened later that afternoon are not clear. Perhaps Walter Tirel fired the fateful arrow, though he swore even on his deathbed that he did not. But his name was quickly attached to the disaster, even after he insisted he was in another part of the forest when it occurred. 'Many people say he stumbled, got caught up in his cloak and diverted the arrow,' wrote Wace.[7]

Perhaps an arrow ricocheted off a stag or a tree. Certainly, though, William Rufus was struck by an arrow, flush in the chest. He instinctively snapped off its shaft in his hands, then fell to the ground, first onto buckled knees, before toppling forward without uttering a word. This impact drove the arrow deeper into him, killing him at once. 'A little earlier [that day],' Henry of Huntingdon reported, 'blood had been seen to bubble up from the ground in Berkshire.'[8] The sudden death of a king was such a catastrophic event that, in the medieval mind, it demanded a supernatural omen as its herald.

Henry's part in the day that changed his life for ever started with a humdrum piece of bad luck. On drawing back his bow, he had snapped its string. 'Henry took the bow in his hand and rode quickly to a peasant's lodgings in order to get twine or thread to mend his bowstring,' wrote Wace. 'While he was delayed over the mending of his bow, an old lady in the dwelling asked a youth who it was who was holding the bow and wanted to go hunting.'[9] When told it was Henry, she prophesied that he would soon be king.

Henry had returned to his brother and his companions by the time the lethal arrow struck. Stunned by what had occurred, the hunting party soon scattered. The period between the death of one king and the coronation of the next was a time of unique insecurity in the land, a vacant throne easily leading to a lawless state. Some of Rufus's lords rushed from his side to secure their possessions. Others took advantage of the temporary vacuum in royal power, hoping to seize what they could while they could.

As shown by the disrespectful way in which William the Conqueror's corpse was treated, death for a king took him from the peak of human power to the depths of undignified irrelevance at a stroke. William Rufus's servants threw a cloak over him and escorted his body from the hunting field, slung over a horse 'like a wild boar stuck with spears', before placing it in a cart.[10] The humble funeral wagon trundled through the forest towards Winchester, where Rufus was buried 'on the day after his perdition'.[11]

Henry and his attendants rode the same path to Winchester, but they were charging ahead, determined to reach the city before news of the royal tragedy got out. Winchester, the second city of England, was the home of the royal treasury, and Winchester Castle had been the repository of Norman kingly power since the year after the Conquest. Whoever controlled Winchester had one hand on the crown.

When Henry arrived, he revealed the death of his brother to incredulous ears. He stated his intention of taking the throne. William de Breteuil, an important nobleman who had ridden with him from the spot where Rufus was slain, was the only man who tried to block Henry's entry into the treasury. De Breteuil, a religious man, felt compelled to remind the prince that both of them, along with the majority of Anglo-Norman barons, had sworn homage to Robert Curthose. Also, he pointed out, Curthose was even then on his way back from the Crusade, where he had fought valiantly for God: this was a further reason, de Breteuil claimed, for submitting to him as the rightful king.

Henry drew his sword and brushed de Breteuil aside. The royal coffers were his and, the following day, Henry was declared king by the barons in Winchester. The last thing they wanted was a delay for, as Wace wrote, 'It is necessary for a kingdom to have a king, for it cannot exist without a king.'[12] The barons hoped the swift installation of Henry on the throne would bring about immediate peace and order.

Henry set off for London to be crowned in Westminster Abbey, in a ceremony combining mysticism and symbolism. Coronation was believed to confer on him the status not only of England's leader, but also that of God's representative on earth. It would make it extremely difficult for another – even his eldest brother – to challenge his right to rule. This transition, from minor princeling to anointed king of the English, was to be achieved within seventy-two hours of William Rufus's death.

So great was the hurry that there was no time to summon the archbishop of Canterbury from exile in Burgundy, or the archbishop of York from Yorkshire. Henry was crowned by Maurice, Bishop of London, a former archdeacon of Le Mans who had been chancellor of England to William the Conqueror in the later years of his reign. The new king was, from the start, eager to connect his rule to that of his late father.

Henry obeyed the traditions of English royal succession by making promises to the country that had submitted to him. His 'Coronation Charter' was a compact with his subjects that he ordered to be read out at each of England's county courts. It consisted of fourteen clauses, the thrust of which was to 'establish a firm peace in all my kingdom', to stamp out wrongdoing and to commit to the upholding of his predecessors' laws. As the chronicler and statesman Abbot Suger noted approvingly from France: 'He gladly restored order to the kingdom of England according to the law of kings of old. And to win the goodwill of his people, he confirmed by oath the ancient custom of the realm.'[13]

Eager for their support, the new king reassured his aristocrats that he would not exploit them as his late brother had done when their families were at their most vulnerable. Someone from a medieval landowning family had a life expectancy of a little over thirty years from birth. This rose to forty-five if they successfully ran the gauntlet of childhood diseases and reached the age of twenty-one. In an era of such short lives, when warfare, illness or perhaps hunting accidents could suddenly carry away even the most powerful, these were guarantees that the aristocracy craved, and felt comforted by.

Henry promised that, when an heir succeeded his father, he would no longer have to pay an exorbitant fee to the crown. Also, when the king stood as the guardian of an heiress, she would not be married off for royal gain. Instead, he promised: 'When one of my barons or other men die leaving a daughter as heir, I will not give her in marriage except according to the advice of my barons.'[14] Equally, a lord's widow would no longer be forced to take as her new husband a man chosen by the king.

Henry wanted to reconnect with the firm rule of his father, the Conqueror, who, remembered Henry of Huntingdon with a nostalgia so misty-eyed that it blurred into fantasy, 'had created such a complete peace that a young girl, laden with gold, could travel unharmed through the kingdom of England'.[15] Henry promised to reassert similar peace in the land. He wanted quickly to set out his stall as a monarch who took the duties of kingship extremely seriously. Henry knew that Curthose would never accept being passed over as the ruler of England for a second time. He would surely soon challenge hard for the crown, so Henry needed to present a brand of kingship to his lords that would stand in contrast to Curthose's dangerous incompetence in Normandy and Rufus's past failures in England.

Henry of Huntingdon noted: 'William was rightly cut off in the midst of his injustice. For in himself, and because of the counsels of wicked men, whom he invariably chose, he was more evil to his people than any man, and most evil to himself; he harassed his neighbours with wars, and his own men with frequent armies and continued gelds. England was miserably stifled and could not breathe.'[16]

Henry was determined to show that, now he was king, nobody would be above the law. He took immediate aim at Ranulf Flambard,* a son of a priest in Bayeux. Flambard had served as one of the compilers of Domesday Book, before rising to become the senior figure in Rufus's corrupt rule. He was William Rufus's chaplain, his leading administrator and (for a time) the main legal figure in the kingdom.

The all-powerful Flambard had pleased his royal master by extracting huge sums from rich and poor alike. Henry of Huntingdon wrote how Rufus's rule was a time of 'not shaving but skinning the English people with taxation and the worst exactions'.[17] Flambard had also seized wealth from the Church, and as a reward for his loyal service, Rufus had given him the wealthy bishopric of Durham. Now, in a clear indication that things had changed under the new king, the hated bishop, the embodiment of Rufus's degenerate rule, was imprisoned for corruption in the Tower of London.

Henry, eager to secure Anselm's backing for his kingship before he could support Curthose's claim, urged the exiled archbishop to return from Lyons and resume his mission in England. Henry

---

* 'Flambard' was a nickname: Archbishop Anselm would explain to the pope that it was derived from Ranulf's famed cruelty which, Anselm explained, burned like an uncontrollable flame.

promised to right the wrongs of his late brother's rule and renounced the 'evil customs' by which Rufus had helped himself to the wealth of the Church. Henry also promised to submit to the archbishop's counsel. Crucially, though, nothing else was agreed between the king and the prelate.

When Anselm arrived back in England, he found himself in a more contrary position to royal power than he had been when he had entered exile. Urban II, instigator of the First Crusade, had issued a papal decree a few months before his death in 1099. In it he determined that any layman who oversaw the investiture of a churchman, or any churchman who accepted investiture from a layman, must be excommunicated. It was the formalisation of the thoughts that Urban had stated a few years earlier: 'No priest shall perform homage to a layman, because it is unseemly that hands consecrated for God and hallowed by holy anointing should be placed between unconsecrated hands, which may belong to a murderer, or an adulterer, or one guilty of some other heinous sins.'[18]

During his time in exile Anselm had attended the papal councils of Bari and of Rome as an honoured guest, and he had fully absorbed Urban II's message as it crystallised into dogma. On his return to England Anselm found himself awkwardly placed between a papacy keen to establish the Church's independence from lay interference and a monarch who was very clear indeed about his rights. 'Your holiness should be aware that as long as I live,' Henry wrote to Urban's successor, Pope Paschal II, 'with God's help, the privileges and uses of the kingdom of England shall not be diminished.'[19] It set the stage for an investiture contest in England along the lines of the one that had pitted pope against emperor for a generation.

But Henry had pressing needs at the outset of his reign which put off the moment when either side would confront such thorny issues. One of Henry's prime duties, as king, was to produce a male heir. Another was to keep peace in his lands. The two obligations were interconnected: there could be no greater danger to harmony than a disputed succession, and no better guarantor of peace than an acknowledged ruler-in-waiting.

Henry had, by this stage, sired a dozen children out of wedlock. For his Norman ancestors, there would have been no barrier to a natural son succeeding his father. But the increasing influence of the Church in England and Normandy since the mid eleventh century had brought a renewed emphasis on the sanctity of marriage. William the Conqueror would be the last illegitimate ruler in Rollo's direct line. Henry's most urgent duty as the new king was to marry, before producing a legitimate male heir as quickly as he could.

Orderic Vitalis tried to put a heroic spin on Henry's now opting for matrimony after a particularly hectic bachelorhood, saying the king's decision stemmed from his 'not wishing to wallow in lasciviousness like any horse or mule, which is without reason'. But Henry would, in time, father many more illegitimate offspring. He was marrying not because he had suddenly been swayed by the lure of sanctified monogamy, but because he had to establish his dynasty.

Henry chose as his bride a princess of Scotland. Born in 1080 in Dunfermline, she was one of two daughters (there were also six sons) of King Malcolm III of Scotland, who was known as Malcolm 'Canmore' – an anglicisation of the Gaelic for 'Great Chief'. She had been baptised 'Edith' at a service where her godparents were Henry's eldest brother, Robert Curthose, and their mother, Matilda of Flanders. But Edith would be known as 'Matilda' – a particularly popular name in royal circles at the time – when she was Henry's queen.

Malcolm's militarily incompetent father, King Duncan, had been killed in battle. His successor Macbeth, the earl of Moray, had ruled as king for seventeen years, with a wisdom and touch far removed from Shakespeare's dark, fictionalised, neurotic. The real-life Macbeth was a devout Christian who attended a papal jubilee in Rome in 1050. Undertaking such an ambitious expedition showed great confidence in the security of his rule back home. He took significant wealth with him to Rome, impressing onlookers with the amount of alms he doled out to the poor. As king, Macbeth insisted on enlightened measures, such as the legal defence of widows and orphans. He governed with a firm hand that ensured order, and he led successful forays over the border into England. His strength of purpose and his vision helped to bring prosperity to his people.

But Malcolm Canmore successfully lobbied the papacy and the English to support him in his bid to become king. After three years of defensive fighting against Malcolm and his English allies, Macbeth was toppled at the Battle of Lumphanan, in north-east Scotland. With defeat certain, Macbeth made a last stand, before being overwhelmed. Near the battlefield is a rock, where Macbeth is said to have been dragged for beheading.

Malcolm Canmore would reign for thirty-five years, before the cycle of violence in Scotland eventually caught up with him. In 1091 he had submitted to William Rufus (just as he had to the Conqueror, in 1072). Two years later he advanced into England to ask why the conditions of his submission had not been honoured by the English king. Malcolm and his son Edward were returning north, still dismayed at Rufus's deceit, when they were caught in an ambush at Alnwick, in Northumbria, and killed.

But, Malcolm's lineage aside, it was Matilda's mother, Margaret, who made her such an enticing match for Henry. Margaret was from the English, West Saxon, royal family that descended through Alfred the Great, all the way back to Cerdic, the sixth-century king of Wessex. Margaret's great-uncle was Edward the Confessor, while her grandfather had been Edmund Ironside, king of England in 1016 until defeat by Cnut cost him half his territory, then – when accosted by an assassin while on his privy – his life.

Margaret's father was Edward the Exile, so called because he was driven out of England after Edmund Ironside's subsequent murder left the entire kingdom in Cnut's hands. Edward was only a few months old when forced to leave. Margaret's brother, Edgar Ætheling, was the teenager who had been proclaimed king by the English Witan after the death of Harold at Hastings. His hopes had come to nothing, though, when William the Conqueror was instead crowned at the end of 1066.

Margaret had been born in Hungary in 1045 during her family's years in exile. She married Malcolm Canmore after her family was shipwrecked on the Scottish coast. The queen was respected for her deep personal piety, sustained in part by her gold-lettered copies of the Gospels. William of Malmesbury noted that Margaret would hear Matins three times a day during Lent, and he claimed that she could recite many of the Psalms from memory. She fasted frequently, gave alms to the poor, championed the protection of orphans and insisted that prisoners be treated humanely. Such Christian devotion would see her canonised two centuries later.

Margaret became gravely ill in November 1093, on hearing of the slaying of her husband and their son Edward. 'Immediately summoning priests,' recorded John of Worcester, 'she went into church, confessed her sins to them, and caused herself to be anointed with oil, and to be strengthened by the holy viaticum.'[20] Then, broken-hearted, she died.

By the age of thirteen, Matilda had therefore been both an orphan and an exile. The *Anglo-Saxon Chronicle* noted that Henry's bride was 'of the true royal family of England'.[21] The prospect of her marrying the king reminded people of the famous deathbed vision of Edward the Confessor. In it he had been warned by two ethereal figures that his kingdom would face great trials in the years ahead. England would only be healed, they said, 'when a green tree, if cut down in the middle of its trunk, and the part cut off carried the space of three furlongs from the stock, shall be joined again to the trunk, by itself and without the hand of man or any sort of stake, and begin once more to push leaves and bear fruit from the old love of its uniting sap'.

One interpretation of this scene gained popularity: it was hoped that the recovery of England, after the protracted trauma of the Norman Conquest, would stem from the marriage of the princess with such an ancient English bloodline to the king descended from warriors of the renown of Rollo, Longsword and the Conqueror.

Although a dynastic marriage, the couple were eager participants. Eadmer observed that they were 'in love', while Orderic Vitalis wrote that Henry had 'long adored' Matilda's 'perfection of character'. Another commentator noted that Matilda was 'not despicable in point of beauty'. But the choice of Matilda as royal bride had its difficulties. On being returned to England in her youth she had been educated at convents at Romsey – under the protection of her aunt Cristina, who was a nun there – and then Wilton. The question arose as to whether she had taken the veil while attending either religious house. If she had ever made her vows to God, she could never marry.

When Matilda understood that she might be blocked from becoming Henry's wife, she appealed to Anselm for help. She explained that she had only worn 'a little black hood' at her aunt's insistence, to protect her from the lust of marauding Normans. 'And when I threw it off,' Matilda protested, her aunt 'would often make me smart with a good beating and a most horrible scolding'.

Archbishop Anselm ordered an investigation, the findings of

which were to be considered by an assembly of leading churchmen and barons at Lambeth. Reports came back confirming that Matilda had not taken the veil, although she had worn one once – when the notorious Alan of Richmond had heard where she was and come to inspect her as a potential bride. To save her teenaged niece from Richmond's unwanted advances, Cristina had disguised Matilda as a nun until he was safely on his way.

Anselm appears to have been sceptical about Matilda's eligibility for marriage, but it was not an issue over which he was prepared to risk his budding relationship with the new king. The archbishop led the marriage ceremony of Henry and Matilda in Westminster Abbey at the end of 1100, less than four months after Henry became king.

FIVE

Consolidation

There will come to the throne a lion of justice. At his roar the
Gallic towers and the Dragons of the island will tremble. In his
day gold will be squeezed from the lily and the nettle, and silver
from the hooves of mooing cattle.

From *The Prophecy of Merlin*, a twelfth-century poem

Henry's successful capture of the throne had been achieved
through many powerful figures quickly agreeing to swear
allegiance to him because he represented an alternative to chaos.
This was particularly relevant while Robert Curthose was still
away on Crusade. But, a few weeks into Henry's reign, his eldest
brother returned from the Holy Land, and he did so with his
reputation glowing.

Henry of Huntingdon was among the contemporary chroniclers who celebrated Curthose's military achievements, recording
how, in 1098, while fighting near Antioch, 'With his sword the
duke of the Normans split open one man's head, teeth, neck,
and shoulders, down to his breast.'[1] Another story circulated of
Curthose striking a Turk so perfectly with his lance that it went

straight through the enemy's shield, and body. Such tales probably owe as much to idealisation as to fact: this was how a Norman prince, coursing with Viking blood, was meant to conduct himself in battle.

Curthose had led his force with distinction, and had fought bravely, in the campaign of 1099. He was present at the capture of Jerusalem by the Christian forces in mid-July, after a thirty-eight-day siege. But nowhere was Curthose's personal courage more noteworthy than at the subsequent Battle of Ascalon, the last major engagement of the First Crusade.

A month after Jerusalem's fall twenty thousand Muslims set out in an attempt to reclaim the city and avenge the subsequent slaughter of their people. Despite being outnumbered by two to one, the Crusaders rode out to meet the enemy at Ascalon. Curthose, one of the commanders of the Crusader centre, made out the standard of the emir facing him across the battlefield: it had a golden apple atop its gleaming silver pole. After both sides had fired thick volleys of arrows to open the engagement, Curthose rode forward, slashing his sword as he drove deep into the enemy ranks. He eventually reached his opposing general and gave him a fatal wound. After this great victory against the odds, when nearly thirteen thousand Muslims lay dead, Curthose retrieved the emir's standard and laid it in tribute beside Jesus's sepulchre in Jerusalem.

Such episodes of Crusader gallantry were quickly recounted across Europe. Wace recorded how, during his time in the Holy Land, Curthose 'received great renown and great honour; many people spoke of him'.[2] The Normans were proud to see their leader finally bringing esteem to their name. 'Duke Robert returned to Normandy in the month of August,' Henry of Huntingdon noted, 'and was joyfully received by all the people.'[3] For now, his subjects were prepared to forget Curthose's past failings as a ruler and welcome him back as a Christian, military, hero.

The duke had left for the Holy Land impoverished, but now he had the wherewithal to mount a proper challenge against his brother. For, on his journey to and from the Crusades, Curthose had passed through Norman-held lands in southern Italy. He had stayed as a guest of Geoffrey of Conversano, a Norman-born count whose landholdings in Apulia included Bari and Brindisi. On the outward journey, Curthose had met and contracted to marry Geoffrey's daughter, Sibylla, and he wed her three and a half years later on his return. The duke was in his late forties while Sibylla was around twenty-one and, wrote Wace, 'a great deal was said about her beauty in many places'.[4] She also represented wealth for Curthose, for her hand in marriage was accompanied by a lavish dowry – William of Malmesbury called it 'an immense sum'.

As Henry had anticipated, Curthose was furious that he had again been passed over for the English throne. On returning to Normandy he immediately reminded his magnates of the homage they had sworn him before his departure and demanded that they help unseat his usurper in England.

Curthose's plans were helped by the first ever escapee from the Tower of London: Ranulf Flambard. Liberally provided for in his captivity by Henry, Flambard encouraged his guards to share the barrel of wine delivered to his quarters one evening. They knocked back so much alcohol that they eventually fell into a drunken stupor. Flambard let himself down the Tower walls with a rope that is said to have been smuggled to him inside the same barrel of wine that had incapacitated his guards.

While the rope was strong enough to support his weight, it turned out to be shorter than Flambard required. The disgraced bishop fell the last part of his descent, hurting himself as he landed. But his waiting men dusted him down and spirited him away to Normandy, where he presented himself as a willing avenger, ready to mastermind the destruction of King Henry.

While Curthose had various powerful lords ready to fight for him, they tended to be as addicted to idle pleasure as he was. In Flambard he had the brains to turn aggressive intent into a focused plan.

Flambard set about organising a new invasion of England from Normandy in 1101. Henry seemed to have little hope: his powerful friend, Hugh, Earl of Chester, who had encouraged Henry to make a stand against his brothers in Mont Saint-Michel a decade or so before, was mortally ill. They had been close since 1090. Although loyal to William Rufus as his anointed king, Hugh had also discreetly supported Henry when he was a landless prince. And the family connection went back further – Hugh's father had supplied sixty longships to Henry's father, William the Conqueror, for his 1066 invasion fleet.

Hugh was remembered as 'a great lover of the world and of worldly pomp . . . always in the forefront in battle, lavish to the point of prodigality, a lover of games and luxuries, actors, horses, and dogs and other vanities'.[5] Food was another of the earl's great loves, which had led to his nickname of 'Hugh the Fat'. He was such a slave to fine cuisine that he rewarded his head cook with the tenancy of two manors. By his mid-forties Hugh was of such a size that, contemporaries noted, he could barely walk. Spent as a military force and as a man, the earl retreated to the abbey he had established in Chester, became a monk there and died in early July.

Other formidable lords who had pledged their allegiance to Henry at the time of his coronation declared for Curthose. Among these was the cruel and erratic Robert de Bellême. He had rushed to swear his homage to Henry the previous year, but now he went back on his word. De Bellême was not alone. William of Malmesbury noted that 'almost all the nobility of this country violated the fealty they had sworn to the king, some without cause, some feigning slight pretence'.[6] Henry of

Huntingdon agreed that 'the leading men of England were roused up against the king, in support of his brother Robert, who was approaching with an army'.[7] Many of Curthose's supporters were kicking themselves for having supported Henry's coronation so impetuously.

Henry felt his best hope lay in sending out a fleet to intercept his brother's forces before they could land on English soil. But many of Henry's ships submitted to Curthose without a fight.

Now Henry's careful courting of Anselm paid dividends. The archbishop stepped forward, insisting that Henry was the rightful occupant of the throne, who must be supported against the invaders. The archbishop reminded the lords that their allegiance to the king was a holy bond and to renege on it would result in their excommunication. Anselm also threatened to excommunicate Curthose, while supporting the deposition of Ranulf Flambard from the bishopric of Durham. Eadmer was correct to write that, without Anselm's support, 'King Henry would at that time have lost the English throne.'[8]

With his reign still so fresh, and his reputation yet to be established, Henry learned that Curthose and his army had landed at Portchester, just north-west of Portsmouth, on 20 July 1101. Even with Anselm as his cheerleader, Henry's prospects looked bleak.

Curthose had intended to strike at Winchester, the administrative and financial heart of Henry's fledgling regime. However, according to Wace, the duke was advised that his sister-in-law Matilda, Henry's wife, was confined there while expecting a child, so he swung his invasion force towards London, hoping to engage his brother in battle. But at this crucial point Curthose discovered that his interests were at odds with those of his nobles.

While the king had many fewer supporters among the senior ranks of the aristocracy than he would have wanted, his immense wealth meant he had still been able to amass a substantial army, with a strong mercenary contingent, against the invaders. If battle were joined a bloodbath was certain.

'The barons realised that things were going badly,' Wace recorded, 'that relative would be killing relative, cousin cousin, and brother brother, and a son his father. They all made up their minds that they would act quite differently, and bring about peace between the brothers and never fight for them.'[9] As the two armies approached one another, at Alton in north-east Hampshire, the lords on both sides told Curthose and Henry not to fight, but to negotiate.

The brothers met and agreed a compromise that was then attested to by a dozen barons from either army. The Treaty of Alton was signed on 2 August 1101, a year to the day after Rufus's death. It brought about peace, as Curthose renounced his claim to the English crown and recognised Henry as its true wearer. For his part Curthose received a share of those English riches that he was otherwise forfeiting. He would be given an annual tribute of three thousand marks of silver. Henry also surrendered all his Norman possessions other than Domfront, whose lord he had sworn to be for ever and which he would never allow to be up for negotiation. The brothers formed a defensive pact, promising to provide one another with a hundred knights in case of attack by a third party. Looking to the future, it was agreed that if either died before producing a legitimate male heir, the survivor's son would rule both England and Normandy unchallenged.

This tidied up the conflicting loyalties of the Anglo-Norman nobility quite helpfully: the Channel formed the dividing line, as it had before 1066; but plans were in place for England and Normandy to be reunited one day, should either of the Conqueror's remaining sons fail to provide a successor. Satisfied, Curthose sailed back to Normandy.

Henry was confirmed in his kingship, but he had no intention of obeying the Treaty of Alton. 'Soothe them with promises,' advised Robert de Beaumont, Count de Meulan, who had been one of William the Conqueror's stalwarts. Once they were pacified, he suggested, Henry's enemies could be caught off guard and be 'driven into exile'.[10]

Henry was aware that the most immediate threat to his rule came from unreliable elements in the upper nobility. Most of his leading aristocrats also held ancestral estates in Normandy. Even if they swore loyalty to him for their English possessions, they remained vassals of his brother in Normandy. Their loyalties were consequently divided in two.

Henry realised early in his reign that, if he was to have peace in England, he must promote those barons who were dependable and weed out those whose allegiance was rooted in sand. The chronicler Eadmer quotes Henry stating this fundamental aim in a clear voice: 'I am not willing . . . to tolerate anyone in my kingdom who is not my man.'[11]

Firmly in Henry's sights was Robert de Bellême, whose enmity Henry had earned when the people of Domfront had replaced him with Henry as their lord, in 1092. Since then de Bellême's already considerable wealth and power had grown enormously. He had inherited all the Norman lands of his father, Roger de Montgomery, on his death in 1094. These lay in a lavish garland a hundred miles or so to the west of Paris. De Bellême had also succeeded in impressing Rufus in warfare, capturing Elias, Count of Maine, and at the same time seizing the key city of Le Mans for the English king. De Bellême obeyed Rufus's instruction to protect the Norman Vexin from French incursions, too. In 1095 he had designed and built the first castle to stand at Gisors, its location and construction revealing its creator's keen understanding of military requirements and architecture.

In a move that had become increasingly common among the Anglo-Norman aristocracy in the years since the death of the Conqueror, Roger de Montgomery had left the extensive English territories gained in his lifetime to his second surviving son, Hugh. Hugh had succeeded his father as earl of Shrewsbury, and he spent the next four years performing the duties that went with the title, defending England from foreign aggressors on its western flank.

In 1098 Hugh seized an elderly priest, Cenned, who Welsh rebels looked to as a wise sounding board when devising their tactics against the English. At Hugh's command Cenned was taken from the sanctuary of his church and terribly mutilated: he was castrated, had one eye removed and had his tongue cut out. A week later Hugh of Shrewsbury rushed to fend off a daring raid on the island of Anglesey. This was mounted by Magnus Barefoot, King of Norway, supported by Harold Haroldson, a son of the Anglo-Saxon monarch slain at the Battle of Hastings. The Norwegians had welcomed the landless Haroldson in gratitude for his father sparing Hardrada's son after the slaughter of Stamford Bridge.

While Hugh was riding through the surf, an arrow fired by Magnus went clean through the eye-slit in his helmet. 'He fell like a stone,' recorded Orderic Vitalis, 'and breathed his last in the waves of the tossing sea.'[12] Many believed this end was fitting reward for having so brutally maimed the priest, Cenned.

Since Hugh died childless, his title and lands were meant to pass to a younger brother. But Robert de Bellême swooped in to steal the inheritance, so consolidating the fortunes and territories of both his parents. De Bellême's English estates alone gave him the astonishing income of £2,430 per year. (The mighty Hugh, Earl of Chester, received just a third of that.) Henry knew well enough that he could never rely on de Bellême, and that he was a very powerful man to have as an enemy, even for a king.

In his growing resistance to Henry, de Bellême had the support of two of his brothers, Roger the Poitevin and Arnulf de Montgomery, each of whom had profited greatly from the favour that William Rufus showered on their family. Roger was lord of a swathe of northern England that covered much of the land between the River Ribble and Cumbria. He had earned further landholdings in East Anglia (including the important feudal lordship of Eye in Suffolk), as well as in three Midlands counties, and in Hampshire. Roger had also, as his full name reveals, extended his influence across the Channel, through marriage to an heiress to the lord of Poitou, in west-central France.

Arnulf, born at the time of the Conquest, the youngest of the six sons born to Roger de Montgomery, had defied his junior position in the family to build up impressive power and status. In his early twenties he had joined his brother Robert in building a castle in Pembroke, to extend royal control into that part of west Wales. Rufus made him lord of Pembroke as a reward, and further repaid Arnulf for his military efforts with great estates in Yorkshire and Lincolnshire, as well as lands in south-west Wales taken from the former kingdom of Deheubarth. Arnulf was readily accepted as a son-in-law by Muircheartach Ua Briain, king of Munster and Leinster, who was by some distance the most powerful ruler in Ireland.

All in all, the de Bellêmes were, at this time, one of the most important families in Europe not to be occupying a throne. The Treaty of Alton had drawn an end to Robert Curthose's invasion of England in 1101, but Henry remained determined, after such a threat to his rule, to terminate de Bellême's power in England.

When de Bellême built a castle at Bridgnorth, in Shropshire, without obtaining a royal licence, Henry struck. Such open contempt for the king's sovereignty was a terrible crime, and it is testimony to de Bellême's arrogance (and to his low regard for Henry) that he pushed ahead with the construction anyway. Henry took a year carefully to compile his case against de Bellême before catching him off guard with a list of forty-five offences that he had committed against the crown. In the face of this unanswerable legal onslaught, de Bellême withdrew and prepared for military action.

He called on his two brothers to help. Their ranks were swollen by Scandinavian mercenaries, ferried over from Ireland, and by forces from Welsh rulers who still bucked at the notion of Norman rule. But few Anglo-Norman barons cared for de Bellême, and plenty regarded him with fear and hatred because of his unspeakable cruelty.

Henry acted with correctness from the beginning, pointing at de Bellême's long list of crimes and insisting he answer the summons issued in his name. De Bellême refused to obey, and it was then that Henry resorted to force. The king set sieges in train, with the de Bellêmes' southern stronghold of Arundel the first to fall, in April 1102, after three months' resistance.

Over the next five months, another three de Bellême castles capitulated in Yorkshire and Shropshire. Henry deployed his wealth as cannily as his weaponry, strategic bribes buying off the Welshmen who had assisted the rebel brothers. When Henry next marched into his stronghold of Shrewsbury, Robert de Bellême recognised that the game was up. He was reduced to appearing in person, humiliated and defeated, and handing over his castle's keys. This was an act of total submission.

Henry cast de Bellême and his brothers into perpetual exile, allowing them safe passage to Normandy, while confiscating their English estates. It was an astonishing reversal for such a mighty family. The rest of the Anglo-Norman barons realised that if this could happen to the most powerful of their number, then it could happen to them, too.

Orderic Vitalis wrote of the reaction to Robert de Bellême's fall: 'All England rejoiced as the cruel tyrant went into exile, and many flatteringly congratulated King Henry, saying,

"Rejoice, King Henry! Give thanks to the Lord God, for you have begun to rule freely now that you have conquered Robert de Bellême and driven him out of the kingdom.'"[13]

Within four years of Henry's accession, the great lords of England had learned to be loyal to him. For the rest of his reign, no one would rebel, or hold a castle, against the crown.

Despite the commitment Henry made at the Treaty of Alton to stay on his side of the Channel, he was intrigued by possibilities in Normandy as the excitement at Robert Curthose's Crusade heroics ebbed away.

An early disappointment to Curthose's people came when he failed to hold on to Le Mans, after it was attacked by the counts of Maine and Anjou. His beleaguered garrison there sent to him for urgent reinforcements. But, to general astonishment, the duke replied that he was 'worn out with the toils of pilgrimage, and more desirous to go to bed than to go to war again'. He recommended his troops make their peace with Elias of Maine rather than fight on, as he had enough to do in Normandy.

The arrival in the duchy of Robert de Bellême after his exile from England brought with it a further undermining of ducal authority. De Bellême was a toxic export, one Curthose had neither the power nor the ability to contain and control. Henry watched his brother's hold on Normandy quickly loosen, and it was not long before he had an excuse to meddle directly in the dukedom.

When one of Curthose's principal followers, William de Breteuil, died in 1102, he left behind no legitimate male heir. This led to his illegitimate son Eustace de Pacy competing for his vast landholdings with de Breteuil's nephews. One of these, Reginald of Grancey, gained a reputation for cruelty that rivalled that of de Bellême: after seizing one of Eustace's strongholds, Reginald had his prisoners of war lined up, then ran his sword through each of them in turn.

Eustace sent to Henry in England, asking for help. The king gave him not only troops, but also one of his natural daughters to marry: Juliana de Fontevrault, Henry's thirteen-year-old child by one of his many mistresses. Such a union, Henry hoped, would secure this corner of Normandy for him, not his brother. This wedding took place at much the same time as another of Henry's illegitimate daughters, Matilda, married an even more important figure for the security of the dukedom, Rotrou III, Count of Perche.

The thickly wooded Perche was a key strategic region just to the south of Normandy. Its neighbours were the counties of Maine and Chartres, as well as the Île-de-France – that power base of the kings of France, who were so frequently at odds with the dukes of Normandy. Perche had maintained its independence thanks to the power and military ability of its ruling family, a tradition continued by Matilda's husband. He had led a battle-hardened life of such renown that he became known as 'Rotrou the Great'.

In his late teens Rotrou had joined the First Crusade, fighting with distinction. During the siege of Antioch, in 1098, he was among the first to scale the city walls by ladder. His further feats, including a heroic role at the Battle of Nicaea, were celebrated in verse. He reached Jerusalem, from where he carried home the frond of a palm tree. This he laid on the altar of a monastery founded by his family. It is believed that he also brought back from the Crusade some Arab horses, which he crossed with those found in his native county. This led to the establishment of the Percheron breed, a form of draught horse that still exists today.

Henry had been pleased to approve Matilda's marriage to this well-placed warrior, who was a bitter enemy of Robert de Bellême and lord of a land from which Henry could mount an attack on Normandy or France. In turn Henry added to Rotrou's Norman power base. But the building of a web of power through illegitimate offspring could hardly compare to the calming effect of producing a true heir to the throne of England. The fallback clause of the Treaty of Alton, whereby Henry would inherit Normandy if his brother had no legitimate male heir, fell away in late October 1102.

Robert Curthose had at least three illegitimate children during his rebellious youth, when he was fighting against his father near the border between France and Normandy. One of his lovers from that time, 'the beautiful concubine of an old priest', came forward many years later with two sons, named Richard and William.[14] She claimed that Curthose was their father and asked him to provide for them both. While Curthose remembered the woman, and their affair, he was sceptical as to whether the young men were his offspring. He insisted she be tested to determine if she was telling the truth. She agreed to undertake an ordeal, which would involve her carrying a red-hot iron in her hand, in front of priests and people.[15] If she could do this without injury, God would be seen to have supported her assertion.

Curthose's former lover completed the ordeal, then showed her hand, which apparently bore no scars from the scalding heat. Curthose accepted the duo as his sons, and they became prominent knights. Orderic Vitalis would later note that they were both 'brave and likeable'.[16]

Curthose also had a natural daughter, whose name is lost to history. She was married to Helias of Saint-Saëns, a powerful Norman baron who received as dowry the county of Arques, which the Conqueror had confiscated from the rebellious uncle who he had cast into perpetual exile half a century earlier.

But a legitimate heir followed.

Despite Sibylla of Conversano's famed beauty, Curthose had sworn to delay consummating his marriage with her until he had had the opportunity to give thanks to God, at Mont Saint-Michel, for his safe return from the Crusade. She proved to be an impressive consort to Curthose, noted for her cleverness: the chronicler Robert de Torigni, writing a generation later, believed that during the duke's absences she administered Normandy with a steadier hand than her husband ever had. Orderic Vitalis, who was withering in his assessment of Curthose, wrote of Sibylla that she was 'endowed with many virtues, and was lovable to all who knew her'.

Sibylla fulfilled her primary dynastic duty, at Rouen on 25 October 1102, when she gave birth to a boy. Curthose gave his son the name of his own father, William, realising how positively it would resonate with the people of Normandy, despite his own battles with the Conqueror. The newborn's status as Curthose's legitimate heir was made clear in the name by which he would always be known, William Clito – 'Clito' being the Norman name for a prince of ducal blood who was eligible to reign after his father.

With William Clito's arrival, Henry and his line were blocked from succeeding to Normandy, while Henry's lack of a son at this time marked William Clito down as the heir presumptive to England.

Clito would remain an only child. Sibylla died in Rouen five months after giving birth. There are two theories as to her cause of death. Orderic Vitalis and Robert de Torigni wrote that Sibylla was poisoned and suggested the culprit was Curthose's mistress, Agnes Giffard, who found herself free to marry the duke following the sudden loss of her own husband. However, Sibylla's end may rather have been the result of an innocent mistake brought about by medical ignorance: it was said that her breasts had been tied too tight by a midwife, causing a fatal infection. William of Malmesbury referred to this when he recorded that she died 'by disease'.

However she may have perished, Sibylla left behind in Clito a pungent legacy. Her son would dictate Henry's foreign policy for the next two decades, acting as a lightning rod for all who opposed the king of England. This, despite Henry at last fathering his own longed-for heir.

SIX

The Heir

He was the only son of the king and queen and had no doubt
that he would be raised to the crown.
William of Malmesbury, Anglo-Norman historian and monk
(c.1095–c.1143), writing about William Ætheling

In 1103, the year after William Clito's birth, Henry and his
queen Matilda welcomed the arrival of their own firstborn
son. He too was christened William after his grandfather the
Conqueror. He was also given a suffix to his first name –
'Ætheling' – that marked him out as eligible for succession to
his father: it was the Anglo-Saxon equivalent of Clito.

Henry and Queen Matilda had already produced a daughter,
Matilda, who was born either in Winchester or in Sutton
Courtenay, near Abingdon, in early February 1102. Perhaps before
her the king and queen had another daughter, who was referred
to by some chroniclers: if that child did exist, it was only for a
very short time, or perhaps she was stillborn.

William Ætheling was born, probably in Winchester, at some
point in the late summer or in the autumn of 1103: Pope Paschal

II wrote to congratulate Henry on the arrival of his heir on 23 November that year, presumably soon after news of the significant birth reached him from England. The *Anglo-Saxon Chronicle* refers to William Ætheling as 'the king's son'. There were many others of those by this time, but William was the only one to be born in wedlock.

William Ætheling entered the world when his father was at loggerheads with his archbishop of Canterbury. Henry and Anselm found that their equally firm but opposing views on the question of investiture had quickly derailed their relationship. In 1102 Anselm had convened the Church Council of London, where he set out his intention to instigate papal reforms throughout England. As well as attacking the sale of ecclesiastical offices and the marrying of priests, Anselm targeted the sodomy, drunkenness and slovenly dress that he was disappointed to find flourishing among the English priesthood.

But it was the intertwined question of lay investiture and feudal homage that caused the split between Henry and Anselm. When the archbishop departed on an expedition to the pope in 1103, which led to Paschal II excommunicating three bishops who Henry had installed, the king blocked Anselm's return to England. The prelate retreated to Lyons to await the pope's instructions on how to react to this, his second exile.

In Anselm's enforced absence William Ætheling was baptised by Gundulf, Bishop of Rochester. In his late seventies, Gundulf was a former monk, who was a favourite cleric of the queen. He also had a gift for architecture: he had designed the White Tower – the keep at the Tower of London – as well as Colchester Castle, for William the Conqueror. This man who was both a bishop and the first ever King's Engineer performed his spiritual role at William Ætheling's baptism, conducting the service as well as taking on the duties of godfather to the prince.

Henry adored William, the son who represented the future,

and treated him with what William of Malmesbury called 'the prudence of [a] truly careful father'.[1] The prince's guardian was Otuel FitzEarl, illegitimate son of the powerful Hugh, Earl of Chester, who was also a confidant of the king: Otuel's signature is visible on important charters from 1114 – when he acted as witness to a significant royal grant of land – onwards.

Otuel was tasked with overseeing William's general education – some school learning, an understanding of good manners and a mastery of the skills of the battlefield. Some of the lessons would have taken place in the Tower of London, the pivot of Norman power in England, where Otuel was castellan.

The king had every hope that the boy would build on his efforts and, in time, perpetuate his dynasty. It had soon become clear that William Ætheling would be the only son of the royal marriage. William of Malmesbury wrote that 'satisfied with a child of either sex, [the queen] ceased having issue'. It was rumoured that Matilda chose a life of celibacy as soon as her queenly, maternal duties were completed. Perhaps this suited Henry, as he looked at the way that he and his royal brothers had spent much of their time at one another's throats: a single legitimate male successor must have seemed a tidy and sensible way forward, by comparison, if he could be kept safe until in time producing his own heir.

Matilda and Henry lived separately, the queen choosing to base herself at Westminster, her court a place of understated pomp, with learning and culture at its heart. Writers, poets and musicians enjoyed the queen's patronage: William of Malmesbury, one of the most learned men of the early twelfth century, began to write *Deeds of the Kings of the English* at her invitation.

Matilda devoted herself to various innovations and good works. The most famous of these was the establishment, in 1101, of a leper hospital at St Giles-in-the-Fields, which then lay on the road between London and Tyburn. It was founded out of the queen's sincere compassion. Her brother David, who had joined the English court as a teenaged Scottish prince the preceding year, recalled witnessing Matilda cleaning lepers' feet, before holding them tight and kissing them on their lesions. She invited David to join her in doing Christ's work in this way, but he recoiled in horror.

Matilda provided the capital with its first public lavatories, and with a bath house for the poor. She built bridges over rivers on roads approaching London, including two at Stratford, to the east of the city, near a spot on the River Lea where she liked to bathe. The larger of these had a single arch which was of a new design for England, and people soon referred to this place as 'Stratford-le-Bow', 'because the bridge was arched like unto a bow'.[2] The other, over a small brook, was called Chanelse (now Channelsea) Bridge. Matilda connected the two by a gravel road, and she gave some manors and Wiggen Mill to the Abbess of Barking to pay for the upkeep of both bridges and their walls in perpetuity. She built another bridge over the River Mole at Cobham, to the south-west of the capital.

To help provide her with an income the queen was given a busy quay in an ancient part of the City of London. Its use goes back to Roman times, but its nine-hundred-year-old association with Matilda is recalled in its name to date, 'Queenhithe'. An important stop off for the corn trade, it provided a revenue that helped Matilda to build yet more. With Anselm's guidance and help, in 1108 she founded a priory in Aldgate on London's eastern perimeter.

While Matilda lived a pious life of self-denial, on her own terms, her husband pursued his political and military ambitions, as well as a bevy of mistresses dotted around his lands. Henry was quick to claim fatherhood to his many illegitimate offspring (there would eventually be twenty-two of them) even though they could have no prospect of ever succeeding to the English throne. The spreading influence of the Church had affected the domestic arrangements of all, including priests and princes, setting bastard stock in a separate, inferior category to children born in wedlock.

Richard of Lincoln's birth was a result of his father's affair with an English widow called Ansfride. She lived in Berkshire and was, according to William of Malmesbury, 'of no rank'. She lost her husband after he was roughly handled while a prisoner in one of William Rufus's jails. Henry was, it was noted, keen 'to support her in her troubles'.[3] His close attention resulted in three children altogether, with Richard of Lincoln appearing in 1100, in the months before Henry became king.

Richard would be well educated, becoming in Malmesbury's eyes 'a youth of intrepidity, and dear to his father for his obedience'.[4] As a boy he shared a classroom with Henry of Huntingdon, who would become one of the great chroniclers of twelfth-century England. Richard was brought up in the household of Robert Bloet, who had served as a clerk to the Conqueror. In 1087 Bloet had performed his final duty for that master, crossing from Normandy to England with William Rufus, bearing the deathbed letter ordering Lanfranc to confer on Rufus the English crown. Bloet had then briefly served as Rufus's chancellor before in 1093 becoming bishop of Lincoln, a position he would hold for thirty years. Despite his holy office, Bloet was known for his rampant promiscuity and his unrestrained enjoyment of the good things in life. Some of his extravagance and taste are still visible at Lincoln Cathedral, to which he devoted a slice of his great personal fortune. Richard was one of a number of young aristocrats who found a vibrant home under Bloet, a man who Henry trusted and enjoyed in equal measure.

Robert FitzRoy was Henry's oldest illegitimate son. There is no definite record of who his mother was, or when or where he was born. However, it seems probable that she was of Norman rather than English birth, given the weight of contemporary references (the generally reliable Orderic Vitalis refers to Robert as being 'of Caen'), and the known whereabouts of his father during 1089–91, the period when he was most likely conceived. At no point in those years was Henry in England.

That background would explain his Christian name too, for this was one of the brief interludes in adulthood when Henry and his eldest brother Robert were on good terms. It is hard to imagine Henry giving such a compliment to his brother when at odds (or, indeed, at war) with him. It may also be significant that when Robert FitzRoy founded a church in Bristol, he dedicated it to St Ouen, a seventh-century saint who had been bishop of Rouen and who remained popular in the Normandy of Robert's lifetime. On balance, the probability is that his mother was Norman, but we cannot be sure.

Otuel, William Ætheling's guardian, had previously served as Robert FitzRoy's tutor. Robert proved to be a willing and able student as a young man, particularly accomplished in reading and writing, and with an appetite and a gift for the skills of warfare.

Robert FitzRoy and Richard of Lincoln were each acknowledged as *filius regis* – a son of the king – and as such were considered active members of the royal family. Their signatures as witnesses on important crown documents from 1113 onwards show how publicly their father valued their presence and support. But they were limited to supporting roles, while their sole legitimate half-brother was destined for centre stage.

William of Malmesbury noted how William Ætheling, 'a youth of delicate habit', was prepared for his future 'with fond hope and immense care'. Henry brought him into the business of kingship at an early age: he was also witnessing his father's royal edicts from 1113, after he had just turned ten years old. When twelve, 'all the free men of England and Normandy, of every rank and condition, and under fealty to whatever lord, were obliged to submit themselves [to William] by homage, and by oath'.[5]

Wace, writing fifty years later, spoke of William Ætheling as an obedient son, with the princely virtue of big-heartedness: 'William, Henry's son, gave and spent generously and dwelt with his father, who loved him very much. He did what his father asked and avoided what his father forbade.' As a result of his position at the very pinnacle of society, his love of fine things, and his glamour, 'the flower of chivalry from England and Normandy set about serving him and had great hopes of him'.[6]

There were other, less generous assessments of William Ætheling at the time. These spoke of a princely sense of entitlement and startling arrogance. It was claimed that he thought of his father's Anglo-Saxon subjects as naturally inferior to the Normans, and some said the prince had boasted that 'he would bend the necks of the Saxons to the plough, and treat them like beasts of burden' when he became king.[7]

While William Ætheling represented the future in England, and William Clito mirrored his purpose in Normandy, the two princes' fathers faced each other with increasing animosity. Divided loyalties on both sides of the Channel kept the tension between Henry and Curthose high. Wace calculated that 'through traitors and slanderers, flatterers and deceivers – may they take a tumble! – the king's and the duke's anger increased'.[8]

Henry of Huntingdon recorded how 'the king and his brother [Curthose] were at odds over several matters. So the king sent soldiers into Normandy, who were received by those who were plotting against the duke, and they caused considerable damage to the duke's property by plundering and burning.'[9] Henry himself travelled to Normandy in 1104 to challenge Curthose, pointing at the disaffection in the family dukedom brought about by his elder brother's weak and rudderless rule. The king contrasted the turmoil in Normandy with the order enjoyed in England, thanks to his strong governance.

Henry was welcomed by many of the barons, including Rotrou, Count of Perche, who had recently become his son-in-law. Increasing numbers of Norman lords became convinced that the purposeful English king represented an attractive alternative to the lazy spendthrift who had been foisted on them by the Conqueror's deathbed concession. Curthose's Crusader heroics were, by now, merely a memory.

Encouraged by the reaction to his reconnoitring the year before, Henry 'crossed to Normandy to make war on his brother' in the spring of 1105.[10] The contrast in the finances of the brothers was stark. Wace noted how Henry arrived in the duchy with a large number of men, and he had so many chests of coins that 'with great barrels and carts he had the money carried with him'.[11] Mercenaries flocked to the king from Maine, Brittany and Anjou. Meanwhile Curthose struggled to pay or feed his men. When they tired of this, many of his mercenaries crossed over to Henry and his dependable paymasters, leaving the duke's dwindling band of loyal knights disgruntled. As Henry's prospects improved, so more and more barons fell in behind him.

One of those who Henry could now call on was William de Warenne, the 2nd Earl of Surrey, who had been among Curthose's most powerful supporters during his invasion of England in 1101. Henry had applied the same punishment to de Warenne as he had to de Bellême and his brothers – confiscation of his English estates. However, realising that de Warenne might be ripe for turning, and that he could be extremely useful as an ally, Henry restored the earl's possessions to him in 1103, cleverly transforming de Warenne into a devotee of the crown. Over the next twenty-odd years, de Warenne would expend much of his wealth and power on Henry's behalf, in Normandy, whenever required.

Curthose had neither the ability nor the means to control troublesome barons in his dukedom. In 1103, his opposition to the exile Robert de Bellême began to unravel. Even shorn of his English income de Bellême remained the most powerful magnate in the dukedom, and he cut a swathe of destruction through central Normandy.

De Bellême fell out with his youngest brother, Arnulf de Montgomery, in a property dispute. When Arnulf managed to gain control of the family's stronghold at Almenêches, halfway between Caen and Le Mans, he gave it over to Curthose, who garrisoned it with his own men. Before long de Bellême appeared, breathing fire. He burned the nunnery of Almenêches to the ground – even though one of his sisters was abbess there – and seized the castle, giving orders for Curthose's captured soldiers to be tortured to death.

Curthose mustered his allies and met de Bellême in a battle near Exmes, the precise location and date of which are unknown. The result was clear-cut, though: utter defeat for Curthose. De Bellême led the charge that decided the day, capturing many, including Curthose's brother-in-law, William of Conversano. The duke achieved peace with de Bellême only by restoring to him all his lands and castles.

Curthose found himself effectively underpinned by the might of the degenerate and loathed Robert de Bellême, which helped Henry's cause further. Orderic Vitalis called de Bellême: 'Grasping and cruel, an implacable persecutor of the Church of God and the poor . . . unequalled for his iniquity in the whole Christian era.' In early 1105 de Bellême incinerated the church of Tournai-sur-Dive; forty-five people were stuck inside and perished in the flames.

'Suddenly the land was in great fear and people were very

much afraid,' Wace noted. 'The war was great, and they were dismayed.'[12] Anarchy sprang up and ordinary people emptied their homes of anything valuable, hiding what they had in graveyards and the woods to keep it safe.

On his arrival that year Henry was greeted as a liberator. The reforming Bishop Serlo of Sées, whose diocese in south-east Normandy contained the charred remains of the church of Tournai-sur-Dive, was in self-exile because of fear of further outrages by de Bellême. The bishop delivered an Easter sermon in Carentan, at the eastern base of the Cotentin Peninsula, in which he urged Henry to free Normandy from Curthose's horrifying incompetence. Henry accepted the challenge: 'I will rise up and work for peace in the name of the Lord,' Henry vowed, 'and will devote my utmost endeavours to procure, with your help, the tranquillity of the Church of God.'[13]

Bishop Serlo seized the moment to attack the long locks, silk clothes and other fashions that had, in the early 1100s, taken the fancy of the Anglo-Norman aristocracy. Short hair had been part of the martial look of the earliest Norman settlers, Serlo reminded the congregation, and he believed a return to the masculine values of that celebrated past was essential. The bishop pronounced that beards gave men 'the look of billy-goats, whose filthy viciousness is shamefully imitated by the degradations of fornicators and sodomites . . . and by growing their hair long they make themselves seem like imitators of women'.[14] Henry chose to bow to the fiery rebukes, because he needed the bishop to bless his campaign against his brother. He allowed Serlo to pause Easter Mass, to cut his hair and that of many of his lords.

Henry proved less biddable with sword in hand. He swung into action in Normandy, with allies from Anjou, demanding the surrender of the episcopal city of Bayeux. Curthose's men refused to lay down their arms, anticipating that time was on their side, for surely Henry's forces would follow convention and settle into a siege? But Henry instead ordered a frontal attack, during which much of Bayeux was set alight. This served as a warning to the rest of Normandy as to what they could expect if they dared to resist.

Henry marched to the east, to Caen, where Curthose occupied the castle that the two men's father had built in 1060. The duke had quickly added a huge ditch to the defences, but neither it nor Curthose's presence at this, the focal point of the duke of Normandy's court, could prevent the city's speedy surrender. Many wanted to avoid Bayeux's brutal treatment, while some of the leading citizens had been compromised by Henry after capture. He offered them the return of their freedom, their lands and possessions if they would secretly work for him. Henry held their sons as hostages while they returned to Curthose's ranks, spreading defeatism so contagious that it helped Caen to fall softly into Henry's hands.

Curthose fled, leaving his two great cities in his brother's possession, with the area between deserted: 'The peasants did not dare till the land, join their oxen together, or plough the fields, and the merchants did not dare go about the town or transport their merchandise,' Wace recorded.[15] Apart from Bayeux and Caen, Henry of Huntingdon noted how King Henry 'also captured many other castles, and almost all the chief men of Normandy submitted to the king'.[16]

The end of the 1105 campaign was not as successful for Henry. He was unable to take Falaise, the place of his father's birth and a fulcrum of Norman power, thanks to desertion from his ranks. This occurred because of a threat that was not military, but spiritual. Since Archbishop Anselm's exile in 1103, Pope Paschal had been contemplating suitable punishment for Henry's continued stubbornness over investiture. Reports that Anselm was setting out to excommunicate Henry in person were enough to convince the pious Elias of Maine (who fasted every Friday, and whose correspondence with Anselm shows profound and humble respect) to cease his alliance with the English king.

Fully aware of the direct connection between his military capabilities and his Christian standing, Henry went to L'Aigle in July 1105 to meet his exiled archbishop. After much negotiation a settlement was agreed between the two, subject to papal blessing: if the king allowed the pope to appoint whomever he chose as England's leading clerics, then he would still be allowed to receive homage from those same men – for their lay possessions only. It was a logical recognition of the dual role of abbots and bishops – as men of God and as grandees in the land. Meanwhile Henry agreed to support papal reforms, particularly the drive against married and cohabiting priests.

Henry returned to England the following month, waiting to learn if Paschal would agree to what he and Anselm had brokered. He was followed in February 1106 by Curthose, who came to see the king in Northampton Castle, 'amicably seeking from him the free restoration of what had been taken from his paternal inheritance'.[17] But Henry refused to return any of his gains to the brother who had treated him with such contempt in the past, and who was so vulnerable now. The two parted on extremely bad terms.

A month later Henry received the welcome news that the pope had agreed to accept the investiture compromise negotiated with Anselm. This settlement would remain, to a large extent, the arrangement between the ruler of England and the pope until the Reformation. Its immediate effect was to free Henry to attack Normandy once more.

Henry crossed the Channel at the end of July 1106, with a large army. He was reaping a dividend from the peace he had established in England: he was able to bring many of his kingdom's most powerful magnates across to fight for him, sure that there would be no trouble while he was gone. Henry struck out towards Falaise again, taking the abbey of Saint-Pierre-sur-Dives en route, before advancing towards the town of Tinchebray, the imposing castle of which was owned by an old enemy, William de Mortain.

This count sat at the junction of several mighty bloodlines: he was a nephew of Robert de Bellême and his brothers. Like them, he had been a great favourite of William Rufus, while also being heartily disliked by medieval historians: the twelfth-century *Warenne Hyde Chronicle* called him 'incorrigibly turbulent', and William of Malmesbury remembered de Mortain for his 'shameless arrogance'.

De Mortain was the son of one of William the Conqueror's half-brothers, who had landed in England to try to depose Rufus in 1088. William de Mortain was therefore a cousin of Henry's, although a hated one. Henry's feelings towards de Mortain pre-dated his own rise from landless junior son to the king of England. As a youth Henry had enjoyed a passion for the coun-tryside and for hunting, going into the woods with his own pack of hounds, without a huntsman, blowing the horn for his dogs to follow. He became known for his skill in catching deer and wild boar, through clever deployment of hides and a keen understanding of prey and habitat.

William de Mortain thought Henry's hunting obsession laugh-able. He felt that his younger cousin had squeezed the aristocratic glamour out of the sport by becoming little more than a hunt servant. He called Henry 'Stag's Foot'. It was a nickname designed to belittle Henry who, de Mortain scoffed, was so well versed in the ways of the forest that he could surely tell how many points a stag had on its antlers merely by studying its hoof prints.

While Rufus reigned Henry had to deal with the taunting as best he could. But a desire to be avenged of his tormentor burned deep within him. When, on Rufus's death, Henry seized the throne so unexpectedly, William de Mortain found himself suddenly exposed to retribution for the years of mockery.

The animosity between the two men had deepened after de Bellême and his brothers were crushed by Henry in England and sent into exile. De Mortain was infuriated after he was also, in Henry of Huntingdon's words, 'disinherited by the king in England because of treachery'.[18] He demanded the return of the titles and lands that had belonged to his father, which included the county of Mortain in Normandy and the earldom of Cornwall in England. He sought his uncle Odo of Bayeux's earldom of Kent, too. But Henry explained that he would never give in to de Mortain's claims, because he did not trust him.

Humiliated and furious, de Mortain crossed the Channel and declared for Curthose. He proved to be loyal to this new cause, the *Anglo-Saxon Chronicle* noting how, in 1106, almost all submitted to Henry's advance through Normandy, 'except for Robert de Bellême and the earl of Mortain and a few other men who still held with the earl [*sic*] of Normandy'.[19]

When Henry's men dug in around de Mortain's castle, at Tinchebray, Curthose came to break the siege with de Mortain and, according to Wace, 'all their good neighbours; they wanted to help the castle and rescue all the equipment inside'.[20] When they could not find a way through Henry's lines, they chose to invite battle in the surrounding fields instead.

The engagement took place on 28 September 1106, forty years to the day after the Conqueror's invasion force landed in England. At a time when the heavens were studied for portents – Henry regularly employed astrologers to help interpret divine messages in the stars – chroniclers would later recall omens that announced this to be a day of divine reckoning. 'A sign of this, a comet,' wrote Henry of Huntingdon, 'had appeared in the same year. There were also seen on Maundy Thursday two full moons, one in the east and the other in the west.'[21]

Before battle was joined Vitalis of Savigny, a holy man, strode out between the armies, urging Curthose and Henry to choose peace over bloodshed. Vitalis knew the ruling family well: he had served as chaplain to Robert de Mortain, Henry's half-uncle and William de Mortain's father. Now Vitalis was a hermit, famed for his religious purity. Whether heeding Vitalis of Savigny's words or not, Henry suggested an alternative to the coming clash. He sent a message to Curthose, offering him a lavish pension for life if he would surrender the rule of Normandy. Curthose indignantly declined.

They lined up, ready for battle, Henry with the larger army, Curthose superior in foot soldiers. The chronicler Henry of Huntingdon noted the distinguished faces in the English king's cavalry ranks, recording he had the support of 'almost all the chief men of Normandy and the best soldiers of England, Anjou, and Brittany. He was therefore,' Huntingdon continued dryly, 'not unprepared.'[22]

'The battle was soon joined,' recalled Wace, 'but it did not last long.'[23] Tinchebray was a battle as decisive as it was brief. The engagement started promisingly for Curthose, with his cavalry making inroads at once, but Henry's men absorbed the shock of the enemy charge and held firm. The action became almost static, Orderic Vitalis reporting of the combatants: 'They were so closely crowded together and were brought to a halt with their weapons so closely locked that it was impossible for them to strike one another, and all in turn struggled to break the solid line.'[24]

It took a sweetly timed flank attack to crack the stationary melee and turn the day. Henry's allies Count Elias of Maine and Duke Alan IV of Brittany (who had served alongside Curthose during the First Crusade) thundered into Curthose's men with an impact so devastating that Robert de Bellême panicked. He abandoned his duty as commander of Curthose's rearguard, and fled for his life without taking any part in the fighting. His men quickly followed in a chaotic flight from the field. The rest of Curthose's army was now exposed, and it too broke. It had taken an hour.

A few escaped, including William, Curthose's surviving illegitimate child from the lover who had undergone ordeal by hot iron to prove her sons' paternity. But four hundred knights were among the ten thousand prisoners taken that day. Among these were Edgar Ætheling, who had been proclaimed king by the English after the death of Harold at Hastings, and William Crispin, whose father had been one of the Conqueror's leading soldiers at Hastings. William de Mortain was also taken, detained by Henry's Breton troops. But the biggest prize was Robert Curthose, captured by Henry's former chaplain, Waldric, who fought alongside his master's knights.

Henry saw no threat in Edgar, his wife's elderly uncle, or in William Crispin, whose loyalty he hoped to reclaim. He released them both. But the prize pair of Curthose and de Mortain were kept prisoner. Before being sent across the Channel Curthose was taken to Falaise, where Henry made him order the surrender of his garrison. Entering the city, Henry for the first time encountered William Clito, Curthose's three-year-old heir. He decided to spare the boy from what he had planned for his father, handing him into the care of Helias of Saint-Saëns, whose wife was an illegitimate daughter of Robert Curthose. Allowing Clito his freedom would be a decision that Henry would come to rue as one of the worst of his life.

Curthose and William de Mortain were escorted to England for imprisonment. This must have been sweet revenge for Henry, being payback for the two occasions that Curthose had committed him to gaol a decade and a half beforehand, and for the mockery William de Mortain had heaped on him as a youth. In a dispatch to Archbishop Anselm Henry acknowledged that Tinchebray was a victory handed to him by God. But Henry had shown tactical superiority in battle, and the triumph owed at least as much to his deft diplomacy in the preceding months. He had settled with the pope in time to avoid the crippling impact of excommunication.

Orderic Vitalis found Curthose's defeat to be the inevitable consequence of his failures as a ruler and as a Christian, because 'all men knew that Duke Robert was weak and indolent . . . he exercised no discipline over either himself or his men'.[25] Henry of Huntingdon saw Curthose's fate as fitting reward for his past failures: 'So God condemned him to everlasting inactivity and perpetual imprisonment.'[26]

Curthose was sent to be prisoner in Devizes Castle, in Wiltshire. It was a motte and bailey structure built by Henry's tutor, Bishop Osmund of Salisbury, in 1080, which the king would have known well. Curthose would eventually take to the quiet of his new existence with ease. While victory at Tinchebray delivered up Normandy to Henry, it also eliminated Robert Curthose as a contender for the English throne. The lands of the Conqueror were reunited.

Henry started his rule in Normandy by setting the clock back to how it had stood at the time of his father's death, nineteen years earlier. Just two weeks after Tinchebray he summoned leading churchmen and barons to a council in Lisieux, an important Norman town and home of a prominent bishopric. There Henry dismantled the carcass of Curthose's failed legacy with the swift, clean cuts of an expert butcher. Haphazard and damaging grants of lands were annulled, Church possessions were restored and castles that had been built without permission were marked down for speedy destruction. At two further Norman councils, in early 1107, Henry re-emphasised how things had changed. When he returned to England, in time for Easter, he was as powerful as his father, the Conqueror, had ever been.

SEVEN

Kingship

He was a good man and was held in great awe. In his time no man dared do wrong against another; he made peace for man and beast; no man dared say anything but good to whoever carried their load of gold and silver.

Anglo-Saxon Chronicle, on Henry I

Henry arrived back in his kingdom eager to build on the peace and order he had established earlier in his reign. 'Thus victorious, and strong for the first time,' wrote Henry of Huntingdon, the king summoned the great men of England and Normandy to his Easter court at Windsor, in April 1107.[1] They 'attended it with fear and trembling. Earlier, when he was a young man and [in the years immediately] after he had become king he was held in the greatest contempt.'[2] He was a different prospect now.

Henry had eyes and ears everywhere, having built up a wide network of spies at home and abroad. Henry of Huntingdon criticised him for using informants to report on the poor, in his constant quest for tax revenue. But the king relied on his spies to bring him every detail of the lives of those who served him closely, as well as of those who might plot against him.

Assisted by this espionage in the field, Henry's administration was based in Westminster and Winchester, with support from officials in London, as well as others working out of his hunting retreat at Woodstock in Oxfordshire. All these different strands fell under the command of one man, Roger of Salisbury, who was the leading administrative force in the land, and who had become so powerful that Henry of Huntingdon rated him as being 'second only to the king' in importance.

Roger had started as a village priest in 'the church of Avranches', in a parish near Caen. According to William of Newburgh, a twelfth-century chronicler from Yorkshire, Henry had happened to hear Roger deliver a religious service with a speed that was intriguing to a busy and impatient man who had campaigns to fight and quarry to pursue. In the early 1090s he invited Roger to join his household, and it is possible that Roger was the chaplain who followed Henry into obscurity in France, in 1091, after Henry was forced to surrender Mont Saint-Michel. Either way, Henry quickly discovered that a speedy dispatch of the Mass was just one of the country priest's startling talents.

Despite an education that left him no more than semi-literate, Roger possessed qualities that cannot easily be taught. With an abundance of efficiency, energy and devotion, he proved to be an astonishingly able administrator. During those years when Henry's financial resources had to be carefully fostered, Roger oversaw the household expenses with scrupulous care. He was particularly alert to unnecessary expense, and in the period before his master's reign he maintained an aversion to outlay on luxuries.

As king, Henry liked to keep close to him those who had shown loyalty before he seized power. A year into his reign he had appointed Roger chancellor, a senior position with close contact to the king and control of his household clerks. This office was often a stepping-stone to greater things, and the prosperous bishopric of Salisbury was entrusted to Roger a year later. He was not consecrated until August 1107, after Anselm and Henry had finally concluded their investiture clash. But the delay in the confirmation of his position affected Roger of Salisbury's importance not at all, since his lay duties continued to dominate, and to grow.

During Henry's long and frequent absences in Normandy Roger held the executive reins, maintaining peace in England while Queen Matilda acted as regent. He was wise enough too to foster good relations with Anselm. These he achieved with the reforming archbishop despite Roger openly keeping a mistress, Matilda de Ramsbury, who was the mother of the couple's son (sometimes referred to as their 'nephew'), Roger le Poer.

Salisbury worked with great effect for Henry, concentrating on what mattered most to the king. Henry had long enjoyed a reputation for personal financial competence, Wace remarking that, as a young man, 'he was skilled at investing money, using it well and looking after it'.[3] The careful weighing of his coin inheritance from his father demonstrated how seriously he took that which was owing to him.

Henry had brought the same care and order to his reign. He ensured that Roger of Salisbury's administration was vigorous, focused on binding the finances and the justice of the kingdom more tightly to the crown. To assist in this, clerks of the Royal Chapel were transformed from a general, courtly role into a dynamic team of secretaries that reported to the chancellor. Roger of Salisbury became Henry's Justiciar, a recently created position that was of unique seniority and trustworthiness. With control of the treasury, the judiciary and the household, the bishop had risen to be, in William of Malmesbury's estimation, in charge of 'the very kingdom'.

Roger was supported in his responsibilities by the King's Court, which was comprised of lords attached to Henry's household. This body had two roles: it sat as the highest court of appeal, and it oversaw the royal revenues. When doing the latter, it was known as the Court of Exchequer.

The Exchequer would be Roger of Salisbury's greatest legacy. The year 1110 saw the beginning of a great audit that revolutionised the management of England's finances. Henry had to raise an enormous sum to pay for the dowry of his legitimate daughter, Matilda. It was so great that a special assessment, called an 'aid', needed to be levied and administered. Out of this extraordinary tax evolved a system, overseen by Roger of Salisbury, the name of which survives as the centre of British government finances today: the Exchequer, so-called because the moneys due to the crown in Henry's time – rents, taxes and fines – were laid out on a large table. It was ten feet by five, with a three-inch rim around its edge to stop anything from falling off.

This counting table was covered with a cloth, on which there was a pattern of horizontal and vertical squares, as would be found on a board for a game of chequers. The columns of squares had different values, starting with pennies, progressing through shillings to pounds, all the way up to tens of thousands of pounds.

The royal accountant set out counters across the top row of squares, representing the sums that he had calculated as being due to the crown. Along the row immediately below this were laid out further counters, showing what had actually been paid in against the debt. In an age of complicating Roman numerals, the employment of what was, in essence, a giant chequerboard abacus reduced payments and debts to their simplest and most digestible form.

'Tallies' were the reports of payments received. The money paid at the Exchequer would be recorded along the length of the wooden tally, which resembled a ruler. Knife cuts would be applied to both sides, to show receipts: this prevented ink forgeries and helped the illiterate to understand the conclusions of the accounting process. The tally would then be split down the middle, with Roger of Salisbury's clerks keeping one half, while the man paying in to the Exchequer kept the other. That man was the sheriff of each county.

When the Normans conquered England, they took over the most centralised system of governance in Europe, with the sheriff the key link between the crown and each county. Responsible for taxation, and for raising troops in time of war, the sheriff also oversaw the shire courts, where Church and lay matters were heard and adjudicated.

During Henry's reign the sheriff had to appear in person twice a year, at Easter and Michaelmas, to pay over the revenue due to the king. Because of the unforgiving grids on the Exchequer's table, any shortfalls would be visible instantly. Explanations would be demanded by Henry's barons of the Exchequer as to where the missing sums might be and when the sheriff would make good his deficit. The clerk of the treasurer sat by, recording the audit on sheets of parchment for Roger of Salisbury's archives. This record was called the 'pipe roll', and while the one for 1130 is the oldest to survive, it refers to Exchequer business earlier in Henry's reign.

Writing a generation later, a treasurer called Richard FitzNeal likened the Exchequer encounters between his office and a sheriff to a game of chess: 'As in chess the battle is joined by kings, so in this it is chiefly between two men that the conflict takes place and the battle is waged, namely, the treasurer and the sheriff who sits there to render his account, while the others sit like umpires to watch and judge the proceedings.'[4]

It could be an ordeal for the sheriff, who was used to pre-eminence in his county. He had to submit to more powerful men who undertook this forensic examination of his honesty, his attention to detail and his ability to perform his duties. Rare was the sheriff who came to the Exchequer with confidence and a clear conscience. One who did was Gilbert, the sheriff of Surrey. The monks of Merton Priory, writing of Gilbert (their founder) in 1125, boasted how: 'When the sheriffs of England assembled at the exchequer and were all agitated and apprehensive, Gilbert was the only man who turned up unperturbed and cheerful. As soon as he was summoned by the receivers of money, he sent the cash in and he promptly sat among them, quite at his ease, as if he were one of them himself.'[5]

The Exchequer had a judicial element, with some of its barons travelling round England on 'judges' circuits', settling local disputes about payments and rents. This legal arm became known as the Upper Exchequer, and evolved into the Judiciary, while the Lower Exchequer developed into the Treasury.

While Roger of Salisbury saw that the income due to the crown was properly accounted for, Henry insisted that Salisbury also guard his currency's purity. The minting of coins had been a lucrative monopoly for the English crown since the tenth century, when King Edgar made it one of his priorities. Edgar had halted a deterioration in the content of coins after recognising that it was undermining confidence in the trustworthiness of financial deals, as well as rewarding counterfeiters.

King Edgar used imports of silver from Saxony to create coinage that became the most desirable in Europe, with a high purity that was regularly checked. His silver pennies were struck in fifty or so mints across England from dies that came from London, in return for a payment to the crown. William the Conqueror had been happy to continue in his predecessors' money-spinning practices.

The coinage changed whenever the king decreed, usually every three years or so, and new coins could be minted only after those applying to do so had paid a hefty fee, called 'seignorage'. The rate was based on the difference between the value of the money and the cost of producing and circulating it.

Henry was clear about the importance of keeping the quality of his money beyond reproach, both for financial reasons and because he viewed any attack on his coins as a form of treason. In December 1100, while Henry was parading with his new wife in their new crowns at his Christmas court at Westminster, one of his first declarations was a warning to anyone caught debasing his coins: they would have their right hand chopped off, and be castrated.

This was no empty threat. At Christmas 1124 Roger of Salisbury would summon to Winchester all those in the land who minted coin, by order of the king. Henry of Huntingdon wrote of the result: 'It is rewarding to hear how severe the king was towards wicked men. For he had almost all the moneyers throughout England have their right hands cut off for severely debasing the coinage.'[6] They were castrated at the same time.

Others tamed by the king's exacting rule were those in the itinerant royal household accustomed to trailing havoc in their wake. Henry had seen for himself the outrages of his two older brothers and their followers, meting out robbery, rape and terror to ordinary people around the kingdom.

Henry insisted that his courtiers' projected movements be advertised beforehand, so neighbourhoods could be forewarned of their arrival, while his senior officers established all logistical needs in advance. The king had Roger of Salisbury establish a table of fixed rates to be paid by his lords and courtiers, in cash, when on the move, to those selling their wares. There was to be no more plundering and no more theft, on pain of death. The punishment for rape was castration and blinding.

The further day-to-day reordering of the royal household under Henry was distilled into a register, called *The Establishment of the King's Household*. This first appeared just after the king's reign, but owed everything to what had been achieved during it. It listed court appointments. It also itemised the provisions that members of the royal household were entitled to, according to their rank. An enormous number of different officers had to be taken into account: Henry's passion for hunting resulted in a multitude of categories for that department alone, including horn-blowers, wolf-hunters, harriers and archers.

The broader list of royal attendants ranged from the chancellor down through ushers (who were, in turn, broken down into ranks, depending on whether they were from the knightly class or of more modest stock) to humble watchmen. The king's kitchen had forty categories of staff, including bakers, larderers, cooks and the operators of the 'roasting house'. There was even a 'napier', in charge of the royal linen, and a 'waferer', to make the sacramental bread needed for consumption at Mass. Each officeholder's individual stipend was set down, including their particular allowances of butter, candles, or even (because they still had value) candle ends.

Henry's reign also saw a void left by his brother and father be filled. They had both failed to produce a recognised and accessible body of law. The *Laws of Henry the First* was an unofficial tract, written in around 1115 by somebody involved in royal administration. Detailing the laws of Henry's reign, based on custom, it applied to the highest in the land down to slaves.*

---

* At the time of the Conquest 10–30 per cent of the English population were slaves. The Normans disapproved of slavery, Archbishop Anselm insisting, in 1102: 'Let no one dare hereafter to engage in the infamous business, prevalent in England, of selling men like animals.'

GVLIELMAS · CONQISTER ·

Known to contemporaries as William 'the Bastard', and later as 'the Conqueror', the most famous Norman of all inherited the warrior spirit of his Viking ancestors.

Top: The *Mora* – the flagship of William's 1066 invasion fleet – was built in Barfleur as a gift for Duke William from his devoted wife, Matilda of Flanders.

Bottom: To the twelfth-century European mind, the sea was an impenetrable place of dark menace, its perils being both real and imagined.

Top: Pope Urban II at the Council of Clermont, surrounded by leading churchmen and laymen. Here, in November 1095, he announced the First Crusade.

Bottom: Anselm was a reluctant archbishop of Canterbury, whose eagerness to implement Church reform led to bitter clashes with William Rufus and Henry I.

le roi et le roiaume de france.
Ci fenist le secont chapitre du premier
roi philippe et commence le tiers.

Ors disoit on que al rois
Guillmes dengleterre qui trop
estoit fiers et orgueilleus. bai
oit a auoir le roiaume de
france. quar li nobles damoisiaus looys
estoit tout seulz demourez dioir hoirs du
roi phelippe. de la noble rome berte qui
sereur estoit robert le conte de flandres.
si auoit il ij. autres fils phelipp et flo

Some contemporaries saw God's hand in William Rufus's sudden death on the hunting field, when he had no time to repent his many sins.

Top: Henry I being crowned in Westminster Abbey, on 5 August 1100.
In his Coronation Charter Henry made profound commitments to his people.

Bottom: Henry I and Queen Matilda with their daughter Matilda and son
William Ætheling. Although Henry would father 22 others, these were his
only two whose birth, and claim to the throne, would be legitimate.

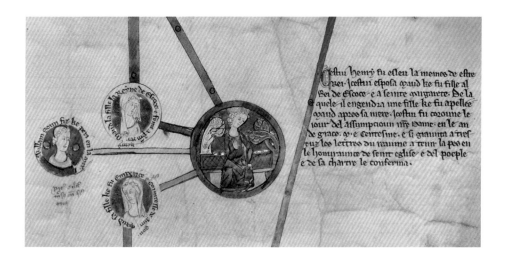

Top: The Battle of Tinchebray, in 1106, saw Henry challenge his brother Robert Curthose for control of Normandy.

Bottom: The tomb of Robert Curthose. Curthose shone as a warrior during the First Crusade, but he found the question of ruling Normandy altogether more taxing.

Opposite: Henry's uncompromising attitude to criminals led a contemporary to claim that 'a young girl, laden with gold, could travel unharmed through the kingdom of England'.

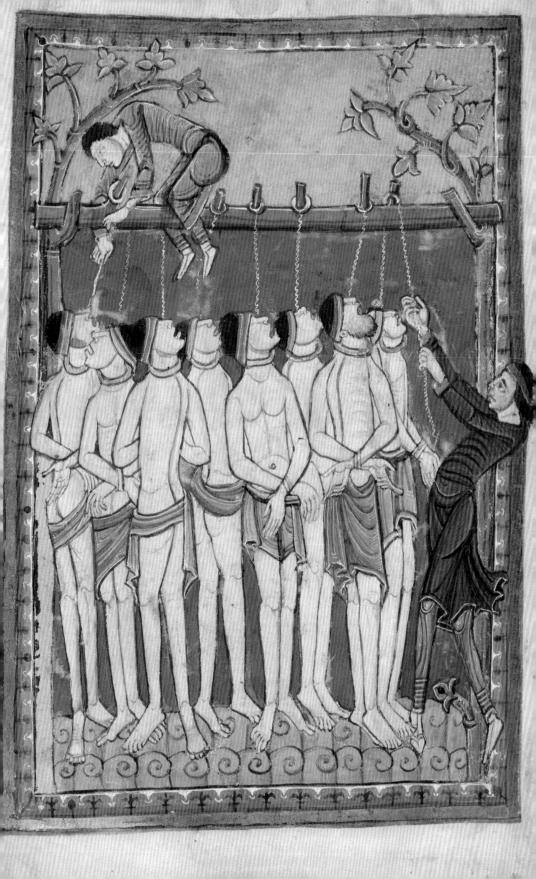

The four men who ruled England between 1066 and 1154: William the Conqueror
(top left), William Rufus (top right), Henry I (bottom left) and Stephen (bottom right).

It set out the punishment to be given for each crime, including death or mutilation for treason, murder, robbery, rape or arson. Written in Latin, after translation from Old English, the tract made understanding of the law possible, wherever it was administered.

The *Laws of Henry the First* established how a seigneurial court could operate. Henry accepted that such a court was the key forum in which a lord's power could be exercised in his locality. It dealt with matters relating to competing claims between lords, and claims between and against the lord's vassals, as well as criminal matters, including murder and theft. There was too the capacity for tenants to counter their lord, bringing complaints to be heard against him or his agents. In the words of Wace, writing in the mid to late twelfth century, Henry 'spared from justice neither high born or low'.[7]

Henry's love of peace and order extended to the royal forests, which he loved as deeply as his father had before him. They were organised and overseen with Henry's customary efficiency. The pipe roll of 1130 refers to a crown visitation of the forests, recording revenue owed and received from this resource. In the reign following Henry's, a chronicler would look back with admiration to a time when, under his rule: 'So many thousands of wild animals . . . overflowed the whole land in numerous herds . . . [as if in] a countless swarm.' They were 'scrupulously preserved in the whole kingdom, as though they had been enclosed within hunting-nets'.[8]

Henry achieved such success with nurturing quarry at something of a cost to his popularity at both ends of the social spectrum. His barons resented him for being miserly in the granting of hunting rights, sometimes forbidding noblemen from enjoying the sport available to them on their own estates, since he preferred to take it for himself. Henry's successor would acknowledge the deep unpopularity of this by swearing in his coronation charter to hand back land that Henry had appropriated during his reign.

Meanwhile those living within the royal forest were bound by strict rules. Any dog owner who lived on the fringes of one of the king's hunting estates had to agree to the animal's feet being mutilated, to prevent it from chasing game. Once, finding peasants looking for firewood in one of his forests, Henry ordered their feet to be chopped off.

Henry's style of kingship suited his personality. He was hardworking, but he liked to balance much effort with plenty of play. We hear from the chronicler Walter Map that Henry chose to divide his days in two, spending his mornings with key advisers, concentrating on important matters – his court becoming, in Map's words, 'a school of virtues and of wisdom'.

This was the part of the day when people sought to gain an audience with the king. From the memorial to Gilbert, Sheriff of Surrey, who died in 1125 after nearly two decades of service, we get a sense of how Henry's senior officers jostled for a moment with their master, relying on the favour of the royal gatekeepers: 'You might frequently see many bishops and other people of the highest distinction hanging around the door of the royal chamber for long periods, begging to go in, but quite unable to get a hearing. But if Gilbert happened to appear the doors were flung open to admit him, as soon as the ushers knew who it was. He was admitted to the royal presence as often as he wanted.'[9] This was what good contacts and good conduct could win you, in Henry's reign – a possible route into royal favour.

After a morning's business, lunch punctuated the royal day. Henry was not a big eater, and in general opted for simply cooked foods. As he aged, his physicians warned him increasingly against rich fare, perhaps because of digestive problems, and maybe because of his expanding paunch. He reportedly treated alcohol with suspicion, preferring the safety of sobriety to loose-tongued drunkenness. After lunch the king liked to take a nap. This could be a noisy affair, with William of Malmesbury's noting that the king 'was heavy to sleep, which was interrupted by frequent snoring'.[10]

The afternoon would be altogether more light-hearted in tone, Map remarking how the royal court became a place of 'hilarity and decent mirth'.[11] Henry could readily adapt to the merriment, remembered William of Malmesbury: 'In season he was full of fun, and once he had decided to be sociable a mass of business did not damp his spirits.'[12]

Henry's court achieved a reputation that spread far and lasted for many generations, a scribe of Edward IV's – writing in the fifteenth century – referring to it as a place that attracted 'every young man on this side of the Alps who wanted the renown of a good start in life'.[13] They ranged from Henry's brother-in-law, David of Scotland, who was brought up there before unexpectedly becoming a king himself, through to princelings of the Roman Empire. One such was a great-nephew of Emperor Henry V, Theodoric, who would sail from Normandy to England with William Ætheling in late 1120.

With regard to how Henry viewed (and used) his own family, Wace touched on the king's Achilles heel: 'Because of his love of women he had many ups and downs.'

Henry remained full of love for his two legitimate children, Matilda and William, whose protection was one of his most keenly felt duties. In the autumn of 1108, as he headed to Normandy once more, he wrote to Archbishop Anselm: 'I entrust to you my son and my daughter, so that you may cherish and care for them with paternal love.'

However, his relationship with his wife, Matilda, was conducted at a distance, the two choosing to exist in parallel. He would never give up the pursuit of other women, but after William Ætheling's birth, the writer of *Gesta Stephani* believed:

'He had dissolved on the flimsiest pretexts the blessing of marriage, which God accepted; as he gave way to adulterous allurements himself, so he winked at such practices in others.'[14]

Throughout history rulers have used their children to build and consolidate political and military alliances. If Henry did this more than most it was because he had quite so many offspring – at least twenty-four, with only Matilda and William Ætheling born in wedlock. In perhaps his least convincing passage, William of Malmesbury stated that Henry was 'completely free from fleshly lusts'. The chronicler put the king's spectacular rate of procreation down to his selfless pursuit of a stately policy that was focused on the betterment of his people's interests: the more royal children there were, the more beneficial alliances he could forge. But this does not fit with either the chronology of Henry's life, or reality.

Most of his twenty-two illegitimate children were born in the two decades before Henry became a king (or a husband), when he was merely the youngest son whose elder brothers were seemingly destined for great things, while he – left no lands by their father, bullied by his brothers – would have to make his own way in the world. These, many children were not born to a king-in-waiting, but to a fourth son with few resources.

In his teens and twenties Henry led the life typical of a young aristocrat of his time, although he enjoyed more attributes than the vast majority of his peers. As a young man of the bachelor knightly class, it was expected that he would sow wild oats among the many prostitutes and camp followers on hand, as well as with the women encountered on the wild marauding of the itinerant court.

Meanwhile, as the son of one king and the brother of another, he found ready sexual partners across the Anglo-Norman territories. But his prospects after the death of the Conqueror, which yielded only a cash inheritance, were modest, and without the wherewithal to provide appropriately for a suitable wife, he set about his privileged royal bachelorhood with earthy delight. Henry took lovers from among the wives, widows and daughters of his family's loyal retainers. The one who seems to have been the most significant for him was the widow Ansfride, who has already been introduced as the mother of Richard of Lincoln, as well as of two other of the king's illegitimate children.

There is no record of the details of the couple's affair, but Ansfride's importance to Henry is shown in her burial spot: in the cloister, in front of the door used by the monks, in Abingdon Abbey. Such a notable place seems to have been secured for her by her appreciative royal lover, with added poignancy because the couple's second son, Fulk, appears to have been an Abingdon monk.

Another of Henry's mistresses was Edith, the daughter of Forne, son of Sigulf. Forne was the lord of Greystoke, in Cumbria, who would serve the king in Yorkshire until his death in 1130. Henry appears to have had two children with Edith: Robert FitzEdith, who was born in 1093, and Adeliza FitzEdith, whose birth date is unknown. In 1120, after the affair had run its course, Henry arranged for Edith to marry Robert D'Oyly, the elder son of a Norman aristocrat who was the commander of Oxford Castle. Henry gave D'Oyly a royal manor in Buckinghamshire, to provide him with income to support his wife and family. Henry and Edith's son, Robert, married Matilda d'Avranches, an eligible heiress four years his junior.

There was also another mistress called Edith, whose background is a mystery. She was the mother of Matilda, Countess of Perche, who accompanied her father the king to Barfleur, in November 1120, ready to cross to Southampton on the *White Ship*.

Henry found romance among the enemy, too. Princess Nesta was the sole legitimate daughter of Rhys ap Tewdwr, the king of Deheubarth, in south Wales, and a leader of resistance to Norman incursions. Nesta was seven or eight years old when, during Easter 1093, her father was killed by William Rufus's army at the Battle of Brecon. She was captured and taken as a hostage to Rufus's court while her younger brother fled to Ireland and two of her elder half-brothers were executed.

A decade later Henry, in his mid-thirties, and king of England, made the teenaged Nesta pregnant. Their son Henry FitzRoy was born at much the same time as William Ætheling, in 1103. The affair with Nesta appears to have been brief, and Henry soon afterwards married her to Gerald de Windsor, a son of the feudal lord of Eton who became the constable of Windsor Castle.

But Princess Nesta's son was not forgotten by his father: the fact that he shared his Christian name, and called himself 'FitzRoy' (which means 'the illegitimate son of the king'), clearly announced his regal roots. The king gave him control of lands in south-west Wales, and it was in his mother's native land that he would serve the English crown, eventually losing his life in his mid-fifties, under a 'shower of lances', when leading an attack against the King of Gwynedd on the island of Anglesey.

Another of Henry's mistresses was Isabel de Beaumont, a sister of the twins Waleran, Count de Meulan, and Robert, 2nd Earl of Leicester. She was the only mistress, of those whose identities we know, who was drawn from the upper reaches of the Anglo-Norman aristocracy. In around 1130, again aiming to provide security once the affair was over, Henry approved Isabel's marriage to the Earl of Pembroke.

While lust was his prime driver, and affection for his children and grandchildren a characteristic noted by contemporaries, when Henry became ruler of England and Normandy he certainly appreciated the usefulness of his offspring's eligibility in furthering his political interests.

Within six years of seizing the throne Henry had disabled the most dangerous men operating in England at the time of his succession. The imprisonment of Ranulf Flambard and the enforced exile of Robert de Bellême had demonstrated that in his reign nobody could behave as they had been allowed to before. Orderic Vitalis also wrote about how the king 'pulled down many great men from their positions of eminence and sentenced them to be disinherited'.[15] The rest, he controlled.

In England, after the royal family, earls were the most powerful laymen in the kingdom. William the Conqueror had employed his earls militarily, to oversee the rooting out of Anglo-Saxon opposition and the bedding down of Norman rule. The Conqueror had created eighteen earls in his twenty-one-year rule, many of them in the first full year of his reign, 1067. By contrast, at the time of Henry's death, only seven earldoms remained in place, three of which he had bestowed, including one to his eldest natural son and another to his brother-in-law, King David of Scotland.[16]

Henry's remaining earls were trustworthy and served the crown well. Richard of Chester, the son of 'Hugh the Fat', had inherited on his father's death in 1101, when aged six. He was as good as family to Henry, having been brought up at the king's insistence in his court, almost as an adopted son or nephew. His earldom comprised the most powerful bloc of power in private land in England, with estates in nearly thirty counties. Alongside very significant landholdings, Richard possessed important duties, being both the chief baronial and the leading public figure in the north-west of England. He had a particularly important role in blocking the rebel Welsh from making incursions into vulnerable Cheshire and its surroundings.

All earls at this time enjoyed a status similar to that of a regional governor receiving 'the third penny' – that is, a third of the profits from administering justice and trade in their lands – but the earl of Chester exercised a form of semi-independent power that made him 'pre-eminent among the magnates' of England.[17] Beyond the hereditary titles, the earl also had notable personal qualities, Orderic Vitalis describing him as 'a young man of great valour and notable kindness'.[18]

The earls in place at the end of Henry's reign were either family or those he trusted implicitly. He chose to add to his magnates' power only if they were entirely reliable. Henry's absolute trust was a rare commodity. It was the same with sheriffs. In 1110 Henry tried to take a more ordered approach to maintaining peace across the land. He jettisoned many of his county sheriffs, replacing grandees who he did not have complete trust in with more biddable men.

The king realised that it was wise to consult his remaining, powerful barons frequently, to make them feel as if they had real influence, and so keep their loyalty. He had spent time as a young man alongside unhappy courtiers, hearing their grumbling about the inadequacies of the ruler, and he had listened to them complain of insulting treatment by the crown. Henry knew that aristocratic disgruntlement was the seedbed of rebellion. He was confident that he could nip such threats in the bud, if he engaged with his magnates and convinced them that they (and their views) really mattered. At the same time, he looked for senior servants outside of the traditional ranks of the Norman nobility to wield, and build, his power.

The career of Roger of Salisbury, who rose from humble priest to supreme power, showed how Henry valued loyalty and merit over entitlement and pedigree. While he tightly controlled the aristocracy, he promoted men from modest backgrounds into positions of trust that the nobility had always thought of as their own.

Orderic Vitalis noted how Henry 'ennobled those of base stock who had served him well, raised them, so to say, from the dust, and heaping all kinds of favours on them, stationed them above earls and famous constables'. Looking at such 'new men', as they became known, Orderic said that they 'have heaped up riches and built lavishly, on a scale far beyond the means of their fathers . . . The king . . . lifted them out of insignificance by his royal authority, set them on the summit of power, and made them formidable even to the greatest magnates of the kingdom.'[19]

It was normal practice for the able, the ambitious and the loyal to be promoted by a grateful monarch: many of the great nobles of William the Conqueror's time had died during Rufus's reign, and Rufus had replaced them with 'certain underlings whom he exalted by the grant of extensive honors [feudal baronies] as a reward for their flattery'.[20] However, Henry's reign is particularly notable for the fluidity of his aristocracy and court, with some great families being dispossessed or exiled and others suddenly finding themselves enjoying extraordinary eminence. These ebbs and flows were not random, but came about as the direct result of individual integrity and royal trust.

Henry's promotions differed from his brother's because they were strategic. Rather than scattering wealth thoughtlessly among his supporters, Henry consciously built up an active ruling class, many of whose participants were parvenus, but all of whom he felt he could rely on.

Valuing fidelity and ability wherever they might hail from, Henry even allowed some to become, in the words of the author of the historical *Gesta Stephani*, 'especial and very intimate friends . . . They were of low birth and had been taken into his service as court pages; afterwards he bound them to him by so remarkable an affection that he enriched them with the most bountiful gifts, endowed them with very extensive estates, made them his chief officials in all the business of the palace, and appointed them as advocates in every case that had to be pleaded.'[21] Some of these men came from families that had made a start up the social pyramid, without getting to the top. Others came from anonymous backgrounds. It was their individual efforts that allowed them to leapfrog some aristocratic rivals, in terms of real power and influence.

Some felt unworthy of the privilege of royal favour. Nigel d'Aubigny told the king: 'In your service and in my own affairs I have committed many great sins and I have done few if any good deeds.'[22] But Henry preferred to rely on the self-doubting, who were ever eager to justify their promotion, rather than on the entitled, who could be greedy and ungrateful.

One of these 'new men' was Geoffrey Ridel, a senior royal official in England, who was perhaps twenty-five at the start of Henry's reign. Although Ridel was born in Wittering, Northamptonshire, his family roots seem to have stemmed from Apulia, the part of southern Italy that the Normans had controlled since the turn of the millennium.

Under Henry the Ridels had risen to prominence in England, with Geoffrey becoming 'a justice of all England': trusted by the king to administer the law (and perform other tasks) in the crown's name, as opposed to being limited to wielding his authority in a stated locality, like the sheriff of a county. Geoffrey also controlled significant landholdings in Northamptonshire, while his brother Matthias had been the abbot of Peterborough, a senior Church position. Geoffrey Ridel had served as a witness to royal documents since 1105 and was part of a panel of commissioners sent to look closely at privileges that the archbishop of York had controversially claimed, the following year.

There had been a significant gap in Domesday Book: the ancient Anglo-Saxon capital of Winchester had not been accounted for in the same forensic way that the rest of England had. Geoffrey Ridel was one of those sent to oversee the filling of this void, gathering the testimony and records of the most eminent citizens of Winchester so that what was due to the crown could be properly recorded in the Winchester Domesday. By discharging such valuable duties with care and honesty, Ridel became a man of importance.

One way for these 'new men' to show off their sudden and dramatic increase in status was to build castles. To be allowed to do this, they needed the king's permission: erecting a castle was the ultimate manifestation of royal trust; one that Henry granted sparingly, and only when it suited his purpose.

Geoffrey de Clinton came from a family of obscure minor landowners from the Cotentin. He probably first met Henry when the future king was, as a young man, count of that part of western Normandy. De Clinton quickly rose through the ranks of the king's household, becoming Henry's chamberlain and treasurer in 1120. Henry also made de Clinton the sheriff of Warwickshire. He knew he could rely on him to keep order in that county in the face of the ambitions of Roger de Beaumont, who was earl of Warwick. De Beaumont and some of his influential family were of questionable loyalty.

Henry gave de Clinton permission to build Kenilworth Castle, with its huge sandstone keep, as a counterweight to de Beaumont's imposing headquarters five miles away at Warwick Castle. The king wanted de Beaumont to know that royal power was operating on his doorstep, and that it was watching him very closely indeed.

EIGHT

Louis the Fat

It is neither right nor natural that the French be subject to the English, but rather the English to the French.

Abbot Suger (1081–1151), churchman, statesman, as well as companion and biographer of Louis VI of France

Prince Louis of France was the eldest surviving son of Philip I, who ruled France from 1060 until 1108. While Orderic Vitalis described Philip as 'indolent, fat, and unfit for war', he had spent much of his long reign busily trying to undermine the power of Normandy, which he had watched rise from being France's troublesome neighbour to a form of imperial status.[1] With the taming of the Anglo-Norman threat his goal, Philip had assisted Robert Curthose against the Conqueror, against Rufus and latterly against Henry.

Louis's mother was the king's first wife, Bertha of Holland. When Louis was a boy Bertha had been supplanted in the king's affections, dismissed as unacceptably overweight after he had fallen in love with Bertrade de Montfort, the wife of Count Fulk IV of Anjou. The chronicler John of Marmoutier, writing in the first half of the twelfth century, said of Bertrade that she was a woman 'whom no good man ever praised, save for her beauty'.

Philip and Bertrade's mutual attraction was a force not to be denied. Pope Urban, who was at odds with the French king over his habit of selling religious offices for huge gain, threatened Philip with excommunication if he failed to return to Bertha of Holland. But Philip instead banished Bertha to Montreuil, in the far north of France. Then, in May 1092, while both were still married to others, Philip and Bertrade wed.

Philip was excommunicated for bigamy in 1094. The pope confirmed the sentence at the Council of Clermont the following year, so preventing the king from taking part in the First Crusade. But the passion between Philip and Bertrade continued, producing two sons, Philip and Florus, and a daughter, Cecile. The arrival of these children of the second marriage presented a threat to Louis. Bertrade was determined that one of her sons should succeed their father in place of her stepson. But Philip was equally resolute that Louis remain his heir: he had recognised him as such when proclaiming him 'king designate' when Louis was four years old.

According to Orderic Vitalis the matter came to a head at Westminster in 1100 when Louis, recently turned nineteen, was a guest of Henry I's at his first Christmas court as king of England. During Louis's stay Henry received a surprising letter, seemingly written by Philip I of France, asking him to detain Philip's son and confine him in an English prison. Henry soon learned that the letter had been penned not by King Philip, but by Queen Bertrade. He persuaded Louis to leave for France at once.

When she found out that her stepson had safely returned from England, Bertrade was said to have employed witchcraft to try to kill him. When this failed, she had him poisoned. But

Louis survived, although the queen's poison was believed to have left him so ill that for the rest of his life he was deathly pale.

This strange episode is the only time that Henry and Louis seem to have been on the same side in anything. As soon as Louis succeeded his father, in 1106, their rivalry erupted, never to subside again: 'After the death of Philip, the French king,' wrote Henry of Huntingdon, '[King] Henry crossed to Normandy to wage extensive war against the new king of France, Louis, son of Philip.'[2] Orderic Vitalis noted how intense the hostility between the two kings was, from the moment Louis ascended the throne: 'Consequently,' the monk recorded with regret, 'there was bitter fighting between them and great harm came to many people.'[3]

The two men met as kings for the first time in early 1109. Following his defeat of Robert Curthose, Henry hoped that Louis would acknowledge him as rightful duke of Normandy. It was not a happy encounter. Henry was outraged by the condescension of Louis's envoys, who made it clear that they considered him to be a mere vassal to their master. Henry left feeling so insulted that he ordered his garrison commanders on the frontier with France to ready their castles for war.

The reason was the same as it had been in Philip I's time: France's need to curb the power of Normandy. The catalyst this time, though, was William Clito, the nephew that Henry had failed to take with him after his victory at Tinchebray, in 1106. Henry had committed William Clito to the care of Helias of Saint-Saëns, hoping the boy would be cared for but not heard from again.

But Saint-Saëns had lofty ambitions for his charge. He persuaded Louis VI to back William Clito's claim to Curthose's Norman dukedom. Clito soon became a popular rallying point for disaffection with King Henry. Belatedly realising the threat to his dynasty that his nephew represented, Henry ordered Clito to be kidnapped and brought to him for safekeeping. But Saint-Saëns learned of the approach of Henry's men and smuggled Clito to safety just before he could be seized.

The botched attempt on Clito's freedom sparked a rebellion, and a war, that lasted from 1111 until 1113. The revolt in Normandy was, in truth, largely a reaction to Henry's increasing hold over the duchy, but proclaiming support for Curthose's son had a more acceptable air to it than admitting to aristocratic self-interest. Similarly the war stemmed from foreign opportunism, with France, Flanders and Anjou forming an international conspiracy to diminish Henry, and break his and his heirs' hold on the southern side of the Channel.

Robert de Bellême, by then in his mid-fifties, was one of the leading rebels. But in 1112 his luck ran out. Long exiled from England, he hoped he could persuade Henry to agree a lasting peace with him in Normandy: he flattered himself that such an arrangement would suit them both. So when Louis VI asked de Bellême to go to Henry's coastal castle at Bonneville-sur-Touques, to see if he could negotiate the release of Robert Curthose, he jumped at the chance. He could act as an envoy while at the same time exploring the possibility of a private truce. This was a monumental mistake.

Despite de Bellême's protected status as an ambassador, Henry had him arrested. De Bellême was charged with failing to obey any of Henry's previous summonses, for acting against him as his lord, and for failing to produce accounts that had been repeatedly demanded of him.

The news of de Bellême's seizure was greeted with excitement around Normandy. Orderic Vitalis wrote: 'The people of God, freed from the bandit's yoke, rejoiced and thanked God their liberator, and wished a long and prosperous life to King Henry.'[4]

Henry had his old adversary detained in Cherbourg before

sending him across the Channel to Wareham Castle, in Dorset. He remained there, in the same state of perpetual imprisonment as Curthose, for the rest of his life. In a repetition of what had occurred in England beforehand, all of de Bellême's estates in Normandy were confiscated, as were those of his powerful brothers.

So complete was de Bellême's fall, from leading rebel lord to close imprisonment that, after a mention of his being alive in 1130, there is no further record of him being so, and we have no logging of his subsequent date of death. He left behind a lasting legacy, though: his infamous cruelty is believed to be the model for 'Robert the Devil', a mythical Norman lord of chilling depravity, who was supposedly the spawn of the Devil.

There were plenty of enemies to take de Bellême's place. When Elias I of Maine died in 1110, the county was inherited by Ermengarde, wife of Fulk V of Anjou. Fulk, now count of two of Normandy's traditional enemies, immediately supported William Clito's cause. And from 1112, Clito was welcomed into the court of Baldwin VII, the nineteen-year-old count of Flanders.

The combination of France, Flanders, Anjou and Maine was too strong for Henry to face with any confidence of success, yet he managed to chisel away at the unity of his enemies through secret talks. His most precious diplomatic asset was the hand of his one legitimate son, William Ætheling, and this he offered to Fulk V for one of his daughters, Matilda of Anjou.

Fulk, eager to advance his dynasty, and to form a political alliance with Normandy, agreed the match. Matilda, aged two or three, and nine-year-old William were betrothed in February 1113, near Alençon. The settlement included the county of Maine as Matilda's dowry when they were old enough to marry. In the meantime it peeled the Angevins away from their alliance with France. Unable to continue his war without Fulk's support, Louis met with Henry at the castle of Gisors, in Normandy, to agree peace.

Louis was obliged to recognise Henry's right to the county of Maine, to the lordship of Bellême and to acknowledge Henry's new influence in Brittany: Maud, one of his illegitimate daughters, had recently married its new duke, Conan III, who had deposed his father the previous year.

With William Ætheling approaching puberty, and with William Clito still at large, King Henry set about establishing his sole legitimate son as his undisputed successor on both sides of the Channel. In 1115, at Rouen, Henry had his most important Norman barons swear loyalty to William Ætheling and publicly recognise him as Henry's one true heir to the dukedom. The following March Henry extracted an oath from the English lords, in Salisbury, acknowledging William Ætheling's right to become the next king of England. The *Warenne Hyde Chronicle*, written some fifty years later, referred to William from this point as being 'assumed to be the future king of the Norman-English'. In contemporary documents, after these twin ceremonies, William is termed '*rex et dux designatus*' – the designated king and duke.

But Louis VI refused to recognise William Ætheling's rights in Normandy, at the same time openly supporting the claims of William Clito once more. Henry tried a bribe to persuade Louis to change his mind, but the French king took the payment while failing to see through its conditions.

Henry crossed to Normandy at Easter 1116, ready to rejoin battle with France. When his nephew Theobald of Blois-Chartres took up arms against Louis, who was his overlord, Henry sent Theobald reinforcements, including some of his more experienced commanders. Henry of Huntingdon noted how these men 'caused considerable damage to King Louis'.[5]

The fighting quickly escalated, and 1117 saw Henry's old

enemies re-forming. The French king and the counts of Flanders and Anjou took an oath to secure Normandy for William Clito. Henry had as allies Blois-Chartres and Brittany. Like the conflict of 1111–13, it would last for two years, and would threaten not just Henry, but also the rights of his son, William Ætheling. Meanwhile the enormous taxes that Henry was raising in England to fund his battles overseas were causing real hardship, and much resentment. But with the future of his dynasty at stake, Henry carried on fighting.

While Henry was engaged in warfare, Queen Matilda preferred to base herself for the most part in Westminster Palace. She was an energetic queen with an enquiring mind who acted as her husband's regent in England while he was abroad: his duties in Normandy had kept him on the south side of the Channel for part of each year between 1104 and 1109, and from 1111 through the demands of this latest war.

Henry was dependent on the wisdom and resourcefulness of his wife who also had to carefully oversee her own household and landed interests. Henry gave her advisers to help her, including Robert Bloet, Bishop of Lincoln, in whose household he had placed some of his illegitimate sons. But during the night of 1 May 1118, Matilda died, of unknown causes.

Henry insisted she be buried in Westminster Abbey, rather than in her preferred choice of Holy Trinity Priory, in Aldgate, which she had founded ten years earlier. He ordered that a candle should burn next to her tomb in perpetuity. Henry of Huntingdon eulogised Queen Matilda thoughtfully: 'Successes did not make her happy, nor did troubles make her sad: troubles brought a smile to her, successes fear. Beauty did not produce weakness in her, nor power pride: she alone was both powerful and humble, both beautiful and chaste.'[6] Her epitaph summed her up as 'a woman for all seasons'[7] while her subjects remembered her as 'Matilda the Good Queen', or 'Good Queen Maud'.

There were thoughts of trying to have her recognised as a saint, as her mother had been, but these were not carried through.

Five weeks later, Henry lost his wisest adviser, Robert de Beaumont. Robert had arrived in England beside Henry's father, in 1066, and despite being a young man then, he had commanded the right wing of the Norman army at Hastings, with, it was recorded at the time, 'the utmost bravery and success'.[8] He had served the first two Norman kings of England with distinction and wisdom. He was in the hunting party that ended in the death of William Rufus, and supported Henry's claim to the throne immediately afterwards. In 1107 de Beaumont was rewarded with the title of 1st Earl of Leicester, and ninety-one manors in the English Midlands and Wiltshire, to go with his extensive ancestral landholdings in Normandy and France.

The death of the warrior-statesman was said to have been caused by shame, after his much younger wife, Elizabeth – a granddaughter of Henry I of France and a niece of Philip I of France – was seduced by William de Warenne, another mighty nobleman. Whether or not that was the reason, the loss of the queen and the earl in such quick succession left Henry without two of the great bulwarks of the first half of his rule in England. The timing was particularly unfortunate because Louis the Fat was preparing for a three-pronged attack on Normandy, with the counts of Flanders and of Anjou.

One of Henry's key allies in this war would be his nephew Stephen of Blois. Stephen operated in unison with his elder brother, Theobald, Count of Blois-Chartres, providing cover when Theobald was fighting elsewhere, and in November 1118 riding to his rescue when Theobald was cornered by the enemy at L'Aigle.

Theobald was keen to regain parts of his family's lands that had been given to Stephen when the family inheritance had been divided among the sons of the family. He brokered their restoration to his, senior, branch in return for Stephen receiving Alençon – an area in the south of Normandy the castle of which their grandfather, William the Conqueror, had captured, before brutalising the troops who had mocked his mother's modest roots.

Always one to take the easy course, Stephen allowed his garrison to run wild in Alençon. Finding their rights and customs trampled on, the people of the area pleaded for help from Fulk V of Anjou. When Fulk arrived to besiege the town, Stephen and his brother Theobald sprang into action. They did so without proper planning and, despite Henry having marched with a force from L'Aigle to fight alongside his nephews, in December 1118 they were comprehensively defeated by Fulk V, who took possession of Alençon. This was the only major military defeat that Henry would suffer during his thirty-five years ruling England, and twenty-nine years as duke of Normandy.

It was such a serious reverse that Henry felt compelled to bribe Fulk to leave his alliance with Louis VI. As part of this new arrangement between Henry and Fulk, both men agreed to breathe fresh life into the betrothal of William Ætheling and Matilda of Anjou: they were to be married. The wedding took place in Lisieux, in Normandy, in June 1119. Wace recorded the momentous union with a simplicity that skipped over the reality of the politics involved: 'The king loved his heir and provided him with a very beautiful wife, the daughter of Fulk, Count of Anjou.'[9]

The county of Maine, so long a target of Norman ambition as it looked to the safety of its southern frontier, was included in Matilda of Anjou's dowry. Fulk also promised that Anjou would pass to William Ætheling and Matilda, if he died while on Crusade. In return Henry gave Fulk a commodity that England had plenty of – money.

Despite removing Fulk V from the ranks of his enemies,

Henry still faced many powerful opponents in William Clito's camp. Amaury III de Montfort was one of Henry's most significant and influential adversaries at this time. A French aristocrat, and an uncle to Fulk V of Anjou, he had encouraged Fulk to fight against Henry. Amaury was also related to Louis the Fat.

Amaury had become seigneur de Montfort in 1104, on the death of his brother, Simon. When Amaury's uncle William, Count of Évreux died in April 1118, with no child to succeed him, Louis the Fat granted his estate to his ally, Amaury. It was a serious blow to Henry, as it meant losing a county inside Normandy to hostile forces.

All this, at a time when many in the nobility of Normandy were beginning to question Henry's power, while being swayed by the claim of William Clito. This led to attempts to extort land and power from Henry: if he did not grant his wavering followers more, they threatened to alter their allegiance. Just such a problem arose for Henry from an unexpected quarter. His illegitimate daughter Juliana – one of three children he had with his favoured mistress Ansfride – had been married to Eustace de Pacy as a thirteen-year-old. Eustace and Juliana now warned that they would join Henry's enemies unless he also gave them the castle of Ivry.

Henry was doubly disappointed by this development: his support had won Eustace the lands of William de Breteuil. In addition, for the king's own daughter to support his son-in-law in an attempt to extort more wealth from him was a devastating paternal blow. Henry tried to stall the couple. He insisted on a hostage swap to guarantee the peace while he looked at their claim. Eustace and Juliana committed their daughters to the custody of Ralph Harnec, who controlled Ivry for Henry, while Harnec reciprocated by sending his son to be held in Breteuil.

Somehow Amaury de Montfort inveigled himself into this delicate situation. He persuaded Eustace to have Harnec's son blinded. When he learned of this outrage, the distraught Harnec looked to Henry for justice. It is, perhaps, impossible to understand how a man as powerful as Henry simply bowed to the conventions of the time, but he did. An innocent hostage from one side had been mutilated, therefore the same horror had to be inflicted on the other.

The king gave permission for his two granddaughters to be blinded by Harnec, who also cut off the ends of the girls' noses. This grisliest of tit for tats prompted Orderic Vitalis to comment: 'Thus innocent children, alas, suffer for the sins of the fathers.'[10] But it was not the end of the matter.

Ignoring her husband's hand in the appalling saga, the inconsolable Juliana focused her torment and fury on her father for allowing the blinding and disfigurement of her daughters. She went to Breteuil, to occupy its castle, in defiance of her father. But the citizens of the town refused to join in her stand against Henry. They allowed him peaceful access to the castle walls, where he laid siege to his daughter, confident of success.

Juliana, seeming to understand how hopeless her position was, suggested the two of them meet, to discuss the terms under which she might surrender. Henry arrived in good faith, but Juliana was there not to parley with her father, but rather to avenge her daughters. All of a sudden she reached for a concealed crossbow and fired its bolt at her father. It missed.

Shocked and furious, Henry left the castle, keeping Juliana holed up in a tower. While he waited for her inevitable surrender, she instead plunged into the moat, with her bare buttocks on display, before escaping to her husband at Pacy, sixty miles to the south-west. The king's vengeance was to take Breteuil from his son-in-law and daughter, and give it to a trusted dependant, Ralph de Gaël. De Gaël's daughter Amice would soon become betrothed to one of Henry's illegitimate sons, Richard of Lincoln.

Amice's engagement to Richard worked for both fathers. Ralph de Gaël was keen to establish closer ties with the victorious king because he was concerned that rival claimants might try to relieve him of his newly acquired lands. Henry was happy to approve a match that set up his natural son with money and power for life. Amice's dowry was a patchwork of Breton and Norman estates.

Meanwhile Richard of Lincoln was Juliana's full brother. Orderic Vitalis recorded him as having gone to King Henry during his siege of Breteuil, where he 'pleaded his sister's cause'.

There was another attempt on Henry's life around this time. The identity of the leader of the would-be assassins is not certain, but we know from Abbot Suger that his name began with an 'H', and that he was a *camerarius* – one of the king's senior household officers, combining the duties of a treasurer and chamberlain. Suger – whose master, Louis VI, was something of an aficionado when it came to swift, royal, justice, having had the entire enemy garrison of Crécy-sur-Serre beheaded – wrote of his appreciation of Henry's mercy. Suger thought it admirably restrained that Henry ordered 'H' to be only blinded and castrated, when execution was surely the correct penalty for such a grave crime.

But Henry was troubled by the vulnerability that 'H' had revealed during his botched attempt. From that point the king increased the size of his bodyguard, slept with weapons to hand and ordered a selection of bedchambers to be kept ready for him, so nobody would know where he planned to spend the night. Having survived an assassination attempt by a trusted servant, as well as his daughter's shot at patricide, Henry was perhaps due some luck in the field of international relations. It came in mid-June 1119.

Ten months earlier, while fighting Henry 'with unrestrained knightly spirit, on the castle of Eu', the corpulent Baldwin VII of Flanders had caught a glancing blow from a lance in the face.[11] Baldwin had insisted it was merely a scrape, not worth worrying about, and 'disdained to take care of so small a wound'.[12] But the cut had turned septic, and when it was clear that the twenty-six-year-old was going to die, the question of succession became urgent: the inheritance had gone down the generations of the ruling family for more than 250 years. Baldwin VII had been married at twelve, but divorced at seventeen, and he had never remarried and had no heir. Baldwin died in June but had time before his death to nominate Charles the Good, an elder cousin, as his successor.

Soon after Charles became count of Flanders, Henry arranged bribes in return for his neutrality. The removal of Flanders from the French-led alliance that faced him ensured that the new peace with Fulk V of Anjou, sealed by the marriage of William Ætheling and Matilda of Anjou (in the same month as Baldwin's death), seemed set to last.

Abbot Suger wrote furiously of how Fulk V 'had earlier allied himself to King Louis by personal homage, many oaths, and even a large number of hostages. But Count Fulk now put greed before fealty, and inflamed by treachery gave his daughter in wedlock to William, son of the English king, without consulting King Louis. He falsely betrayed his sworn word to be an enemy of King Henry and joined himself to the English king by ties of friendship of this kind.'[13]

Without Anjou and Flanders, France was left as Henry's sole aggressor, supported only by barons hostile to his rule. These Henry now treated with uncompromising aggression. In 1119 Reginald de Bailleul, a twenty-four-year-old nobleman, demanded an audience with Henry at which he sought to be released from his homage. This, Henry appreciated, was a prelude to de Bailleul's attaching himself to William Clito as his lord instead. Henry said he could agree to the request only if de Bailleul returned the properties that he had received from him in return for his homage. When he refused to do this, Henry simply seized them, filling de Bailleul's castles with his own troops.

With the recent threats to his life reminding him of his mortality, Henry set about preparing his son for his own reign. In 1119 we see increasing signs that William Ætheling was being taught the governing and military duties of medieval kingship. He had been by his father's side throughout that summer, witnessing a royal document in Rouen with a signature that, underneath, had the proclamation: 'by the grace of God the designated king'. The previous year the prince, after his mother's death in the spring, had been given increased responsibilities in England, acting as regent.

William also prepared for combat in the climactic engagement between his father and Louis the Fat. The Battle of Brémule would take place sixteen miles south-east of Rouen, in the centre of the Norman Vexin, on 20 August 1119. Alongside William Ætheling were two other of Henry's sons – Robert FitzRoy and Richard of Lincoln. By now these were both experienced in battle, and Orderic Vitalis calls them 'excellent soldiers'.

Richard of Lincoln had commanded a fortified position in the village of Le Grand Andely, in 1118. Its defences were betrayed by a turncoat, and Richard made a stand with his men in the village church. With no hope of rescue, they had been forced to surrender to the French. Richard had been released by Louis the Fat. Being always in the thick of the fighting, he was nearly captured by the enemy again soon afterwards but was rescued by one of his father's military champions just in time. Richard then fought alongside his father during the siege of Évreux.

The three royal half-brothers commanded the third line of the Anglo-Norman army, which was comprised of foot soldiers, with the king directing the battle from the second line on horseback, surrounded by his household knights. His most important nobles were drawn up in front of him.

Louis was supported by many of the great French magnates, as well as the sixteen-year-old whose cause they were there to support, William Clito. Robert Curthose's son had grown into a charming and promising young man, who had been knighted by Count Baldwin of Flanders when only fourteen. The talismanic Clito commanded the front line, with Louis and his finest men in the second.

Looking back on the fateful day, Abbot Suger contrasted the actions of the two kings as they prepared for and engaged in battle. He noted how, 'Setting fires that would leap up and throw him into disarray, King Henry made his armed knights dismount so that they might fight more bravely on foot, and wisely busied himself taking whatever military precautions he could. King Louis and his men, however, deemed it unworthy to plan carefully for battle and rushed against the enemy in a bold but careless attack.'[14]

The undisciplined French, led by Burchard de Montmorency and Guy de Clermont, broke the English front line of barons and knights, some of whom fled the field. But they then encountered King Henry's well-ordered ranks of foot soldiers, drawn up in a strong position. These infantry units withstood the force of the enemy's charge before counter-attacking. It was a furious encounter, Henry of Huntingdon recording how: 'The royal lines struck out at one another, and there was fierce fighting. Every spear is broken. They carry on with swords.'[15]

Henry was fighting against the nephew who he had unwisely allowed to be free. His life was now nearly ended by another whose liberty he had too readily granted. William Crispin, let go after being captured fighting for Robert Curthose at Tinchebray, thirteen years earlier, struck Henry twice on his head with his sword. The king's armour held, but the impact forced his helmet down into his head, causing blood to gush out. Chroniclers claimed that Henry then knocked Crispin and his horse down with a mighty blow, but it was a lord called Roger FitzRichard who saved the king's life by unseating Crispin. He was captured at Henry's feet.

At this point the third line of the Anglo-Norman army, including the king's three sons, rushed forward on foot, with lances levelled, settling the day. The French fled, but many nobles 'were captured and brought to the king's feet. He then returned to Rouen amid the sounds of battle-cries and the chanting of the clergy, and glorified God who is the Lord of hosts.'[16]

William Clito and Louis the Fat were among those to flee successfully from Brémule. In his one-sided biography of the French king Abbot Suger wrote: 'The sight of his host falling back astonished the King, but as he usually did in bad times, he relied on his own hardy fighting spirit to help himself and his men.'[17]

This is something of an exaggeration. Louis cast off all the insignia of his kingship so that he might slip away unnoticed, to all appearances just another refugee from a battle lost. A peasant, unaware of who he was, helped him on his way, and eventually Louis made it to the safety of his mighty castle at Les Andelys, which Clito also reached.

Still reeling from the completeness of their defeat, the French king and Clito were surprised to be reunited with the magnificent warhorses that they had abandoned in their flight. These had been returned as gifts from Henry and William Ætheling respectively. This was chivalry of such a supremely high order that it bordered on the insulting. Henry did, however, hold on to the French royal standard, captured on the battlefield that day.

The Battle of Brémule was, in military and dynastic terms, the high point of Henry's reign. As far as the king of England and his heir were concerned, they surely had nothing further to fear from their defeated enemies. Henry must have looked forward to spending more time in England: his frequent campaigns in Normandy had been firefighting operations, putting out the flames of rebellion lit around Clito's perfectly valid claim to his father's lands. Now, surely, it was over.

In October 1119 Louis applied to Callixtus II, the recently elected pope, who was presiding at the Council of Reims, to have Henry condemned for offences against him. This pope was particularly well qualified to judge such a highborn contest, in that he was a son of the count of Burgundy and a relative of the kings of France and of England. Henry was, Louis insisted, guilty of four feudal outrages: invading Normandy, imprisoning Robert Curthose, disinheriting William Clito and encouraging his vassal Theobald of Blois-Chartres to rebel against France.

As part of his education as a king-in-waiting, William Ætheling accompanied his father to Reims and witnessed international diplomacy in action. Henry successfully sought a fresh audience with the pope and his council, not in French Reims, but rather in Norman Gisors. Henry's advocates at the November hearing explained to Pope Callixtus how completely Curthose had failed as duke of Normandy. Henry presented his brother 'as a noble pilgrim, worn out with many troubles, reposing in a royal citadel (*in arce regia*), with abundance of delicacies and comforts'. Meanwhile William Clito was described as an ungrateful nephew, who had declined to take up Henry's invitation to join his royal court.

The king's men detailed how Henry had, during his thirteen-year rule, worked tirelessly to restore Normandy to the lawful ways it had ultimately enjoyed under his father, the Conqueror. The pope and his councillors refused to find against Henry on any of Louis's four points. Instead they declared that Normandy was justly his, and recognised William Ætheling as his rightful heir. It was a diplomatic triumph every bit as forceful as the military one achieved at Brémule. So it was that, by 1120, Henry finally achieved all that he had proposed to Louis the Fat five years earlier.

It was agreed, thanks to the help of Henry's sister and nephew, Adela and Theobald of Blois, that the king of England would not have to give homage to his French counterpart for the dukedom of Normandy. Instead, this would be performed by the males of the next generation. Louis's three-year-old son, Philip, received the homage from William Ætheling. This formal recognition of William Ætheling's claim extinguished any hopes William Clito can have had of further French support.

Recognising the scale and the finality of his defeat, Clito humbly sought the release of his father. He promised that, if it was granted, Curthose and he would live out their lives in Jerusalem, and they would never again venture north of the Alps. Henry could see no benefit in this suggestion so rejected it.

The dominant question of Henry's rule – who would eventually succeed him, in each of his realms? – had been resolved. The answer was quite obvious now: William Ætheling, his position secure as future king of England and duke-designate of Normandy. Henry's main duties appeared to have been achieved: he had produced an heir and, by guaranteeing William's dual inheritance, had paved the way to a future that promised peace and security for both his peoples.

PART TWO

DISASTER

NINE

Contemplating Rewards

In the year of grace 1120, when all were subdued and pacified in Gaul, Henry joyfully returned to England.

Henry of Huntingdon

O rderic Vitalis opened the long chapter of his history for 1120 with an epic sweep: 'King Henry, who had now, after tremendous toil, settled affairs admirably in Normandy, decided to cross the Channel, pay generous wages to the young champions and distinguished knights who had fought hard and loyally, and raise the status of some by giving them extensive honors [feudal baronies] in England. He commanded a fleet to be made ready at once, and numbers of knights of all ranks to accompany him.'[1]

Those sailing to England with the king were to rendezvous in Barfleur, the coastal town that lies near the tip of the Cotentin, on the north-eastern side of that stubby thumb of a peninsula that points up from Normandy towards England. The perfection of Barfleur's natural harbour, held tight between two protective arms of shoreline, made it irresistible to mariners and to shipbuilders, keen to keep their vessels safe from the whims of wind and waves.

Due south of the Isle of Wight and Southampton, Barfleur was a favoured arrival and departure point for voyages across the Channel. In ancient times it was the landing site for iron and tin brought across from Britain. Legend has it that King Arthur set off to fight the Allobroges, a warrior race that inhabited modern-day Burgundy, from Barfleur. By the Middle Ages it had long been established as the preferred Norman port for those crossing to and from the southern English coast, a journey that would take ten to twelve hours in decent weather.

Henry's retinue comprised not only the victorious fighting men mentioned by Orderic Vitalis, but also leading lords, churchmen and courtiers, some accompanied by their wives and daughters. Many of those descending on Barfleur were of the highest rank. These were the people who would accompany Henry home, to celebrate his ultimate triumph after two decades of focused rule.

The king of England who entered Barfleur in November 1120 was now in his early fifties. His frame was still powerful but stout, his increased weight emphasised by his lack of height: William of Malmesbury diplomatically estimated Henry to be 'more than short, but less than tall'.[2] When younger, Henry's dark hair had been thick enough to flop forward over his forehead. But it had long since receded and what was left was greying.

By the standards of the time the ageing king was preparing for his upcoming voyage with a clean sweep of regal success to his credit: an acknowledged heir, peace across his lands and a rich reservoir of loyal support. Indeed, it must have seemed that Henry had not only honoured the astonishing scope of his father's Anglo-Norman ambitions but that he had finally set his victorious legacy in place for generations to come.

In those who followed Henry into Barfleur that late autumn we see living examples of the winning system of kingship that he had constructed over the previous twenty years. These were the human tools with which he had fashioned such a lofty pinnacle of success. First in importance was his heir, for whom all was now, finally, settled. Henry had undertaken his many struggles and reforms in England and Normandy in order to rule as he wished. But, equally, all his achievements had been pursued with the aim of passing on his realms, in the finest of order, to William Ætheling.

In Barfleur, as elsewhere, there was a flurry of excitement around the prince. As many of his entourage as could do so would travel with William Ætheling on the upcoming sea crossing to England. William of Malmesbury pictures them abuzz, 'almost all the young nobility flocking around him, from similarity of youthful pursuits'.[3]

They jostled for favour, eager to suck from the flower of his youthful glamour, while quietly conscious of the majestic power that would one day be his by inheritance. For now, they attempted to catch the eye of a prince who was himself dazzling.

To flaunt their status and wealth, the extremely affluent and influential coveted the finest silks, and William Ætheling was not slow in showing off his worth. Henry of Huntingdon wrote of how: 'We saw William, the king's son, clothed in silk embroidered with gold, surrounded by a throng of servants and guards, glittering in a glory all but heavenly.'[4]

This snapshot of the prince reveals his social pre-eminence, through both his luxurious wardrobe and the size of his retinue. As William of Malmesbury remarked, the seventeen-year-old now, 'by his father's indulgence, possessed everything but the name of king'.[5] Drawing on the aristocratic fashions of the time, we can guess how William Ætheling was turned out when he waited in Barfleur to make his sea passage home. If we picture him swathed in the finest silk shirt and tunic, with a fur-trimmed brocaded cloak thrown over his shoulders – to combine magnificence with warmth – we are probably not too far from the truth. If, in addition, he was following the fashion that had taken root during his grandfather's rule of England, and was still in vogue, his shoes would have been long, with pointed toes.

William Ætheling's bodyguards would have remained close enough to keep their precious charge safe at all times. It is fair to assume that these guards had increased in number and in vigilance since the abortive attempt on the king's life a year or so earlier.

Several of Henry's natural children were also accompanying the king at this time. Two of his elder illegitimate sons, Robert FitzRoy and Richard of Lincoln, were there. The half-brothers had served as their father's military commanders, and after performing well at Brémule they were acclaimed for their leadership and bravery in the field.

Not long before setting off for Barfleur, and the triumphant return to England that beckoned, Richard of Lincoln had got engaged to Amice, the only child and heiress of Ralph de Gaël – he who had been made lord of Breteuil by Henry the previous year after his daughter Juliana's attempt on his life with the crossbow. But in Barfleur Richard awaited his voyage to England alone: Amice was not to travel with him, perhaps out of a wish to stay with her family until royal marriage demanded she start a new life abroad. Richard of Lincoln was wearing clothes so fine that they were remembered clearly by those there who saw him – a princely peacock, happy to dazzle, proud of the admiring glances he attracted.

Henry's eldest natural son, Robert FitzRoy, one of his father's favourite children, had also agreed a wealthy match. The king had taken care of FitzRoy's future, marrying him off to Mabel

FitzHamon, another substantial heiress, praised for her beauty. Her father, Robert FitzHamon (who had been in the hunting party that witnessed the death of William Rufus) had died in 1107, having received brain damage two years earlier supporting a failed attack by Henry on the city of Falaise.

Since their marriage Robert FitzRoy had taken full control of his wife's estates. Later, Mabel was applauded by a chronicler for fulfilling the list of limited expectations imposed upon a lady of her noble pedigree, for she was 'a lovely and noble woman, a lady who was both obedient to her husband and blessed in being the mother of numerous and very fair children'. Mabel's landholdings made Robert FitzRoy particularly powerful in south-western England, where he commanded Bristol, Gloucester and Tewkesbury. Robert was also strong in Wales, as lord of Cardiff and Newport, and his wife brought with her estates in Normandy, too.

Another of Henry's illegitimate brood was in Barfleur. Matilda was the product of Henry's relationship with the lover we know nothing about, except that she was called Edith. Matilda had become the second wife of Rotrou III, Count of Perche, in 1103. When, in 1114, Henry had finally defeated his implacable enemy, Robert de Bellême, the king had given the confiscated lordship of Bellême to Rotrou both for safekeeping and as a reward. Henry had further built up Rotrou's power and wealth in England, giving him property in Wiltshire as Matilda's dowry.

The investment had paid off. Just as Rotrou's father had fought alongside the Conqueror at Hastings, Rotrou had ridden with Henry during his gloriously victorious campaign of 1119. We know he was in Normandy with the king during 1120 too, but he chose to remain at home rather than join in the triumphant voyage north. Matilda and Rotrou's two daughters seem to have stayed with their father. In late 1120 Philippa was seven years old, and Félicie was four.

Also in Barfleur that late autumn were other grandchildren of the Conqueror. Stephen of Blois, a son of Henry's beloved sister Adela, was there, his serious military reverse at Alençon already a receding memory in the otherwise successful four-year war with France.

Many of the great families of Mortain, where Stephen was count, had opted to cross on the *White Ship* with him. He was a popular figure who was known for his approachability as much as for his bravery as a warrior. Among these travelling companions was Hugh de Moulins, a celebrated soldier who was a cousin of Stephen (and of the king's) through the Conqueror's mother.

Alongside Stephen was his twenty-three-year-old sister, Lucia-Mahaut of Blois-Chartres. She was heading to England with her husband Richard, Earl of Chester, who had succeeded his father, 'Hugh the Fat', as the head of a distinguished Norman family, the senior nobleman in England and as a great royal favourite.

Richard of Chester had shown the value of his power in 1114, when aged just twenty. He had led one of the armies deployed in a three-pronged expedition into Wales, helping to quell a serious rebellion in Gwynedd. Henry of Huntingdon wrote of how Richard 'had been brought up in the greatest splendour in the full expectation of being his father's distinguished heir, [while] still a beardless youth'.[6] The insinuation was that, with full maturity, even more could be expected of Hugh's promising successor.

Accompanying Lucia-Mahaut and Richard in Barfleur was Otuel FitzEarl, one of Hugh of Chester's illegitimate children – and therefore Richard's half-brother. This was the same Otuel who had been the tutor of Richard of Lincoln and the guardian of William Ætheling, while also serving as castellan of the Tower of London.

One more preparing to sail from Barfleur with a blood link to the mighty Chester earldom was William of Rhuddlan. His father, Robert of Rhuddlan, had been Hugh's first cousin, and a courtier to Edward the Confessor who had successfully navigated the Conquest. Presumably he achieved this because he was of Norman blood. In 1072 Robert had become the commander of Hugh of Chester's troops, with Wales as his field of operations. He built a castle on the north coast there, near Rhuddlan, which gave him and his son their title. William of Rhuddlan was the second cousin of Richard of Chester and of Otuel FitzEarl.

The tight mesh of intermarriage that bound the Anglo-Norman upper classes so closely was further evident in the rest of the group preparing to sail together on one ship from Barfleur to Southampton. Richard of Chester and Otuel FitzEarl's paternal aunt, Judith d'Avranches, had married the lord of L'Aigle.* The de L'Aigle family was more powerful than the unexceptional size of their ancestral landholdings might have suggested. They were not especially rich, but their estates formed a strategically intriguing bloc in the south-eastern corner of Normandy, near the border with Maine, where three important rivers converged. The location made them people of influence and this they had parlayed into a series of beneficial marriages, connecting them to many great families including that of the king of Navarre and Aragon, and of Rotrou of Perche.

The de L'Aigle family had a proud tradition of fighting for the dukes of Normandy. One of their number died at Hastings, the only notable aristocrat lost by the Normans that day. His son had also perished in battle, a generation later, again in support of the Conqueror. In the next generation Engenulf and Geoffrey de L'Aigle had been on recent campaigns with Henry in Normandy, serving him well, and they were now ready to accompany the king from Barfleur to England.

---

* The surname allegedly came about after an eagle was seen making its nest in the masonry of the family mansion, as it was being built.

With them would sail Gilbert, Viscount d'Exmes, a senior figure in the de L'Aigle family and a noted force among Henry I's leading warriors. He had fought alongside Henry during the bloody riot of Rouen that had culminated in Henry hurling the rebel ringleader Conan from a tower to his doom.

Engenulf and Geoffrey de L'Aigle were heading to England with high expectations. After their father's death a couple of years earlier they had been left as heirs to the family's English lands near Pevensey – the beachhead of the Norman invasion. But instead their brother Richer had snapped up this estate, insisting he be allowed to retain it. If not, he threatened Henry, he would give his support to Louis VI of France. This would have left south-east Normandy vulnerable to further French inroads, so Henry had very reluctantly agreed to Richer's theft of his brothers' inheritance. But Richer's blackmail had soon been overtaken by events when the de L'Aigle lands in Normandy were captured by Louis VI. Henry, having nothing to gain from continued links with Richer, had promised to make over Pevensey to Engenulf and Geoffrey, the rightful heirs. All that stood between them and possession of their English estate was the upcoming voyage.

Other distinguished young aristocrats returning with hope in their hearts were Ivo and William de Grandmesnil, grandsons of another of the Conqueror's leading warriors at the Battle of Hastings (who was also called Ivo de Grandmesnil) and sons of one of the most powerful barons in Anglo-Norman society.

This senior Ivo had a somewhat controversial military record. He was believed to have disgraced himself during the First Crusade. After a brutal and bloody day's fighting in Antioch, which convinced him that he must soon be put to death by the enemy, Ivo and a posse of other likeminded Crusaders had let themselves down the city's walls by rope in the dead of night. The fugitives reached Antioch's port of St Symeon in a wretched state, with the flesh from their hands and feet stripped to the bone. They sailed for safety, but they would afterwards be referred to with contempt for their cowardice as the 'clandestine rope-dancers'.[7]

On returning to England, things had got even worse for Ivo senior. At a time when the new king was keen to root out magnates whose loyalty was questionable, Henry had prosecuted him for waging private warfare around his stronghold of Leicester, and for destroying his neighbour's crops – which was, Orderic Vitalis noted, 'an unheard of crime . . . and can be atoned for only by a very heavy fine'.[8] The forfeit had been huge, and the confiscations swingeing.

To raise the money demanded, Ivo de Grandmesnil had mort-gaged his lands for fifteen years to a powerful count, Robert de Meulan, who was in turn a close friend of the king's. But de Meulan reneged on the agreement at its stated termination, in 1116. It was only with de Meulan's death in 1118 that things changed. Henry had decided to resettle the English lands on the two de Grandmesnil sons, who had served him well in the royal household. Now they were finally heading home to receive what was due to them.

Many of those in Barfleur that late November may not have shared the same rarefied status as the royal and aristocratic names already mentioned, but they were also valued members of Henry's Anglo-Norman elite. They included representatives of that class of powerful 'new men' that Henry had chosen to reward for their merit and loyalty. They owed everything to his patronage, unlike the powerful hereditary lords, and the king knew he could rely on them totally.

One of these, whom we have met already, was Geoffrey Ridel. Ridel had risen from modest family roots in Apulia to become a 'justice of all England'. He became prominent enough to be named by Henry of Huntingdon as one of those men from lowly birth who had reached the pinnacle of power and position under Henry's patronage. His increasing importance had won him the hand of Geva, an illegitimate daughter of Hugh of Chester. Perhaps for this reason, Ridel chose to sail to England with the rest of the eminent party attached to the Chester earldom.

Another beneficiary of the king's meritocratic favour was William Bigod. He was the eldest son of Roger Bigod, who had served as sheriff of Norfolk and Suffolk. The Bigod forebears were impoverished Norman knights, and it was only when William Bigod's grandfather Robert ('le Bigot') revealed a conspiracy against the life of William the Conqueror that the family achieved social advancement: Robert's reward was a senior position in the king's household. William had built on this start to become royal steward.

A further senior courtier expecting to make the voyage to England was Robert of Mauduit. From Domesday Book we see that Robert's father, William, held land in Hampshire in 1086. Given his surname we can deduce what William's senior function in the household was: 'Mauduit' was the nickname given to the king's chamberlain, being the name of the officer with that role in the legends of King Arthur.

Robert of Mauduit's specific role was chamberlain of the treasury, where he ultimately answered to Roger of Salisbury. He had been born in Portchester, in Hampshire, a couple of years after the Conquest (so he was the same age as the king), and had served as a senior courtier since the early years of Henry's rule. Now in his early fifties, he had no sons and one daughter, called Constance.

Lower down the royal bureaucratic scale was Gisulf, one of Henry's scribes, who was accompanying his master back to England. Gisulf was unusually wealthy among his peers, being a property owner in his own right. Some of his possessions were in London, while in 1110 he had acquired a tenement in Winchester.

An important contingent among the many people milling around Barfleur, waiting for the wind to turn so they could head for England, was made up of leading soldiers. They were, as Orderic Vitalis pointed out, ready to reap all that was due to them for the dangers they had been exposed to on Henry and William Ætheling's behalf. Chief among them was Ralph the Red of Pont-Echanfray. As a young man he had served in the small but effective army of Bohemond, Prince of Taranto, an ambitious Norman warrior who had joined the First Crusade in 1097. Ralph the Red had accompanied Bohemond to Constantinople and Jerusalem, fighting with notable skill and success.

Ralph had also distinguished himself in the recent wars against France, attacking one of Henry's chief opponents in his head-quarters at Évreux, and racing to the aid of Breteuil when it was threatened by Louis's forces. In 1119 he had saved the king's illegitimate son Richard of Lincoln from what would have been his second capture by the French in a short time, at the fortress of Les Andelys. This rescue had resulted in Ralph's own imprisonment, but he was not long detained, the ransom for the royal champion being quickly paid by Henry. Ralph was expected to receive substantial rewards for all his valiant efforts when the king was safely back in England, with titles and estates believed to be already earmarked for him.

Similar was true of Edward of Salisbury. His father, who was half-Anglo-Saxon, had been a justice of Edward the Confessor as a young man, before serving as sheriff of Wiltshire for thirty-five years. During this time he had also become the tenant-in-chief of Chelsea, near London. Edward of Salisbury grew up in Wilcot, near Pewsey, in Wiltshire, where his family had an impressive manor house with its own vineyard. Edward had fought with merit in the 1119 campaign against the French and was in the body of distinguished knights who stood to be well remunerated for their efforts.

The well-connected William de Roumare was another awaiting a ship home from Barfleur. He was the twenty-four-year-old son of the Lord of Bolingbroke, who had estates in Lincolnshire (where William was born) and in Normandy. He had served as constable of Neuf-Marché Castle, successfully holding it for Henry in 1118 during a dangerous rebellion. Through his mother he was yet another who was closely related to members of the earl of Chester's family.

Perhaps the humblest figure heading towards Barfleur harbour had no royal or noble blood, no bureaucratic skill and no known military pretensions. He stood out because his clothes were not the silks and furs of courtly fashion, but wool and leather – the offcuts of his trade – and his name was Berold.

'This Berold was from Rouen,' recorded Wace, 'he was a butcher and sold meat. To get what was due to him he was following the court, for he had sold his meat to a number of people on credit.'[9] Having travelled nearly a hundred miles from Rouen to Barfleur, Berold was determined not to be left out of pocket. He would have his money, even if it meant pursuing his well-bred debtors on to the ships that lay waiting to take them away across the seas where, in the medieval mind, danger always lurked.

TEN

The Sea

Little he dreams that drinks life's pleasure,
By danger untouched in the shelter of towns
Insolent and wine-proud, how utterly weary
Oft I wintered on open seas.

> From *The Seafarer*, an Old English poem
> from the eighth or ninth century

Wace, the twelfth-century poet and historian, was brought up on the Channel island of Jersey, fifty or so miles to the west of Barfleur. Through constant immersion in the maritime world he had developed a feel for the sea and had closely observed those who crossed the waves in peacetime and in war.

The scene in Barfleur harbour in mid to late November 1120 can have differed little from the vivid description that Wace gave of Southampton – Henry's English destination in the coming voyage – in his *Roman de Brut*:

There the ships were gathered
And the troops assembled.

You would have seen many ships being prepared,
Ships moored, ships anchored,
Ships beached and ships launched,
Ships being pegged and nailed together,
Cordage spread out, masts raised,
Gangplanks put over the side and ships loaded
Helmets, shields, hauberks carried,
Lances raised, horses led,
Knights and servants boarding,
And one friend calling out to another.
They exchange many greetings,
Those who are staying behind and those departing.
When all had gone aboard the ships
And they had the tide and a fair wind,
Then you would have seen anchors raised,
Cables hauled, shrouds tied down,
Sailors clambering around on board,
Unfurling canvas and sails;
Some strain at the windlass,
Others with the sail pin and tacking spar;
Aft are the helmsmen,
The best of the master steersmen.
Each one is attentive to his navigation
At the rudder that steers the ship;
Tiller forward if running to port,
Tiller back to starboard.
In order to gather the wind into the sails
They brace the leech-spars to the fore
And fix them solidly into the leeches.
There are some who pull the buntlines,
And lower the yard slightly,
So that the ship may run more smoothly.
. . . They check the wind and the stars,

And trim their sails according to the breeze;
They lash the brails to the mast
So that the wind does escape past it;
They run under two reefs or three.
Very bold, very gallant was he
Who first built a ship
And set sail down wind,
Seeking a country he didn't see
And a shore he didn't know. [1]

Barfleur on that November day nine centuries ago would have shared the soldierly feel that Wace depicts in the earlier section of this passage: an army was coming home. But Barfleur would have had an added splash of luxury and elegance, thanks to the presence of the many aristocratic ladies and leading courtiers accompanying the king and his knights across the Channel.

Two aspects that would have been shared by Wace's Southampton and Henry I's Barfleur were the nautical procedure before and after the vessels set sail, and the nervous buzz of people embarking for a Channel crossing.

In the final five lines quoted Wace touches on the bravery that was needed to board a ship and chance your life on something as temperamental, unpredictable and powerful as the sea. To the medieval mind the sea was a place of beauty, majesty and bounty, but also of constant fear and horror.

Shipwrecks were not uncommon, as we have seen: Harold had been cast upon the shore of Ponthieu, before being ransomed to the Conqueror; Margaret's ship had been dashed against the Scottish shore, leading to her marriage to Malcolm Canmore; and John of Worcester recorded how, in the summer of 1091, Rufus had set off with an invasion force to fight that same king of Scots: 'But, before he reached Scotland, almost all his fleet was sunk.'[2] As a result terror of the sea is frequently shown in medieval texts.

The author of *The Voyage of Saint Brendan the Abbot* wrote with distrust even of the deep when calm, referring to it as 'the sea, dormant and dead'.[3] Its was a latent threat, ready to spring alive. The sheer scale of the sea made it troubling to the twelfth-century mind, the anonymous writer of *Parthenopaeus de Blois* losing courage when pointing out:

> See the sea which goes on so far
> That we cannot see the end of it.[4]

While the limitless horizon provoked its own fears – of where the destination actually lay, and what storms or hidden rocks might be en route – the twelfth-century poet Benoît de Sainte-Maure found the impenetrability of the depths terrifying:

> Sluggish was the sea, black and hideous,
> Murky and ugly and dark.[5]

What horrors and dangers might be lurking in that grim, soupy swell? According to those maps that survive from the era of the *White Ship*, the answer was a thick concoction of monsters: sea serpents, sea dragons, sea lizards, sea bears, aquatic lions and elephants (the latter probably drawn from sightings of walruses), wolf-fish and even sea goats.

The monk and cartographer Matthew Paris, active in the mid thirteenth century, wrote alongside his representation of Scotland: 'This part between the North and South looks out on a vast sea where there is nothing but the abode of monsters. But an island is found there that has many rams.' Even if sailors were able to avoid the monsters, it was believed that sirens would do all they could to lure them to their rocky ruin.

Most of those undertaking medieval voyages felt they were embarking on such a dangerous activity, involving constant fear of unknown forces above and beneath the waves, that it was sensible to commit to God's protection. An anonymous thirteenth-century author wrote:

> Oh God, I very much have to doubt myself
> And be afraid in case I fall
> And tumble into this deep sea.[6]

The author of *Li Romans de Bauduin de Sebourc* reflected the general fear of the medieval seafarer:

> The man who enters the sea, on a journey,
>   enters into great danger!
> This water must be greatly feared, for it is so
>   horrible, lengthy and wide.[7]

In *Le roman de Troie*, an epic twelfth-century poem about Ancient Troy, Benoît de Sainte-Maure has one of his characters state baldly: 'The sea greatly scares me.'

De Sainte-Maure's sea contains other dangers, terrifying because of their immovability and strength:

> The rock is smooth and rises straight upwards.
> The terrible and deep waves of the sea pound
>   it on three sides.[8]

Rocks caused drowning, and drowning was considered one of the very worst ways to die: in an era when almost nobody could swim, it was an end that combined imaginable panic with unimaginable pain. Adenet le Roi, writing in the thirteenth century, presented one of his female characters as being in such overwhelming agony that: 'She was suffering more from the heart than if one were submerged in the sea.'[9]

The seasons played a part in the calendar of fear. Winter sailing was seen as doubly menacing, the fourteenth-century chronicler Jean Froissart writing: 'The sea is cold and proud in the month of December.'

Henry and his companions were set to sail a few days before that most dangerous month for navigation was upon them, but there was already ice in the air. In Barfleur as winter approached even King Henry, who had crossed the Channel two dozen times, must have wondered how his voyage would fare. Nobody sensible took such things for granted. Only the most brave, foolhardy and arrogant chose to ignore the perils of the sea.

There is a tale, popular with twelfth-century chroniclers, of how William Rufus – who was indeed brave, foolhardy and arrogant – was enjoying a hunting trip in the New Forest, near Clarendon, in July 1099. He was sought out there by Amalchis, a messenger sent by Robert de Bellême. Amalchis informed the king that his key stronghold in Maine was beset by enemy forces. These had dared to rise up against Rufus's rule a year after swearing loyalty to him.

'Le Mans has been taken by treachery,' Orderic Vitalis quotes Amalchis as saying: 'My master is holding Ballon* and the royal household troops are resolutely defending all the fortifications in their charge; they urgently look for relief by the royal army against the enemy force surrounding and assaulting them.'[10]

Wace recorded Rufus's reaction:

'Tell me', he said, 'if you can, how . . . I could get to Le Mans by the straightest route. Let each man turn his face in the exact

---

* Ballon is a fortress twelve miles to the north of Le Mans of such strength that it was known as 'The Gateway to Maine'.

direction he thinks Le Mans is.' They turned aside and made the calculation, then pointed to a wall, saying that Le Mans was over there, so he said he would go that way. For a hundred marks of silver, he kept on saying, he would not stray from [the route to] Le Mans by a hundred feet from the point at which he was standing when he heard about the crisis. Then he had the wall, which was very fine and complete, knocked down; the wall was knocked down and the exit made so large that King Rufus and his vassals all passed through it on horseback. The king spurred on to Southampton and summoned his people from all sides; he asked for sailors and gave the orders for them to cross the sea.[11]

But the conditions were clearly against a Channel crossing. The only ship available for the king was old and it had not been fitted out for a voyage. The sailors protested in fear of their lives:

'My Lord', they said, 'have mercy in God's name! We do not have a good breeze; we do not have a favourable wind. It is dangerous to sail against the wind. The sea is cruel and we are afraid of the weather; we do not dare set sail.'

William Rufus thought their protests absurd, and scolded them:

'I have never heard of a king', he said, 'who was drowned at sea. Have your ships drawn out into the deep and see what you can do.'

To do the king's bidding, they agreed to what he asked. They carried the king into the vessel, along with those he wanted to take with him. They drew in the boats and anchors and had people sit quietly and turned the ship toward the wind. They strengthened the shrouds and hoisted the sail; the man who took up his position at the helm headed directly for the wind. With the corner of the mainsail and the spritsail forward, they sailed to Barfleur and in the early morning they arrived at Barfleur on the Cotentin; then the king continued his journey and did not halt until he reached Maine.[12]

The king was adamant that God would never claim the life of the most eminent in the land. Drowning at sea was common, but it was surely a fate reserved for commoners? Rufus completed his voyage safely, as he had felt sure that he would, then summoned a great army, which forced the rebels to abandon Le Mans to him. He found the city in ashes, but he was in time to rescue his fortress garrison.

It remained to be seen if Rufus was correct, and God really did protect the highest born when they braved the sea.

———

As Henry settled into Barfleur awaiting a favourable wind to England, he was approached by Thomas FitzStephen. He was the son of Stephen FitzAirard, the captain of William the Conqueror's flagship, the *Mora*, which had sailed at the head of the invasion fleet of 1066.

FitzStephen began his audience by offering Henry a gold mark, a valuable coin worth six pounds (which was more than a labourer would earn in three years). This, he explained, was payment that he was happy to make in return for a repeat of the royal favour conferred on his family half a century before: 'Stephen son of Airard was my father,' FitzStephen explained, 'and he served your father at sea during his lifetime, for he carried him in his ship to England when he set out for England to fight against Harold. He earned your father's favour by performing this service for him to the end of his days, and received many gifts from him which raised him to high honour among his companions. I ask you, my lord king, to grant me this fief: I have a vessel which is aptly called the *Blanche-Nef*, excellently fitted out and ready for royal service.'[13]

FitzStephen made a point of mentioning how 'aptly' his ship was named. Presumably this is because she was 'blanche' – white – not so much in terms of the colour of her sails, but in the unusual paleness of her timber. There are seventeen hues associated with Viking decorative painting, and white was a particularly important colour in Scandinavian culture: it denoted high status, and celebration.*

Perhaps the *Blanche-Nef* had been treated with a liming wax, or maybe chalk paint (or actual paint) had been used. Whatever the method, the result was clearly evident enough for FitzStephen to refer to it when in the king's presence. FitzStephen was submitting his handsome vessel for Henry's consideration, clear in the understanding that in her whiteness her design was strikingly different from the rest of the great ships of the fleet. She was therefore suitable – in the Viking tradition, still so alive in the longship design of the *Blanche-Nef* – for a king returning to his kingdom with great victories to report.

FitzStephen added further weight to his plea for royal favour by pointing out that the *Blanche-Nef* had fifty skilled oarsmen, and so possessed the speed to get him to England ahead of any other vessel in Barfleur. The wind could not be relied upon, so she kept this full complement of oarsmen to power her forward in the stillest conditions, or to make headway

---

* Recent excavation of the royal, Viking, hall in Lejre, in eastern Denmark (believed to be the real-life model for Heorot, the palace from the opening scenes of *Beowulf*) reveals that it was painted white. The remains of another Danish feasting hall, in Tissø, show a similar whitening, from limewash, of the timber there.

when the wind or tide were against her. FitzStephen was boasting not only of his ship's appearance, but also of her powerful turn of pace.

Henry thanked FitzStephen for his suggestion but explained that he had already made all his arrangements for the Channel crossing, on what he knew to be 'a fine ship'. He did not want to change plans, and so would still take his chosen 'esnecca' – the term for the traditional Viking ship of the leader, derived from the Norse word for 'serpent'.

However, the king consoled FitzStephen by saying that other members of his family, and many of the most trusted members of the nobility and court, would travel in the *Blanche-Nef*. Henry was sure they would enjoy the speedy voyage while he carried on as planned in a less eye-catching ship. Henry was impressed enough by the strength of FitzStephen's vessel to entrust his treasure chests to her hold.

The king planned to sail that afternoon, to leave FitzStephen and his crew – including the fifty rowers – to follow with their human cargo of more than two hundred of the most important people in England and Normandy. These included Henry's sons William Ætheling and Richard of Lincoln, his nephew Stephen of Blois, and his niece Lucia-Mahaut of Chester.

In addition the *Blanche-Nef* would take Richard of Chester and Otuel FitzEarl, and the long list of their cousins and associates, including the de L'Aigles and the de Grandmesnils; as well as Ridel and his fellow 'new men' Bigod, Mauduit and Gisulf. Alongside them would be the great warriors Ralph the Red, Gilbert d'Exmes and the younger soldiers whose careers were on the rise, such as de Roumare and Edward of Salisbury. Others who opted to board her included a bevy of leading churchmen, a relative of the Roman Emperor and the butcher Berold, still in dogged pursuit of his debtors.

Henry had never before crossed the Channel later in the year than September. But the weather was set fair, and as long as a southerly wind could be harnessed, it looked like an uneventful voyage was in store on the *Blanche-Nef* – a name that, when translated into English, becomes the *White Ship*.

ELEVEN

Bound for England

There in the harbour stood the ring-prowed ship,
The prince's vessel, icy, eager to sail.

From the epic poem Beowulf

Henry and his travelling companions had waited for several days for the conditions to come right for the voyage north to Southampton. On the early evening of 25 November, which was dry and bitterly cold, the fleet's captains told them to board their ships to take advantage of the wind, which had started to blow in the right direction, and the tide, which was set to rise.

William of Ætheling's bride, Matilda of Anjou, aged nine or ten, and perhaps considered too young to be exposed to a night of debauchery alongside her husband and his entourage, would travel with her father-in-law. She and the others sailing with the king on his 'esnecca' said goodbye to those travelling on the other ship, sure they would all see one another the following day after a night-time of sailing across the Channel.

Henry's fellow passengers, who included 'a body of noble knights of the king's company', embarked. Orderic Vitalis recorded that their launch took place 'in the first watch of the night', and William of Malmesbury agreed that this was 'just before twilight'. They slipped out of Barfleur, the helmsman steering carefully to avoid the few, well-known, rocks just outside the harbour, the ship powered by its oarsmen until reaching the open seas, where the sails were dropped, 'and the wind that filled his sails conducted him safely to his kingdom and extensive fortunes'.[1]

William Ætheling and his companions – who John of Worcester called 'a large crowd of nobles, knights, young men, and women'[2] – were in no hurry to follow. Orderic Vitalis reported that the *White Ship*'s sailors, on learning the prince would be their passenger, 'were delighted, and fawned on the king's son, asking him for wine to drink'.[3] Stirred by the men's flattery, William ordered an enormous quantity of wine to be brought aboard for them as well as for his travelling companions – this was the only cargo the *White Ship* was to carry, other than the king's treasure and the passengers' personal possessions.

Now that Henry had departed, William Ætheling and his fellow travellers set about fully enjoying themselves, with the prince's wine fuelling the festivities. All were confident that they could give the king a generous head start and still reach Southampton before him. The crew were encouraged to join in the fun. The company downed three massive casks of wine, and Orderic reported that 'too much drinking made them [all] drunk'. He noted with further disapproval how the marines serving on the ship were so inebriated that they forgot their station and began showing off mercilessly, occupying some of the seats reserved for passengers and 'paying respect to almost no one'.[4]

This breakdown of order was ominous. The *White Ship* was embarking on a journey with her crew and key personnel intoxicated, while William Ætheling's hangers-on were contemplating the speeds they would achieve in the voyage ahead. They had little time for the normal religious protocols on leaving a major port in such a fine vessel.

Given the general fear of the sea at this time, passengers liked to call on monks or priests to bless their vessel before setting off, in order to harness God's protection. But when monks appeared with holy water to bless the *White Ship* the more high-spirited passengers chose to chase them away, shouting insults. This made the drunken spectators aboard howl with delight.

Roger, Bishop of Coutances, had travelled to Barfleur to bid farewell to one of his brothers, his 'three distinguished nephews' and his son William, who was one of the quartet of chaplains who paid the closest daily attendance to the king's soul. Roger wished them a safe crossing and added a formal blessing of their passage but, Orderic Vitalis claimed, 'they made light of it'.[5]

To the superstitious this rejection of religious blessing – whether offered by the monks or the bishop – left the ship and all travelling on her dangerously exposed to the vagaries of the sea. With the *White Ship* about to cast off and set sail a few passengers disembarked. Among them were: two monks from Tiron; Rabel, the son of Henry's chamberlain, William de Tancarville; William de Roumare, the son of the lord of Bolingbroke; and Edward of Salisbury, who had fought with distinction during the previous year's campaigns against the French.

Some would later say that they had been concerned by the raucousness of the inebriated crew, while Orderic Vitalis reported that, rather than feel confident that the crossing would go well, 'they realised that there was too great a crowd of wild and headstrong young men on board'.[6]

Henry's nephew, Stephen of Blois – whether from an illness that he had already contracted, or as a result of drinking too much that day – also got off the ship just before she sailed, 'because he was suffering from diarrhoea'.[7] Two of Stephen's knights – one of them Robert de Sauqueville, who was steward of his household – disembarked with him, in order to look after their master.

By the time William Ætheling and his companions and crew were ready to leave Barfleur, the evening chill had started to cool further, into a frost, and the new moon meant that it was dark. High tide on 25 November 1120 would have been at 10.43 p.m., making the water deep enough for the *White Ship*, with her two-metre draught, to sail from 8 p.m. Yet Thomas FitzStephen, being the master-steersman, would have waited till the tide slackened, to avoid his vessel being driven south on departing the harbour. The *White Ship* probably set sail a little before midnight.

As FitzStephen gave the order to cast off, he could be heard by the large body of onlookers to shout out his aim of overtaking the king before he reached Southampton. It was a refrain taken up by the passengers, many of them intoxicated after hours of drinking. The excitement of going to England in triumph, added to all the alcohol, made for a fevered atmosphere. Yells of wild encouragement to up the oars' tempo rang out in the cold night air. 'It was dark,' wrote Wace, 'and the light was not good; the sailors had been drinking and had not worked out the correct course. They had left the jetty and already spread the sail.'[8]

The fifty oarsmen bent their backs, falling into a quick rhythm. William of Malmesbury recorded how, after the *White Ship*'s departure: 'She flies swifter than the winged arrow, sweeping the rippling surface of the deep.'[9] The problem was, the helmsman seems to have been as drunk as his crew. It appears likely that the alcohol clouded his senses, leading him to underestimate the considerable distance his ship had covered in a very short time, thanks to the oarsmen's efforts and the premature dropping of the sail. How else to explain his negligence around the infamous rocks that all those steering ships into and out of Barfleur knew to avoid?

The *White Ship* was about one nautical mile out of the harbour, halfway between Barfleur and the Pointe de Barfleur, after which lay the open sea. In the darkness there came the shocking noise and impact of a mighty collision. The *White Ship* had run very hard into the Quillebœuf rock, a well-known local hazard, impaling her port side.

The impact splintered some of the rowers' oars, and staved in two of the clinker-built ship's planks. Water rushed through the deep gash. Sailors sprang onto the deck and, as those around them cried out in panic, they tried to push the *White Ship* clear of the Quillebœuf with boat hooks.

This attempt to extricate the vessel went on for some time, but without success. While struggling to prise the stricken ship free, some of the crew were washed away, the first casualties. Worse, the sailors' efforts only succeeded in further opening up the wound in her side, allowing more water to pour in. The weight of this fresh influx crashed down upon more of the crew, who also drowned.

Wace recorded how the *White Ship* then 'split completely and floundered; [and] the sea entered in several places'.[10] Impaled, askew, on her treacherous perch, and with the wind still filling her large mainsail, the *White Ship* teetered briefly before rolling hard, sideways.

As she tipped over, the passengers and the remainder of the crew began falling into the cold black water, screaming loudly. This was, most likely, the cry in the night that reached those still chatting in the port before heading off to sleep. They assumed that the party on the *White Ship* had merely reached new heights of drunkenness and abandon. Similarly, the cry could perhaps have made its way to Henry's vessel. But neither group recognised the sound as a sign that tragedy had come calling.

The guards responsible for William Ætheling rushed to get him away to safety. They launched the *White Ship's* only rowing boat, bundled him into it and pushed off in the direction of the shore, half a mile away. Their focus was the prince, and they left the rest of the ship's passengers to the mercy of the sea.

Almost all of the nearly three hundred people on the *White Ship* died within minutes, the cold of the Channel in late November causing shock so intense that it quickly killed them. Orderic Vitalis wrote: 'The passengers and crew raised cries of distress, but their mouths were soon stopped by the swelling waves, and all perished together.'[11] His narrative is written for dramatic effect, but it happens to be an accurate description of the effect on the human body of unexpectedly ending up plunged into extremely cold water.

The first reaction would have been what is known now as 'cold water shock'. This is a gasp reflex, frequently accompanied by hyperventilation and muscle spasms. It is common for victims of cold water shock to inhale water while in this state, and to suffer dramatic changes in their pulse and blood pressure.

This lasts two or three minutes in water of fifteen degrees Celsius or less – and the Channel, on a late November night when we know there was frost in the air, would have been touching zero. Many would have drowned or died of shock by the end of this very short time frame. Advice to someone in this perilous situation today would be to focus on their breathing, and to try to control it by consciously slowing down the rate of inhalation and exhalation. The last thing to do is panic. But the occupants of the *White Ship*, partying uproariously one moment, cascading into the sea the next, with very few (if any) able to swim, must surely have panicked.

Many might have clung to the nearest person to them, desperately hoping this would keep them afloat, but in the process guaranteeing the death of themselves and the one they had latched themselves on to. According to Berold the butcher, Richard of Lincoln was hugged tight in the waves by Otuel FitzEarl, his former tutor. This has been presented as a romantic, chivalric, act by chroniclers of the shipwreck, interpreting Otuel's action as a wish to die with one he held so dear. But it is more likely that Otuel was reacting in panic to his imminent drowning, and that he hastened the death of his former pupil by taking him down with him, while seized by a state of terror.

Those who somehow managed to stay alive beyond this initial period would, after anything between three to thirty minutes of immersion, have lost sensation and strength in their hands and feet. Even those who knew how to swim would no longer have the ability to do so. Hypothermia would have claimed those who did not drown.

There were very few survivors after that point. When the ship capsized, Berold struggled through the water. He came across a piece of broken masthead and scrambled onto it, his rough animal-skin pelisse retaining some heat even in the cold of a November night: wool, even when wet, preserves its ability to insulate. There was no better material to wear, if seeking warmth in cold water.

By getting onto the fragment of wood, Berold was able to stave off hypothermia: staying in the Channel would soon have drawn his body temperature down to that of the water itself. Berold was drenched, but conscious, and he was just warm enough to counter the shock of the extreme cold. He could now concentrate on survival.

Berold was joined on the spar by Geoffrey de L'Aigle, one of the pair of brothers who had been anticipating the return to England that promised to deliver up to them their rightful inheritance in Pevensey. Geoffrey was renowned to be one of Henry's braver soldiers, and he needed all his reserves of courage now.

Soon after the pair had found their place of safety, they saw the head of Thomas FitzStephen bobbing above the waves, heading towards them. 'The king's son!' he shouted. 'What has become of him?'

Berold told the captain what he had seen: William Ætheling had been bundled into the *White Ship*'s solitary rowing boat by his bodyguard. This small boat had been making its way towards the shore, and safety, when the prince ordered the oarsmen to stop. He had heard his half-sister, Matilda of Perche, screaming for him to come to save her from death. William of Malmesbury claimed she was 'shrieking out that he should not abandon her so barbarously'.[12] Given the weight of her dress, if this episode did happen, it must have been while she was still aboard the wreck of the *White Ship*, for once in the water she would have been taken below the waves very quickly.

William Ætheling had, Berold reported to FitzStephen, ordered his men to turn back so they could rescue her but, as they made their way through water frothing with the thrashing of survivors desperate for life, many of those drowning tried to clamber aboard the small craft, and it was swamped. It had given way under the weight of so many figures trying to heave themselves out of the bitingly cold water, and it had gone down. The prince had perished along with all the others, Berold told the captain, including the sister he had been unable to save.

FitzStephen's worst fears had been confirmed. Realising that, if he lived, he would be held responsible for recklessly causing the death of the heir to the throne, he accepted the hopelessness of his situation: 'It is vain for me to go on living,' he said.[13] These were his last recorded words. Rather than face a furious and distraught king, seeking answers as to how the man he had entrusted with his son's life had so fatally let him down, FitzStephen allowed himself to slip below the waves to his death.

The butcher and the aristocratic warrior were the sole survivors of the *White Ship* now. They held on to the spar together through much of the dark, frosty night, trying to shore up one another's morale. They prayed, and they submitted to God's will.

Shivering in his fine clothes, Geoffrey de L'Aigle managed to stay alive for several hours. He seems to have suffered from hypothermia, remaining conscious but withdrawn. If so, he would have started to speak with a slur, then would have become increasingly tired and weak, before the cold finally claimed him. His last words were a blessing on Berold, after which he fell unconscious. He slid into the sea, never to be seen again.

'Beroul [*sic*] alone escaped,' wrote Wace. 'He grabbed hold of a piece of wood and clung on to it, holding on firmly until he reached the shore when people came who lifted him out.' These 'people' were three fishermen, going about their business early the following morning. They spotted the butcher who, although frozen and exhausted, was soon able to talk. 'He revealed and explained how the king's son [died] and how the ship had broken up.'[14]

It quickly became clear to the people along that stretch of coastline that the butcher – perhaps the poorest of all aboard; John of Worcester dismissed him as a 'villein . . . not worthy of being named'[15] – was the sole survivor of the passengers and crew who had set off on the *White Ship* in such high spirits the previous night. He was a unique eyewitness to the terrible loss, and one who it seems Orderic spoke to and got to know: 'When he was somewhat revived,' the monk recalled, 'he told the whole sad tale to those who wished to learn, and subsequently lived for about twenty years in good health.'[16] How great the temptation was to exaggerate any of his tale, it is hard to know from this distance.

Local seafarers got to the wreck of the *White Ship*, which was lying broken on the rock, and entered the timber carcass. They found Henry's treasure intact and safely ferried it ashore. The passengers' personal possessions were also largely still there. All that was missing were the people who had set off in such high spirits on the fateful night. Not one corpse was found on the ship.

The people of Barfleur and surrounding ports scoured the shores for others who might have made it to land, but they found only bodies washed up on the beaches and swirling among the rocks. These had for the most part been carried a long way from the wreck site by the tide and were discovered several days after the Quillebœuf had been struck.

Among them was Richard of Lincoln, who had been in the water long enough to lose his features, whether these had been eaten, had rotted, or had been lacerated by the rocks. He was identified not by his face, but by the distinctiveness of his fine clothes. It was possible to lay him to rest.

Churchmen at the time were suspicious of the morality of those who indulged in showy rather than conservative dress, and who flouted convention in other ways. Preoccupation with a flamboyant wardrobe was seen as the signal of a deeper moral malaise, closely aligned to sexual perversion. 'All of them, or nearly all, were said to be tainted with sodomy,' wrote Henry of Huntingdon of those who drowned that night. 'And they were snared and caught. Behold the glittering vengeance of God! They perished and almost all of them had no burial. And so, death suddenly devoured those who had deserved it, although the sea was calm and there was no wind.'[17]

Most of the dead were never found. William Ætheling was one of the many who simply disappeared. The designated ruler of England and Normandy, the apple of his father's eye, vanished in the dark of the night-time sea, never to be seen again: 'The head which should have worn a crown of gold,' Henry of Huntingdon wrote, 'was suddenly dashed against the rocks;

instead of wearing embroidered robes, he floated naked in the waves; and instead of ascending a lofty throne, he found his grave in the bellies of fishes at the bottom of the sea.'[18]

The king did not know it yet, but his family and his twin realms would never be the same again.

TWELVE

Reaction to Tragedy

Sinners in their guilty blindness cannot see or understand the things which the heavenly king rightly ordains for his creation, until sinful man is captured like a fish on a hook or a bird in a net and entangled in sufferings beyond hope of escape.

Orderic Vitalis

Henry reached Southampton safely on the morning after he had set out from Barfleur. On disembarking the king moved twenty miles inland to a favourite royal hunting lodge at Clarendon, in the New Forest. He was keen to get away from the bustle of a port where many other vessels were disgorging passengers recently arrived from Normandy. There he awaited the arrival of the passengers of the *White Ship*.

Back in Southampton it gradually became clear that the *White Ship* was the one vessel out of all those that had recently set off for England that was unaccounted for. In the absence of a storm, which might have hindered her or blown her off course, or of a sighting by any of the many ships that had crossed that night and the following day, the fear slowly grew that the *White Ship* might have sunk. News that she had indeed done so came across the Channel, brought by people shaken by the enormity of what they had to report.

With confirmation of the tragedy, nobody wanted to tell the king what had happened. He was daunting when happy, but terrifying when upset, and all who had direct dealings with him knew how very close he was to his children – especially to William Ætheling, his cherished heir.

At court many were grief-stricken at losses among their own families, friends, colleagues and comrades-in-arms: 'O God,' recorded Wace, 'what a catastrophe and what sorrow there was!'[1] Orderic Vitalis wrote of the 'deep mourning and countless tears' shed for the 'terrible disaster'.[2] But those in attendance at Clarendon kept their heartache hidden from the king, knowing he would ask its cause and learn of the tragedy that had hit him more forcefully than any other.

A day after settling into the lodge Henry began wondering aloud when he would be reunited with his son. His vague concern soon changed to escalating anxiety. It was clear that the truth would have to be laid out to him in all its ghastliness: somebody had to tell the king what had happened.

It fell to Theobald of Blois-Chartres, one of Henry's nephews, to transmit the awful news. Theobald was already mourning the loss of two siblings in the shipwreck: he believed his sister, Lucia-Mahaut, and his brother, Stephen of Blois, were among the dead. (He was yet to learn that Stephen had left the *White Ship* through sickness.)

Weighed down by his own heartache, and eager to avoid the wrath and woe he feared would erupt in his formidable uncle, Theobald persuaded a boy to pass on the horrifying report. The child was old enough to understand the misery he was charged with passing on. He came to the king in tears and threw himself down at Henry's feet, blurting out in a torrent what had happened off Barfleur.

Grief trumped anger as Henry also fell to the floor, screaming in agonised disbelief at the realisation that he had lost his beloved son and heir, as well as two other children, a niece and nephew, and a huge number of his closest and most loyal advisers and supporters. In shock, he was helped up and led away to a more private place, to lament and digest his colossal loss.

With the king at last informed of the shipwreck, those others affected by it no longer had to pretend that all was well. Many sobbed openly. Orderic noted that, as news of the loss of William Ætheling and 'the flower of the highest nobility' spread throughout England, 'all the people of the realm could give rein to their tears, and this mourning lasted for many days'.[3]

The death of William Ætheling represented the cruel snuffing out of a life that had, for seventeen years, kindled Henry's hopes of passing on a hard-won legacy to the next generation and beyond. The settling of peace and order in England, the victories over rebels and over the king of France, the sidelining of his nephew's claims to the duchy of Normandy – all had been turned to dust by maritime catastrophe. William Ætheling had, as Orderic noted, 'both the love of his father and the hope of his people fixed on him'.[4] That hope had, like the prince, been lost at sea.

In France Abbot Suger wrote of Henry: 'His sons and daughters were shipwrecked, and they changed their physical forms after being eaten by the fish of the sea.'[5] Referring to Henry as 'the Lion of Justice', Suger saw the shipwreck as validation of Merlin's prophecy that: 'The cubs of the lion will be changed into fish of the sea.'[6]

Soon after he heard the news that would alter everything in his life so profoundly, Henry's grief turned to denial. In this state, wrote Wace, 'He sent men round all the ports, and had the shorelines searched to see whether his son and his ship had come and whether they could hear any news of him.'[7] But there was none.

Despite the late November cold, local men who dived for lost anchors and snagged nets were lured by the possibility of riches if they could locate anyone trapped beneath the rocks near the shoreline. 'Men hurried to and fro along the beaches, eagerly looking for the bodies of the dead,' recorded Orderic Vitalis. 'But as they failed to find them they were disappointed of the rewards they hoped to receive. Wealthy magnates assiduously sought for experienced swimmers and famous divers, and promised them high wages if they could recover the bodies of their dear ones so that they might be given honourable burial.'[8] The deaths were made all the more ghastly because sudden drowning allowed no possibility of final penance and redemption.

Some consolation arrived for the king when it was learned that Stephen of Blois had sidestepped the disaster through illness. He arrived safely in England to join a court in grief. Accepting the truth of his losses, Henry took to his bed, crying at the enormity of the disaster. Apart from family members, he seems to have been particularly affected by the deaths of the heroic Ralph the Red and Gilbert d'Exmes, 'and frequently described their deeds of courage, weeping as he related them'.[9] It seemed both absurd and cruel that these men who had survived the dangers of so many battlefields and sieges should end their lives in something as commonplace as an accident at sea.

An anonymous writer of the time penned a verse, trying to make sense of this unprecedented calamity:

The fatal hour came; Thomas's doomed vessel,
Badly steered, struck a rock and broke to pieces.
Tragic disaster! For all that young nobility
Sank in the sea and shared the same misfortune.
Noble scions of kings were hurled into the ocean,

Those for whom dukes weep were devoured by the sea
  monsters.
O grief unspeakable! Neither wealth or lineage
Brings back to life those whom the sea waves swallow.
Purple robes and home-spun rot in the deep together;
He whom a king begot became food for the fishes.
So fortune betrays those who trust in their own strength;
Now gives, now takes away; now raises, now crushes.
What could a great retinue, or wealth, or earthly glory,
Or your own beauty, William, do there to help you?
Royal splendour decays; and the ocean obliterated
Equally what you have been, and what you were going to be.
Damnation threatens all those lost in deep waters
Unless mercy from heaven is willing to spare them.
If, though, their bodies are drowned, their souls received
  gladly
The gift of salvation, sorrow would be far away from us.
Sure salvation of the soul is a cause of true gladness
To those who cherish the memory of their own dear ones;
But human minds cannot know, to their grievous sorrow,
If eternal rest comes to those whom the sea waves cover.

The full list of the *White Ship*'s dead took some time to establish and confirm. It contained eighteen women of the rank of countess, including Matilda of Perche and Lucia-Mahaut of Chester.

The loss of Matilda of Perche inspired Rotrou III, Count of Perche, to choose an isolated rural valley, deep in the woods near Soligny-la-Trappe, in Normandy, as the site of a small chapel. Built as a memorial to his dead wife, it was open for prayer, and the Virgin Mary was its holy patron. Soon afterwards Rotrou added a monastery to his foundation, which he placed under the control of the austere Order of Savigny – originally a hermitage founded by Vitalis of Savigny, the holy man who had failed to broker peace between Henry I and Robert Curthose just before their armies clashed at Tinchebray.

La Trappe Monastery would become an abbey in 1140. Soon afterwards, along with the rest of the declining Order of Savigny, La Trappe Abbey would be absorbed by the Cistercians. It flourished for two centuries before falling victim to the destruction of the Hundred Years War and then a conflict in the mid fifteenth century between Louis XI of France and an alliance of regional aristocrats eager for independence. However, La Trappe received new life in the mid seventeenth century when a godson of Cardinal Richelieu became its abbot and led a reform of the Cistercian Order. In the process he made the name of La Trappe highly regarded for its purity and principles.*

Also drowned that historic November night was Theodoric, a great-nephew of Emperor Henry V through a child of his sister, Agnes, and her husband Frederick, Duke of Swabia. Theodoric had most likely been attracted to the king of England's court because of its fine reputation among the royalty and nobility of northern Europe. He must have hoped that time there would further his knightly prospects, but this ambition cost Theodoric his life.

The de Grandmesnil brothers – Ivo and William – had died, too. The deaths of William Bigod, Geoffrey Ridel and Robert Mauduit all left chasms in Henry's bureaucratic complex, as did the loss of Gisulf, the king's property-owning scribe.

William Bigod, who had no children, was replaced by his twenty-five-year-old brother, Hugh: the office of steward of the

---

* Solitude, silence and contemplation are key parts of the Trappist way of life, wedded to the three vows of stability, fidelity to monastic life and obedience. Today there are 168 Trappist convents and monasteries, the thriving offshoots of the humble oratory that was established by a grieving *White Ship* widower to celebrate, for all time, the memory of his wife.

royal household seemed to have become hereditary in the Bigod family. Hugh clearly became a success in his role, Henry showing his appreciation of his loyalty and ability by making him constable of Norwich Castle in 1122.

In 1140 Geva, widow of the justice Geoffrey Ridel, and daughter of Hugh of Chester, founded a priory at Canwell in Staffordshire, for her soul, as well as those of her forefathers and relatives, many of whom had died on the *White Ship*.

The death of Robert Mauduit also saw a passing sideways of his role as the king's chamberlain. Robert had probably inherited the position from his father, William Mauduit. At Robert's death he had a daughter, Constance, but no son to continue the direct line of chamberlains in the family. Instead, Henry passed this senior role on to Robert Mauduit's younger brother, William, who was fifty in 1120.

With the loss of his brothers Engenulf and Geoffrey, Richer de L'Aigle was able to hold on to the disputed family lands at Pevensey. But any hopes that he had of being restored to royal favour came to nothing. He had infuriated the king with the blackmail he had deployed to steal his brothers' inheritance, and there was no way back from that. Henry was only too aware how it felt to be deprived by a sibling of what was due. Indeed, Richer seems only to have attended Henry's court once during the remainder of the king's reign.

Apart from the ecclesiastical members of the bishop of Coutances's family, the Church also lost Geoffrey, the archdeacon of Hereford. His power had been greater than his office suggested because there had been no actual bishop of Hereford since early February 1119, when the previous incumbent, Geoffrey de Clive – formerly one of Henry's chaplains, who had become infamous for his lack of generosity to the poor – had died. Meanwhile Thurstan, Archbishop of York, wrote of having lost 'so many friends'. Several of these were churchmen.

There was a need to give such an unfathomable disaster – one that had played out not in a storm, but in still seas – a divine explanation. Those critical of William Ætheling's adolescent arrogance chose to see it as having been conjured up by God as punishment for the prince's failings. 'The proud youth!' wrote Henry of Huntingdon. 'He was anticipating his future reign, but God said, "Not so, thou impious one, it shall not be."'[10]

Some also talked of the shipwreck being Henry's penalty for the severity of his rule, and questions arose about the late queen: had she, in fact, married the king despite having taken an unbreakable vow to God while a girl in a convent? If so, she had invited this disaster. 'It changed everything,' wrote William of Malmesbury of the impact of the sinking. This included royal custom: Henry never again used Barfleur for his voyages to and from Normandy. And the title of 'Ætheling' was not held again by an heir to the English throne.

———

Henry had been in his bed for days, so inconsolable with grief that he had eaten nothing, when William de Tancarville decided to intervene. De Tancarville was fortunate: his son Rabel had been one of the original passengers to board the *White Ship*, but he had disembarked before she set sail because he was worried by the drunken state of the crew.

William de Tancarville's record of service to the king was extremely distinguished. A baron, he was the latest in a long line of noble courtiers provided by his family to the dukes of Normandy: his ancestor, Tancrède, had raided France with Rollo, and his father, Raoul, had served Robert the Magnificent and William the Conqueror. In this generation William de Tancarville had been chamberlain of Normandy to Robert Curthose during the nineteen years of his dukedom. However, his true loyalties had long been with Henry: they had been brothers in arms as far back as 1089, and de Tancarville was still to be seen fighting alongside Henry thirty years later, at Brémule.

Now de Tancarville recognised the time had come for him to serve his master once more, not as soldier or courtier, but as trusted friend and counsellor. He approached Henry as he lay poleaxed by grief and gave him the advice that no one else would dare to convey.

'My lord, get up!' Wace reported de Tancarville urging. 'Go and eat, do not delay any longer! You would make your enemies happy if you continued to grieve. They would be delighted by your distress. Women should lament and weep, women should express sorrow, but you should take comfort and advise us all. Those who are dead and have drowned will not live because one mourns them, a son cannot recover a father, nor a father a son, by displaying grief. There is no escape in tears. Get up at once and go and eat! The sorrow is intense, the loss great, but you would regret showing any sign of it.'[11]

Wace reported that Henry accepted de Tancarville's bold appeal, first by sitting up in bed, then ordering his barons to join him at his dining table. Although grief must have been clawing at his innards, he understood the need to project an image of dignified, regal authority. He chose to face undreamed-of distress with what looked very like courageous acceptance. In time, thoughts of the future flickered into focus.

There was not a part of Henry's Anglo-Norman realm that remained shielded from the impact of the catastrophe. It was not simply the loss of royal, aristocratic and other leading figures from the court and the Church but the direct effect of death on such a scale among the ruling, Anglo-Norman, class. Yet the greatest loss remained the most obvious: with William Ætheling dead, Henry was without an heir to the kingdom of England or the duchy of Normandy.

After the *White Ship* sank it was noted how the king quickly sought distraction from the pain of his losses through promiscuity: 'He took his pleasure with, and devoted his attention to, noble and beautiful women and courtly maidens; this is a game which brings much pleasure,' Wace noted.[12] But the death of his sole legitimate heir demanded that he marry for a second time and produce another son.

Exactly a month after the tragedy Henry spent Christmas at his hunting lodge at Brampton, in Huntingdonshire. Theobald, Count of Blois-Chartres, who had shirked from directly passing on the news of the sinking, was among those in attendance. This time he rose to the challenge of telling his uncle what he needed to hear.

Being the king's senior nephew, Theobald was one of the strongest contenders to be heir to the crown. But Theobald urged his uncle to remarry in order to produce a son. This proposal was further endorsed by Henry's nobility when he arrived in London, after Christmas. The same advice seems to have come from Robert FitzRoy, who knew his own illegitimacy was a permanent barrier to ever succeeding. Robert's frequent presence at court at this time shows how his father leaned on him during this most terrible of political and family crises.

In fact, a few months before the *White Ship* catastrophe, Henry had been in discussions with a powerful figure in the Lowlands and Germany to marry his young daughter. Godfrey, Duke of Lotharingia and Count of Louvain, was an imposing, bearded, warrior, who was an ally of Henry's son-in-law, the Roman Emperor. Godfrey's power stretched from Lower Lorraine – the westernmost part of the Roman Empire – to Antwerp and Brussels. He had authority in parts of modern-day Belgium, France and Germany. Furthermore Godfrey's wife, Ida of Namur, descended from the greatest emperor of the Early Middle Ages, Charlemagne. This blood link to ancient monarchy appealed to

Henry, just as his first wife's Anglo-Saxon ancestry had helped to seduce him two decades earlier. In late 1120 it had been eighteen months since Queen Matilda's death.

Adeliza of Louvain had made a very good impression at the imperial court at Aachen because of her combination of fine character and striking looks, which had one eyewitness write of her as being 'a maiden of great beauty and modesty'. Henry cannot have failed to be struck by Adeliza's physical appeal, which was pronounced enough to earn her the nickname of 'the Fair Maid of Brabant'. Henry of Huntingdon, dazzled by her appearance and what he could make of her character, would write asking for her patronage:

> O queen of the English, Adela [*sic*], the very muse who prepares to call to mind your graces is frozen in wonder. What to you, most beautiful one, is a crown? What to you are jewels? A jewel grows pale on you, and a crown does not shine. Put adornment aside, for nature provides your adornment, and a fortunate beauty cannot be improved. Beware ornaments, for you take no light from them, they shine brightly only through your light. I was not ashamed to give my modest praise to great qualities, so be not ashamed, I pray, to be my lady.[13]

King Henry and Adeliza were married at Windsor on 24 January 1121, two months after the loss of William Ætheling. The wedding was officiated by William, Bishop of Winchester, because Ralph, Archbishop of Canterbury,* had suffered a stroke in 1119, after which he found it hard to speak. But the archbishop was able to oversee the king and queen's coronation, and they

---

* Anselm had died in his mid-seventies, on Holy Wednesday – 21 April – 1109, after six months of debilitating illness, during which he insisted on daily being carried to Mass.

appeared at court in London together in May, both wearing their crowns.

The speedy installation of Adeliza threw into relief the awkward position of Matilda of Anjou, the girl who had been expected to succeed as queen within a few years. Others who had lost loved ones on the *White Ship* quickly readjusted their dynastic sights: Amice de Gaël, the daughter of Ralph de Gaël, had been betrothed to Richard of Lincoln. She had the fortune not to have sailed with her fiancé. The next year she went on to marry Robert de Beaumont, 2nd Earl of Leicester, the twin brother of Waleran de Meulan.

But Matilda of Anjou was of an altogether greater importance. The peaceful relationship with Anjou, which had secured coveted Maine for Henry's line, had been cemented by her marriage to William Ætheling. Their brief union was now ended and, given that she had been widowed so young, there were no children of the marriage. Indeed, she was still a child herself.

Matilda's father, Fulk V of Anjou, had gone on Crusade soon after securing his daughter's dynastic marriage. He had become a supporter and sponsor of the Knights Templar, a military order founded in Jerusalem in 1119 whose aim was to protect pilgrims to the Holy Land. Fulk was still on Crusade when the *White Ship* sank. As far as he was concerned, the deal between him and Henry had died with the prince. On returning to Anjou, a year or so after the loss of the ship, Fulk insisted the county of Maine be returned to him. When Henry refused the two men's historic hostilities resumed. In 1123 Fulk married another of his daughters, Sibylla, to the man who was most likely to succeed Henry to the English throne, William Clito. With her hand, Sibylla of Anjou brought as her dowry the county of Maine.

Meanwhile Henry was adamant that his widowed daughter-in-law should stay in England for as long as she wished, as a highly favoured member of his court. Orderic Vitalis recorded that Matilda of Anjou was treated like one of the king's daughters. Henry wanted to keep her close and her loyalties English, and he offered to marry her to any one of his most eligible lords. He promised that, when she did so, he would be 'heaping on her wealth and honours which would have raised her above all her family'.[14]

Matilda of Anjou remained in England for several years before homesickness took her back to Anjou. Henry sent her on her way with 'splendid equipment and vessels of gold and silver, palfreys, warhorses and a large amount of money', both as a symbol of his regard for her and to show off his great wealth.[15]

On returning to Anjou Matilda found that her father and brother wanted to find her another strategically useful husband. She declined to take part in any such dynastic arrangement, Wace recording her as saying that: 'She did not want to debase herself or demean herself through marriage; she was to be queen on Earth, and since she could not be so and had failed in this she did not want to take a lesser husband; since she could not have a king, the son of a king, she would not take a husband of lower rank. She said and avowed that she would have no other husband than God.'[16] In 1128 Matilda joined Fontevrault Abbey, near Chinon, in Anjou. The woman intended to be queen of England and duchess of Normandy would remain there for the rest of her life, as a nun.

It was not just the relationship with Anjou that suffered with the sinking of the *White Ship*. Henry had brought order into south Wales with a campaign in 1108, when he had taken allies from Flanders to settle around Pembroke. In 1114, provoked by insurrection in mid-Wales, Henry had led an army to impose his authority, while Alexander, King of Scotland (who was both Henry's brother- and son-in-law), attacked from the north, and Richard, Earl of Chester's third force advanced into Wales from the south. As Henry built up his defences there, particularly along the marches that ran along the Anglo-Welsh border, it had seemed that Wales was settled.

But Richard of Chester's death on the *White Ship* encouraged renewed rebellion, Symeon of Durham recording how: 'The sons of the Welsh king heard about the drowning of Richard, Earl of Chester, and set fire to two castles, killing many. Some places of the county were heavily plundered.' This uprising was directed by the seventy-four-year-old prince Maredudd ap Bleddyn, a former ally of Robert de Bellême, who would be acclaimed as 'the beauty and safety of all Powys, and her defender'.[17] Maredudd had been Henry's prisoner of war for five years early in his reign, before managing to escape in 1107. He now raided Cheshire, supported by three sons of his brother, Cadwgan ap Bleddyn, prompting Henry to lead a retaliatory expedition into Powys, to root out the incursion at its source.

Fighting on behalf of the drowned earl nearly cost the king his own life. Welsh military strength lay in its archers, which soon tested the fine quality of Henry's suit of armour. During one engagement on this campaign it successfully withstood the impact of an enemy arrow, sending it flying away without injury to the king. But it was a close enough call to induce Henry to shout out in surprise, 'By our Lord's death!'

Maredudd was unable to find allies powerful enough to help resist Henry's advance, and he was eventually subdued by the king's army. He was forced to pay a penalty of ten thousand cows and to hand over hostages to guarantee future peace. It would be the last time that Henry needed to lead an army into Wales.

If the Welsh were settled, the succession was most certainly not. Many viewed William Clito as next in line to the kingdom of England and the dukedom of Normandy. Henry of Huntingdon was one of those who saw no alternative, writing that Clito 'was now the king's sole heir, and judged worthy in the expectation of all'.[18] It was all there in the 1101 Treaty of Alton: if either Curthose or Henry died without a legitimate male heir, the eldest legitimate son of the other would be in line for both inheritances.

There were numerous powerful men in Normandy who had long believed that William Clito should be their duke. The sudden death of the young prince who had blocked Clito's way persuaded many others to back his claim, too. In 1122, encouraged by the continued absence of another royal heir, a clique of leading Norman nobles renewed their support for Clito, with the support of Louis VI of France.

Learning from his spies that Amaury III de Montfort was plotting to lead a rebellion in the dukedom, Henry sent substantial forces to meet the threat the following year. The king entrusted command of his troops to Ranulf le Meschin, Earl of Chester and to his own son, Robert FitzRoy. These two men were among the beneficiaries of the *White Ship*. Those voids of power brought about by the sinking had to be addressed by the king. The loss of Richard of Chester, without a male heir, left Henry free to choose a successor from the earl's cousins. He had selected Ranulf le Meschin. The promotion came with a price attached, Henry taking from Ranulf his lordship of Carlisle as the royal fee.

Equally the death of William Ætheling had persuaded Henry to increase the power and wealth of Robert FitzRoy, knowing he could rely absolutely on this able and loyal member of his natural family. FitzRoy was created earl of Gloucester soon after the *White Ship* disaster – in 1121 or 1122 – as Henry bolstered the position of those relatives he could count on during this period of grief and instability, when he and Adeliza had produced no son, and William Clito's claim to be the king's heir seemed unassailable.

Chester and Gloucester arrived in Normandy to face Clito's followers, led by Amaury III de Montfort, who was supported by his nephew, Fulk V of Anjou. Around de Montfort and Fulk was a tightening knot of influential men who also asserted Clito's claims to Normandy, while confidently anticipating that Clito would soon produce an heir to trouble Henry into another generation. These included three powerful aristocrats: Waleran de Meulan, Waleran's brother-in-law Hugh de Châteauneuf-en-Thymerais and Hugh de Montfort. Crucially, though, Louis VI of France had been unable to offer support to his allies, because he was distracted by an imperial army advancing towards Metz.

Fulk V and William Clito invaded Normandy from the south. Henry, with Robert of Gloucester, countered by besieging the castle of Montfort-sur-Risle, a de Montfort family stronghold twenty-five miles east of Deauville, which soon fell.

Henry was at Caen when his army fought against the rebels in a small-scale but far-reaching action south-west of Rouen, in late March 1124. What followed is known as the *Battle* of Bourgthéroulde but, in scale, it was really little more than a skirmish: Waleran de Meulan led a charge at the head of just forty knights, having dismissed Henry's forces as mere 'country bumpkins and mercenaries' who were no match for noble men of war.

The bumpkins trounced the knights, thanks to the skill of Henry's archers – some of whom were deployed while mounted. Their volleys dispatched the horses of the enemy knights before they could engage. Most of the leading rebels were captured, including Waleran de Meulan, Hugh de Châteauneuf-en-Thymerais and Hugh de Montfort, with thirty men-at-arms. Waleran was imprisoned in Rouen, supposedly for life. Three of William Clito's knights – Odard du Pin, Geoffrey de Tourville and Luc de la Barre – were among the captured. Henry sentenced them to be blinded, prompting Charles the Good of Flanders to point out that prisoners 'taken in the service of their lord' should be spared cruel recriminations.

Henry strongly disagreed. 'I act rightly, lord count, and will prove it to you by good reason,' he said. 'Geoffrey and Odard rendered me homage with the consent of their lords, and in violating their faith to me they perjured themselves of their own free will and have thus incurred the penalty of death or mutilation.'

De la Barre was, Henry continued, a different case, though still deserving of the same penalty. A twenty-four-year-old known for his *joie de vivre* and mischievous sense of humour, de la Barre's crime had been to write satirical verses about Henry. The king objected to how the 'jesting songster composed mocking songs about me, insulted me by singing them in public, and often raised mocking laughter against me from the enemies who sought my undoing. Now therefore God has delivered him into my hands for punishment, so that he may be forced to give up his evil practices, and so that other men who learn how his rash folly was cut short may mend their ways in time.'[20] Orderic Vitalis noted how the count of Flanders had nothing to say in reply: by the standards of the time, Henry's actions were justified, if harsh. Just as his father had shown when having the hands and feet removed of the defenders of Alençon, Henry believed personal mockery deserved the direst of consequences.

Luc de la Barre was horrified by his sentence. Unable to face the agony that was coming his way, he repeatedly smashed his head against the walls of his cell until he succeeded in killing himself.

The leader of the rebellion, the silk-tongued Amaury III de Montfort, had also been captured by one of Henry's knights, William de Grandcourt, at Bourgthéroulde. He managed to talk de Grandcourt into not handing him over to the king. His captor escorted him away from the defeat, then released him.

Henry continued to contest Clito's claim wherever he could. He appealed to Pope Callixtus II to have Clito's marriage to Sibylla of Anjou annulled, on the basis that they were too closely related to be allowed to be man and wife. This is ironic since the two were related in precisely the same degree as William Ætheling and Matilda of Anjou, a match Henry himself had helped to arrange. But the pope agreed with Henry's argument, and Clito and Sibylla of Anjou were forced to part in 1124, a year after they had wed, and before they could have a child.

Henry still hoped to father a male heir to his realms. Until then his only legitimate child remained his daughter, Matilda.

THIRTEEN

The Empress

We choose as lady of England and Normandy the daughter of
a king who was a peacemaker, a glorious king, a wealthy king,
a good king, without peer in our time, and we promise her faith
and support.

Findings of a council headed by Henry,
Papal Legate and Bishop of Winchester, 1141

Henry's first wife, Matilda, commissioned William of
Malmesbury to write the *Deeds of the Kings of the English*.
Long after the queen's death, when he presented a copy to her royal
daughter of the same name, William of Malmesbury assured her:
'In it you can discover that none of those chronicled in the present
book has a more royal or more glorious claim to the hereditary
crown of England than yourself.'[1] Yet young Matilda would add
greatly to her meticulous bloodline through a spectacular marriage.

The preoccupation of the court held at Westminster over
Whitsun 1109 was the splendour of a mission recently arrived
from overseas: 'Envoys remarkable for their massive physique
and magnificent apparel were sent by the Roman emperor, to

ask for the king's daughter in marriage with their lord.'² The ambassadors wanted to secure Princess Matilda as a match for Henry, King of the Romans and the designated Roman Emperor.

Matilda's suitor was the son of Henry IV. Henry IV had been crowned king of the Germans when a few months old, in 1051, and had become king of Italy and Burgundy as a six-year-old. During his minority reforming elements in the Church had taken advantage to reclaim the right to appoint the pope – a prelude to their aim of controlling all Church appointments and of blocking lay rulers from dictating the selection of bishops and abbots.

After Hildebrand, a Tuscan archdeacon, became Pope Gregory VII in 1073, the prelate's reforming zeal began to collide with the views that Henry IV – by now a man in his early twenties – had of his rights and status. He wrote a letter to Gregory with the introduction: 'Henry, king not through usurpation but through the holy ordination of God, to Hildebrand, at present not pope but false monk.' It was the opening salvo in the investiture contest, a conflict that only intensified after Henry was crowned Roman Emperor in 1084. This clash would see pope and emperor at various times announce the deposition of the other, recognise an alternative holder of their enemy's office, and be held in harsh captivity. It also sparked what was effectively a civil war that gripped German lands for nearly half a century.

Henry IV suffered turbulence with his family, too. Both his wives would complain of repeated sexual humiliation. At the bidding of Pope Urban II the second of these, Empress Adelaide, made public her shocking accusations: the emperor kept her imprisoned, she said; before her escape he had repeatedly forced her – a Ukrainian princess, who had been plucked from life in a convent by Henry because of her beauty – to partake in sexual orgies; and he and his intimates had practised black magic on her naked body. Chroniclers built on this picture of decadence, claiming Henry IV encouraged his elder son, Conrad, to have sex with his mother during one of his depraved gatherings – an invitation that Conrad, they wrote, had recoiled from in horror.

Despite Henry IV sharing authority with them at different times, both his sons turned against their father. Things had reached such a state with Matilda's suitor, the future Henry V, that at the end of 1105 Henry IV had felt compelled to abdicate. It was that or, he felt certain, his son would murder him. The deposed emperor died suddenly the following August, after a lifetime of conflict.

Conrad had predeceased his father in 1101, so Henry V was the sole heir in the direct line to the Roman Empire. Yet, because of the ongoing investiture contest, it would be several years before he would be crowned as such. The ceremony could only be performed by the pope, and he would not anoint his adversary. As King of the Romans Henry still controlled the Roman Empire, and so he remained one of the most commanding figures in Europe. His patchwork of territories extended from northern Germany down to Rome, and its span stretched from Lyons to Vienna. For Matilda to secure the hand of such a ruler was a great compliment to her father. It lent prestige and recognition to King Henry I, at the head of his Anglo-Norman realm. It also provided England with a potent ally against France.

King Henry had to pay for the acquisition of such a distinguished and valuable son-in-law with a colossal dowry: he had agreed to sweeten the prospect of Matilda's hand in marriage with a settlement of ten thousand marks – a sum so large it necessitated a one-off tax across the realm: 'The king accordingly took 3s. from every hide* in England,' noted Henry of Huntingdon.[3]

---

* A hide was an Anglo-Saxon unit of land thought necessary to support a medieval family or household. Its size varied, since the quality of the land was taken into account when the assessment was made: a small acreage of fertile soil was therefore equivalent to a larger area of poor land.

Matilda became engaged to the would-be emperor, by proxy, in 1109. This allowed her soon afterwards to witness one of her father's charters with words that displayed her new status: 'Matilda, betrothed wife of the king of the Romans'.[4] She was seven years old.

The Church allowed children to be promised in marriage at such a tender age – and even younger if peace between two hostile parties could be preserved or brokered as a result, as had been the case with William Ætheling and Matilda of Anjou. But even a union involving this blending of imperial and royal blood was barred from taking place before maturity: when the groom was fourteen, the bride twelve, and each had to give what was notionally their consent to the contract.

Matilda had set off across the Channel to Boulogne with a large retinue of English nobles and churchmen, before continuing on to Liège where she met the twenty-four-year-old Henry for the first time, in February 1110, the month of her eighth birthday. They were formally betrothed in Utrecht during Easter 1110, and her coronation as queen of the Romans took place in Mainz late that July. Matilda was so small that she had to be cradled in the arms of the Archbishop of Trier while being anointed.

Matilda now submitted to the training required of a princess sent off to forge a new life in a foreign land. While waiting to become old enough to rule as queen she learned to speak and write German, and she was educated in the customs of her new people.

Henry was finally crowned emperor in 1111, and in early January 1114, when she was approaching her twelfth birthday, Matilda and Henry married in the cathedral at Worms. The service – led by five archbishops and attended by the greatest of the imperial leaders – was so magnificent that, it was said at the time, nobody alive, no matter how great their age, could remember witnessing or even hearing of anything to rival it.

But, despite the expectations, Matilda was destined never to become empress. Such an elevation would have necessitated the pope performing the coronation, and he and Henry V continued to butt heads in the investiture contest. The only occasion on which Matilda definitely wore the crown of the empress, it was placed on her head by an excommunicated archbishop during Pentecost of 1117, in St Peter's Basilica, in Rome. This felt so close to an actual coronation that it tempted Matilda to style herself 'Empress' from then on. Many accepted her as such, for the rest of her life. Her enemies never did.

Whatever her true title, Matilda wielded great power on her husband's behalf, when required. In 1118, when she was sixteen, Henry V left Matilda in charge of his Italian territories while he set off to confront a rebellion in Germany. We find her sitting in judgement over a land dispute between a bishop and an abbot. When she delivered her verdict (in favour of the abbot), she did so with an imperial decree attached, forbidding anyone from questioning her ruling. In the Roman Empire this firmness was seen as strength – her husband was ruthless and decisive, and she reflected those qualities. But Matilda's apprenticeship as a ruler taught her a different set of rules from that which she would have encountered in England.

In late 1120 the sinking of the *White Ship* left Matilda as King Henry's only surviving legitimate child. It is hard to gauge the extent of Matilda's grief for William Ætheling when news reached her of his death. She had last seen her brother when she was eight and he was six. But we do know that she had remained in touch with Henry despite their physical distance.

Matilda planned to visit her father in England during May 1122, when he was under severe pressure from the range of

enemies who had declared their support for William Clito.
Henry moved to Kent to greet her on her homecoming. But
Charles the Good, Count of Flanders, concerned that any help
offered to Henry and his family might anger Louis VI, refused
to give Matilda safe passage across his lands to a ship bound for
England. The reunion between father and daughter was successfully blocked.

Three years later, in May 1125, Emperor Henry V died of
cancer in Utrecht, the city where he and Matilda had been
betrothed fifteen years earlier. He was aged thirty-eight and,
according to William of Malmesbury, 'in the very flower of his
age and victories'.[5] His body was taken on a three-hundred-mile
voyage along the Rhine, before being laid to rest beside his
ancestors in Speyer Cathedral.

Matilda had no surviving children* with the deceased emperor.
This, critics claimed, was because the marriage was cursed –
either because Matilda's mother had, in truth, been a nun before
marrying Henry; or as repayment for Henry V's daring to fight
the pope. Orderic Vitalis wrote: 'The Emperor loved his noble
wife deeply, but on account of his sins he failed to have an heir
to the Empire, so that at God's command the imperial line
passed to another family.'[6]

Henry V left his insignia to his twenty-three-year-old widow,
but she was quickly relieved of these by the archbishop of
Mainz, who stepped into the void left by the emperor's death.
The archbishop presided over an election that saw the electors
forgo Henry's favoured relative, Frederick, Duke of Swabia, and
entrust the office to Lothar, Duke of Saxony. Matilda realised
that she had no role to play in the new regime. She added her
husband's imperial crown, lance and sword to the items surren-

---

* One chronicler claims Matilda lost a baby, soon after its birth; but, if so, we
do not know its gender or name.

dered to the archbishop, and declined the lands that Henry V had left for her in his will. The new emperor offered her the choice of several German rulers as a second husband, but she announced her intention to return to her father's side, initially in Normandy.

Matilda did not leave entirely empty-handed. She brought with her treasures, including two golden crowns, one of which was so heavy that it required bearers to support its weight, on two rods, to prevent it from crushing the wearer's neck. She also took the embalmed left hand of St James the Greater, which had been removed from that Apostle's grave in the fourth century. (Matilda had been crowned at Mainz on the feast day of St James, in 1110.)

The widowed empress left Germany with a reputation for wisdom and piety that would see her remembered there as 'the good Matilda', just as her mother was remembered as 'Matilda the Good' in England. Orderic Vitalis noted that she chose to leave for home despite being 'greatly loved abroad'.[7]

In September 1126 Henry returned to England after more military triumphs in France. He brought with him Matilda, who had not set foot on the land of her birth for more than sixteen years. Matilda's widowhood opened up dynastic possibilities for Henry. She was twenty-four, supremely eligible, and also a woman whose beauty (even allowing for the inevitable flattery of chroniclers) was much written about.

The king began to look to Matilda to fill the successional chasm left by William Ætheling's tragic death. After five years' marriage to Adeliza, he was still without another legitimate child. The young queen travelled everywhere with the ageing King Henry, but this constant proximity had yet to translate into a royal pregnancy. It was a worrying situation that would, in time, prompt Hildebert, Archbishop of Tours, to write to Adeliza: 'It has not been granted to you from Heaven that you should bear a child to the King of the English.' With clumsy presumption, he concluded: 'Perhaps the Lord has closed up your womb.'*

By the end of his Christmas court of 1126, held at Windsor, Henry had quietly decided who his next son-in-law would be: Geoffrey of Anjou, the eldest son of his old enemy Count Fulk V. Geoffrey was known as 'le Bel' ('the handsome') because of his good looks, which a contemporary recalled as 'glowing like the flower of a lily, with rosy flush'. Such a union, of the Anglo-Norman and the Angevin dynasties, would echo the design behind the brief, doomed marriage of William Ætheling to Fulk V's daughter, Matilda of Anjou, a few weeks before the prince had perished on the *White Ship*: securing Normandy's southern frontier, while depriving Louis the Fat of a powerful and able ally.

Henry knew that there was much hostility among his aristocracy towards the Angevins, given the fraught historic relationship between Normandy and Anjou. He entrusted the clandestine negotiations over Matilda and Geoffrey's marriage to three of his closest supporters, including his eldest natural son, Robert, Earl of Gloucester. He was in great favour for his role in quashing Norman rebels in 1123, and for dealing with rumbling agitation in Wales with ruthless efficiency.

Henry even chose to keep Roger of Salisbury – whose unique power and influence had only increased after the deaths of the queen and William Ætheling – ignorant of the secret dialogue with Fulk V. The king knew from his spies that the bishop headed the court faction secretly favouring William Clito as the next Anglo-Norman ruler. Worries about Roger of Salisbury's trustworthiness on such an important question prompted Henry, in late 1126, to move his imprisoned brother Robert Curthose

---

* There was nothing wrong with Adeliza's capacity to reproduce, as seven children from her second marriage would prove.

from Roger's custody to the more dependable watch of Robert of Gloucester. Curthose was taken to Cardiff Castle, where he passed time learning the Welsh language and writing poetry, including a piece about an oak tree he could spy from his prison window.

On 1 January 1127, on Roger of Salisbury's recommendation, Henry called together the great men who were preparing to depart his Christmas court at Windsor. 'And there,' the *Anglo-Saxon Chronicle* recorded, 'he caused archbishops and bishops and abbots and earls and all the thegns that were there to swear to give England and Normandy after his death into the hand of his daughter.'[8] The king openly accepted that the loss of his heir on the *White Ship* had been a national catastrophe, leaving his sole legitimate daughter as the only person fit to succeed him. Each of those present was commanded to pledge to acknowledge Matilda as his successor, and to protect her against any rival claimant to the throne after his death. They also had to recognise any sons that she might bear as Henry's eventual heirs. There is no record of anybody objecting to Henry's requirement.

The individual oaths followed, overseen by Roger of Salisbury. The prelates went first. The first layman to step forward was Henry's brother-in-law, David, King of Scotland. His oath was immediately followed by a spat between Henry's nephew, Stephen of Blois, and his son Robert of Gloucester, as to who should go next.

It was 'a noteworthy contest', William of Malmesbury recorded. Each wanted to show his superior status, as well as to advertise his eagerness to support the king's wishes. Stephen who, his supporters claimed, 'was by far the dearest of all the nephews' that Henry had, won the dispute.[9] After all the other noblemen present followed the lead of this eminent trio, Henry felt able to pursue Matilda's marriage to Geoffrey of Anjou openly. But several Norman lords would later complain that they had not been consulted about such a controversial union, with their historic Angevin enemies.

—

William Clito remained the great threat to Matilda's succession. In January 1127 Louis the Fat gave him land in the French Vexin from which to launch raids into Normandy. At the same time Louis approved Clito's marriage to Joanna of Montferrat, his wife's half-sister.

Henry entrusted his nephew Stephen of Blois with the important job of cementing alliances against the French and William Clito. Stephen forged agreements with a bevy of senior aristocrats, including Henry's father-in-law Godfrey, Count of Louvain. This successful diplomacy prompted a letter of protest from Clito to Louis the Fat: 'He [Henry] has brought together innumerable knights and vast sums of money; and out of pure spite he labours to take away from you and ourselves a section of the most faithful and powerful men of your realm, confident in the number of his men and still more in the quantity of his money.'[10]

In April 1127 Henry was at his hunting lodge at Woodstock, in Oxfordshire. This was the place, above all his royal palaces and castles, where Henry chose 'to live a retired life'.[11] It had been here, in 1110, that he had ordered a seven-mile wall of Cotswold stone to be constructed – some of it reclaimed from the flattened homes of local people forcibly moved from their land – to extend his private hunting estate. At Woodstock he had also built up a menagerie of exotic animals given to him by foreign rulers and noblemen. This included a porcupine – 'a kind of hedgehog, covered with bristling spines' – sent by William V of Montpellier, who in 1114 had helped to rid Majorca of the Moors. The porcupine lived alongside camels (admired

Top: The Battle of Brémule, in 1119, saw Henry I defeat Louis VI so decisively that the French king was forced to recognise William Ætheling as duke of Normandy.

Right: William Clito, eldest legitimate grandson of the Conqueror, and charismatic son of Robert Curthose, was the lightning rod for those disaffected with Henry I and his ambitions.

Bottom: Louis VI of France. Louis 'the Fat' was Henry I's most enduring enemy. Both men lost their male heirs in accidents.

A nineteenth-century depiction of the shipwreck, painted by Princess Louise, the sixth child of Queen Victoria.

Henria natu pelago peyerunt adaquatam
Filia que remanet imperiale tenet

Henricus Rex filius   conquestoris genuit

Gillm
qui peyit
in mari

Bren
qui peyit
in mari

Ria
fit impat
as qui
obiit

Matl
dam Imp
attem

Regis
Henria
scdi

Opposite: Henry I mourning the loss of William Ætheling and his other children, after learning of the fate of the *White Ship*.

Top: Adeliza of Louvain, who as a teenager wed the fifty-three-year-old Henry I weeks after the loss of the king's only male heir. The marriage was childless.

Middle right: The wedding feast of Matilda and Emperor Henry V, following a ceremony so magnificent that nobody present could remember witnessing or hearing of anything to rival it.

Bottom: Henry I during a stormy Channel crossing. The king promised to stop an unpopular tax, and to honour St Edmund, if spared by God.

Top: The Empress Matilda reigned on her husband's behalf during his absence. The idea of a woman ruling in England with similar decisiveness was too much for many to bear.

Bottom: The remains of Reading Abbey, which Henry built as his burial place. The abbey was destroyed by Charles I. Henry's body still lies there, most likely under a school building.

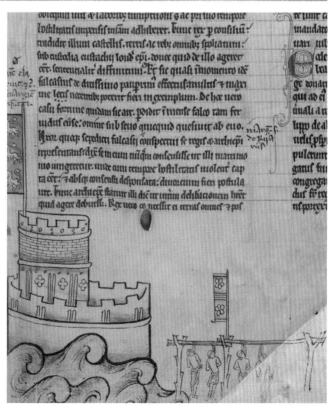

Top: King Stephen (fourth from right) watching on as his men prepare to fight the Battle of Lincoln. He would be captured later that day.

Bottom: The Anarchy claimed countless civilian and military victims. Here five eminent prisoners of war are hanged outside Bedford Castle.

Overleaf: Henry II and Thomas Becket, with a list of some of the king's Plantagenet descendants.

by the Crusaders for their ability to work hard, in the merciless desert), leopards, lynxes and lions.

Woodstock had been the place where, as a younger man, Henry conducted several of his romantic liaisons. From the few details we know about his lovers, they seem to have been local ladies of gentry status and little wealth, some of whom mothered several of his twenty-two illegitimate children.

But now a messenger arrived with news that followed the shocking report received a month earlier that Henry's friend and ally, Charles the Good of Flanders, had been murdered in St Donatian's Cathedral, in the Flemish capital of Bruges. The assassins that day had been knights, and their weapons were swords: the count had been saying his prayers, holding a service book in his hand and lying on the stone floor of the church in humble supplication when he felt the steel of a blade held lightly against his neck. Charles began to raise himself up, in astonishment at the interruption. Burchard, the man entrusted with the murder, raised his sword and brought it down hard, decapitating the count with a single blow. The assassins next slaughtered the count's bodyguard and all of his noblemen that they found in and around the church, before filling Bruges's castle with supplies and holding it as their own.

A cousin of Louis VI, Count Charles was judged by Abbot Suger to have 'governed the well populated land of Flanders with valour and care'.[12] But he had made enemies along the way. His killers' paymasters were the Erembald family. They had been found guilty of hoarding grain, in order to profit from the poor during a time of famine. The count had punished them by reducing them from the ranks of the wealthy to the status of serfs. This was their revenge.

The messenger arriving at Woodstock informed Henry that Louis VI had announced that William Clito would be the next count of Flanders. Louis had pointed to Clito's blood claim to the title, which came through his grandmother, Matilda of Flanders – Henry's own mother. Henry of Huntingdon wrote that the king was 'much distressed'[13] to learn of this elevation of his nephew. Flanders was the perfect base from which to launch assaults on Normandy.

The king of France had advanced into Flanders soon after the assassination, with a large army, seeking vengeance while asserting his dominance as overlord. His forces surrounded the castle where the assassins and their supporters had taken their stand. Burchard, who had wielded the fatal blade, tried to slip away, but was caught. He was tied to a tall wheel, where ravens pecked out his eyes, before his body was riddled with countless arrows and spears, launched by Charles the Good's furious citizens.

A man identified as the assassins' ringleader, named Berthold, was handed over to Louis VI by his own men. 'He was hung from gallows next to a dog,' Abbot Suger recalled, 'and whenever someone struck the dog, the animal turned its anger on the man, eating up his whole face with its biting. Sometimes, horrible to say, it even befouled him with excrement. And in this way, more wretched than the most wretched, he ended his miserable life.'[14]

Louis marched his men seventy miles south, to Arras, in order to concentrate the minds of the Flemish representatives entrusted with selecting Charles the Good's successor. They duly proclaimed William Clito the new count of Flanders. This forced Henry to cross to Normandy in 1128.

Henry was prepared to wage war not only on the battlefield, but also through commerce. The wool trade with Flanders had grown greatly during Henry's rule and now he threatened to impose tariffs on the Flemish. Meanwhile William Clito's rule had lost some of its popularity because of his relentless torture and execution not just of people suspected to have had a hand in the assassination of his predecessor, but of their innocent associates, too. His succession to the county was quickly challenged by Thierry of Alsace, a grandson of a previous ruler. Four of the main Flemish cities recognised Thierry as count, as did King Henry.

Clito and Thierry clashed at the Battle of Axspoele, to the south of Bruges, on 21 June 1128. On the day Clito showed soldierly qualities that his grandfather, the Conqueror, would have been proud of. 'The fighting was fierce,' recorded Henry of Huntingdon. 'Count William made up for the small size of his forces by his inextinguishable prowess. All his armour stained with enemy blood, he hacked into the enemy's squadrons with his lightning sword. The enemy could not withstand the awesome weight of his youthful arm, and took flight in terror.'[15]

With Bruges regained, Clito moved forty miles south-west to try to subdue Aalst, an important imperial city near Brussels. He began a siege which paid dividends at once, a chronicler recording how the garrison 'would have surrendered the following day'.[16] But fate intervened. Clito received a minor wound from a splinter in his hand. It turned septic. He died soon afterwards, aged twenty-five. His body was taken to France, and laid to rest in the abbey of St Bertin, in Saint-Omer.

It was a sudden and curiously muted end to a life that had both promised and threatened so much. William Clito, Curthose's heir, had caused his uncle, King Henry, huge concern in the years either side of the *White Ship* disaster. He had attracted a wide array of self-interested allies to his cause, but he had also dazzled many with his personal charm and generosity. Wace said of Clito that 'he was greatly loved by [his] knights and willingly gave them gifts', while Henry of Huntingdon was more general in his praise: 'In his short life this most noble of youths earned eternal fame,' he wrote.[17]

The prime focus for aristocratic revolt against, and foreign aggression towards, King Henry died when William Clito submitted to his gangrenous wound. Despite two short marriages, he had left behind no children, and his father, Robert Curthose – now in his late seventies – had long resigned himself to seeing out his days as a captive in Cardiff Castle.

Henry, long assured in England, finally felt secure in Normandy. He released Waleran de Meulan from prison and gave him back his lands (although not his castles), before inviting him and his twin brother, Robert of Leicester, to take their places at court.

By such deft manoeuvres – as he had previously managed with William de Warenne – Henry was able to turn former enemies into powerful supporters. The pair would become leading lights among Henry's aristocrats, assisting his rule with the same zeal that they had previously reserved for opposing it. With William Clito gone, they appreciated that continued opposition to Henry was pointless.

In June, the month before Clito's death, Henry had knighted Geoffrey of Anjou. This rite of passage, embracing military manhood, was a prelude to the boy marrying the king's daughter. On 17 June, in Henry's presence, twenty-six-year-old Matilda and fourteen-year-old Geoffrey wed in the recently consecrated cathedral of Le Mans. The couple were then acclaimed with huge excitement by the citizens of Angers, the capital of Anjou.

Matilda had been a reluctant bride, but she had fallen in line with her father's foreign policy requirements. She had balked at her demotion to the rank of countess (although she would continue to call herself 'Empress'), and she also struggled with marriage to a much younger husband – particularly one who had such a difficult, petulant, temper. However, Matilda and Geoffrey soon had much to distract them.

Fulk V of Anjou's wife, Ermengarde, Countess of Maine, had died in 1126. The following year King Baldwin II of Jerusalem, a veteran of the First Crusade, approached Fulk to see if the count might marry his eldest daughter and heir, Melisende. Baldwin wanted to leave her and her inheritance in strong and capable hands, and he greatly valued the wealth of Anjou, as well as Fulk's fighting qualities. William of Tyre, a twelfth-century archbishop and chronicler, recorded that Fulk was 'an experienced warrior, full of patience and wisdom in military affairs'.[18] The count left to marry Melisende in 1129, passing the rule of Anjou and Maine to his son Geoffrey, while he became king of Jerusalem in 1131.*

In the same year Louis VI had his eldest son Philip declared the junior king of France, in order to secure the succession. Contemporary writers considered Philip to be highly promising. Suger commented on the boy's charm while Orderic admired the sweetness and simplicity of his character. This was a time of 'peace in France, Flanders, Normandy, Brittany, Maine, and Anjou', which happy state meant Henry 'returned joyfully to England'.[19]

But, in October 1131, Louis the Fat suffered a family loss to rival that of Henry, eleven years earlier. Fifteen-year-old Philip was riding fast through the Greve, a market area in the suburbs of Paris, when a black pig that had been foraging in a dung heap shot under the young king's horse, tripping it up. Philip was flung forward against a rock and his horse rolled on him, breaking bones and sending him into a coma. The co-ruler of France died the next day, without having regained consciousness.

In a passage that could have been written about the loss of

---

* In 1143, Fulk was mortally injured in a hunting accident. His head was crushed and, recorded William of Tyre, 'his brains gushed forth from both ears and nostrils'. Fulk died shortly afterwards.

the *White Ship*, Abbot Suger recorded: 'So great, so astounding were the grief and sorrow that struck his father, his mother, and the leading men of the kingdom that Homer himself would have lacked the skill to express it.'[20]

Two months before this, in August, Henry and his daughter Matilda had experienced their own brush with death. Having lost patience with her husband, Matilda had separated from him and travelled to Rouen to be with her father. Soon afterwards the two sailed in a ship bound for England. The pair suffered a dangerously rough crossing, in the teeth of a summer storm that surely reminded Henry of the agonising loss of his son a decade earlier. The *Chronicle of John of Worcester* contains an illustration of the king on his ship, perched precariously on the crest of a huge wave, its mast flailed by the gale. Henry lifts his hands in a plea for help from God.

We know that Henry offered up a deal to the Almighty: if He would spare him and his daughter, the king promised to halt the collection of 'danegeld' – an unpopular land tax, histor-ically levied to pay for defence against the Vikings – for seven years. Henry also threw himself on the mercy of St Edmund, the ninth-century English martyr-king. The storm duly abated and Henry and Matilda made it safely to England. Henry saw through his promise, stopping the danegeld and issuing royal favours to the town of Bury St Edmunds the following year.

This scare at sea once again brought into focus Henry's decade-long concerns about what would happen after his death. The king presided over a great assembly at his castle in Northampton, on 8 September 1131, surrounded by his mightiest prelates and lords. Those who had yet to take the oath binding themselves to Matilda's succession were made to do so, while those who had done it already were obliged to repeat their vows.

At the same meeting of his mightiest subjects, it was decided that Matilda must return to Geoffrey of Anjou, who was keen to have his wife restored to him, and Henry and his supporters were eager that she agree: they needed her to give birth to a male heir as quickly as possible. Chroniclers report that when Matilda went back to Geoffrey, he honoured a promise he had made to his father-in-law by receiving her with great shows of pomp, as befitted her rank. She fell pregnant in the summer of 1132.

Over Christmas 1132 Henry was at Windsor, very ill. He recovered by the time Matilda gave birth to a son, in Le Mans, on 5 March 1133. The auburn-haired baby was sturdy and bonny. William of Malmesbury would write: 'The boy is called Henry, recalling his grandfather's name. Would that he may one day recall his prosperity and power!'[21] Orderic Vitalis expressed similar hope, from his monastery, noting how Matilda gave birth to 'a son called Henry, to whom many people look as their future lord, if almighty God, in whose hands all things are, shall so ordain'.[22] In light of the *White Ship*, it was dangerous to presume the natural order of things.

Fifteen months later, in Rouen, Matilda gave birth again, but nearly died while doing so. Her final wishes were recorded as she lay near death, while her father prayed for her survival. She pulled through, as did her second son, Geoffrey.

In February 1134, by now in his early eighties, Robert Curthose died in Cardiff Castle, where he had spent the last eight years of the life imprisonment imposed after his defeat at the Battle of Tinchebray. Curthose had outlived his heir William Clito by five and a half years. The former duke of Normandy's body was laid to rest in Gloucester Cathedral, where he had been a generous benefactor.

That same year of 1134, Henry of Huntingdon recorded: '[King] Henry stayed in Normandy to rejoice in his [Angevin] grandsons.'[23] The king's relationship with Matilda had grown fraught. The old man wanted to return to England, but he was kept from doing so by the new energy in his daughter and son-in-law's marriage. Romantically ill-suited, they found common cause in contemplating their sons' futures, and in plotting for their benefit.

Geoffrey demanded assurance that, after Henry's death, he and Matilda would rule the Anglo-Norman realm alongside his own Angevin lands. But not only had Henry given him no encouragement to expect such a bequest, he had yet to hand over the frontier castles that had been promised to Geoffrey as dowry when he had married Matilda six years earlier.

Geoffrey insisted he would need these forts after his father-in-law's death, so he could guarantee Matilda's Norman inheritance. He and Matilda claimed they were only acting in the best interests of their sons, who would in time be Henry's heirs. The king stood firm, believing that if he handed over Normandy's castles he would effectively be surrendering the dukedom to his son-in-law.

Countering Geoffrey and Matilda's demands and intrigues kept Henry in Normandy, angry and frustrated. He checked his defences across the wide military front that faced Anjou. At the end of the campaigning season he retreated to a hunting lodge at Lyons-la-Forêt, twenty miles to the east of Rouen. The ageing king was in need of rest, having been drawn to new levels of exhaustion by the sad tensions in his family.

PART THREE

CHAOS

FOURTEEN

A Surfeit of Lampreys?

When King Henry, the peace of his country and father of his people, came to his last moments and paid his debt to death, the grievous calamity made the entire aspect of the kingdom utterly disordered.

From *Gesta Stephani*, a mid-twelfth-century, anonymous, history

Lampreys are ancient water creatures with a passing resemblance to eels. But they have no jaws, instead sucking on their prey, before ingesting what they take in through a throat bristling with teeth. Lampreys have to be washed and prepared for human consumption carefully: the mucus on them and the serum in them are toxic.

In the Middle Ages, despite their ugliness and inherent dangers, lampreys were much prized in royal and aristocratic circles for their rich and meaty flesh. They were, as a result, particularly sought after in Lent, when meat was banned by religious practice. Lampreys became the cloying, base, ingredients for dishes that the royal kitchen liked to serve laced with heavy sauces comprised of spices, fats and blood.

Perhaps Henry had had a dangerous reaction to this dish before? This could explain why his physicians had told him never to consume lampreys again. But, Henry of Huntingdon tells us, after a trying year with his daughter and son-in-law, and in the company of his hunting friends, the king ordered lampreys to be served. He got stuck into the rich dish, consuming an excessive amount of them – in a phrase that will be linked for ever to the tail end of Henry's life story, he ate 'a surfeit of lampreys'.

This gorging on rich foods was in contrast to his usual taste for simple dishes in modest portions, and Henry felt ill almost at once. It quickly became clear that he had been a fool to ignore his physicians. It fast became serious. 'So this meal brought on a most destructive humour,' Henry of Huntingdon learned, 'and violently stimulated similar symptoms, producing a deadly chill in his aged body, and a sudden and extreme convulsion. Against this, nature reacted by stirring up an acute fever to dissolve the inflammation with very heavy sweating.'[1] Such a severe reaction suggests that perhaps some of the lampreys had not been properly cleaned before being served so plentifully to the king.

It is conceivable that Henry of Huntingdon was mistaken, in blaming the lampreys: it is impossible from nine hundred years' distance to know the precise cause of death. But, within two days of falling so sick, it was clear the elderly Henry was not going to survive. The archbishop of Rouen wrote from the king's deathbed: 'God give him the peace he loved.' He prayed that Henry would be granted a gentle exit from the world.

Henry knew he was dying, and for one final time he turned his attention to the issue that had preoccupied him during the fifteen years since he had learned of the death of William Ætheling on the *White Ship*: his succession.

At Henry's bedside as he awaited death was a select group including his eldest son, Robert of Gloucester, as well as the powerful twins won over by the king's mercy, Waleran de Meulan and Robert of Leicester. Also there was a reminder of the tragedy that had wrecked the high point of his reign: Rotrou, Count of Perche, widowed by the loss of his wife, Matilda – Henry's daughter. The countess's cries had stopped William Ætheling from continuing to safety in his rowing boat, and persuaded him back, into a sea writhing with the drowning and desperate, whose weight had taken the small craft down.

Henry had recently commanded Robert of Gloucester to move the bulk of the royal treasury in Winchester to the imposing ducal castle at Falaise, for safekeeping. The dying king now instructed Gloucester to dip into his coffers, and extract £15,000, the sum to be used to pay any of his household knights who were owed money, with the rest earmarked for distribution as alms to the poor. Henry passed Falaise Castle to his son too, so he could use its strength in support of his sister's claim to Normandy. Such were the king's final thoughts.

On the night of 1 December 1135, after a week of painful illness, Henry breathed his last. He was sixty-seven years old. Archbishop Hugh of Amiens, one of the senior churchmen in attendance at the end, insisted all the lords present swear to watch over Henry's body and see to its safe and dignified passage back to England. There was to be no repeat of the unseemly desertion of the king's corpse that had followed the deaths of the Conqueror and of Rufus.

The dead monarch was taken to Rouen, the great city from which he had administered his dukedom, where he was welcomed at the cathedral. Here Henry was disembowelled, his innards being spirited away while the rest of him was embalmed, 'Lest it should rot with lapse of time and offend the nostrils of those who sat or stood by it.'[2] He was then washed in a scented essence, and salted, before being taken to lie in state next to the black marble that covered the Conqueror's tomb, in the abbey of Saint-Étienne, in Caen. It was forty-eight years since Henry had stood by that same spot, as a grieving youngest son, in the congregation at his father's chaotic and grisly funeral.

A month later Henry's body made its final journey. John of Worcester wrote of how he was laid out on a hearse, before being committed 'with great honour' to his tomb in front of the high altar of Reading Abbey. The king had founded Reading in June 1121, a few months after the loss of three of his children in the *White Ship* disaster.

Henry had been clear as to his new creation's purpose: 'I have founded a new monastery at Reading,' he explained, 'for the salvation of my soul and those of King William, my father, King William, my brother, and my son William, and Queen Matilda, my mother, and Queen Matilda, my wife.'[3] The location had been chosen with care, for it lay 'between the rivers Kennet and Thames, in a place calculated for the reception of all who might have occasion to travel to the most populous cities of England'.[4]

Henry had selected Christian relics for the abbey, to give immediate importance to his new foundation and to attract pilgrims whose donations would offset many of its costs. The hand of St James the Greater, given to Henry by his daughter Matilda towards the end of his life, was the most important of these. It was kept in a bejewelled case that was in the shape of an arm. Alongside it were objects whose highly suspect attributions were accepted by the faithful without question: one of Jesus's sandals, a hair of the Virgin Mary, pieces of bread left over from the Feeding of the Five Thousand, a sliver of the Holy Cross and the foreskin of Christ (one of seventeen being venerated around Europe at the time). As soon as it opened as a place of worship, Reading attracted a throng of visitors, William of Malmesbury writing that 'the guests arriving every hour, consume more than the inmates themselves'.[5]

Reading was a Cluniac monastery, drawn from the order that had been founded in 910 by William, Duke of Aquitaine, as a result of the guilt he felt at his role in a murder. King Henry had long been a generous benefactor to the mother priory, and had monks for his new foundation brought over from Cluny itself. The first abbot of Reading was Hugh of Amiens, the man who had taken charge of the king's body after death. Hugh had been recruited by Henry from the first Cluniac foundation in England, the Priory of St Pancras, in Sussex.

Writing half a century later, Robert Wace rather underplayed things when he called Reading 'a very worthy abbey'. It was one of the largest monasteries north of the Alps, constructed at enormous expense using limestone brought from Taynton, in Oxfordshire, and across from Caen, in Normandy. Inside it was colourful, boasting decorative architecture of the highest order: its carving 'Coronation of the Virgin' is believed to be the oldest representation of its kind in the world. But it was not simply the construction and the scale of the abbey that made Reading stand out; it was also its purpose.

Henry had ensured that he and the souls of his ancestors and successors had a final resting place as grand as his ambitions had been, even if his life's great tragedy had seen to it that he had no legitimate son to one day lie beside him for eternity. Henry's second wife, Adeliza, ordered that a candle should burn beside his tomb permanently, and she saw to it that the care of the abbey, and of her husband's tomb and memory, were funded in perpetuity by the settlement of estates with suitably sizeable revenues.

It was a dignified and considered departure for the man who had ruled as England's king for thirty-five years, and as Normandy's duke for twenty-nine, displaying a rare talent for governance in both of his realms. Yet Henry's death without William Ætheling to succeed him left the Anglo-Norman territories without a rudder, in a violent sea. 'At his death', wrote

Robert Wace, in Caen, 'there was great sorrow.' But there was also consternation. His rigid control of the English aristocracy – punishing the disloyal with dispossession, exile or extended imprisonment – had helped to lay down a third of a century of peace there.

When the pope wrote, on hearing of Henry's death, he mentioned the 'happy tranquillity' of England and Normandy, and Henry's 'just severity' that had brought it about.[6] Henry of Huntingdon identified the God-given qualities that had under-pinned the successful reign: 'The Almighty Lord freely gave him three gifts: wisdom, victory, and wealth.' They were useful accom-paniments to his hardnosed focus.

But who could continue Henry's commanding style of rule now? Without Henry present, there was no shortage of disgrun-tled men ready to take advantage of a relaxation of the reins, eager to regain what they could of their power and ancestral lands. Who would maintain the order that England and, to a lesser extent, Normandy had enjoyed under the late king? As Walter Map wrote of Henry: 'His greatest glory he reckoned the peace of his kingdom and the prosperity of his subjects.'[7] This peace had been exacted ruthlessly at times.

Only after Henry's death did a dark secret emerge: the king had, according to Henry of Huntingdon, had William, Count de Mortain, blinded while he was a prisoner in the Tower of London. Mortain had taunted Henry when he was younger, and we know from the later sentence of blinding inflicted on Luc de la Barre for his mocking verse how unforgiving Henry could be in the face of ridicule. Equally de Mortain had broken his homage to the king in 1104, then had fallen captive at the decisive Battle of Tinchebray in 1106. Blinding was a truly shocking punishment for a royal relation to suffer, but it was the standard one for treason.

In an age when the crown was expected to punish the bad,

ruthlessly, and protect the weak, diligently, perhaps England needed a similarly uncompromising guardian of peace and prosperity now. John of Worcester lamented how: 'After Henry's burial . . . it was not long before there was much discord throughout England and Normandy, and the bonds of peace were torn. Each man was against his fellow . . . The strong violently oppressed the weak.'[8]

It happened straight away, across the land: on hearing of the king's death, people in Pontefract murdered William Maltravers, a lord who Henry had given them to replace the De Lacys, a powerful family dispossessed in 1106 for their support of Robert Curthose. They gave the lands back to a De Lacy and awaited the consequences – only to find there were none, because their crime had taken place at a time when no king ruled, so no king's peace had been broken.

In Normandy, where Henry had spent more than half his reign striving to keep control of volatile lords, he had also managed to lay down the law, again harshly. As Abbot Suger wrote: 'He calmed the land, renewed the laws, and imposed peace on the subdued. To those who planned [discord] he promised nothing but the ripping out of eyes and the swing of the gibbet.'[9] Henry's death had immediate, calamitous results. 'For on the very same day that the Normans heard that their firm ruler had died,' wrote Orderic Vitalis, 'they rushed out hungrily like ravening wolves, to plunder and ravage mercilessly.'[10]

This was the legacy of the *White Ship*, just as Henry had feared it would be. Once he had failed to father a son with Adeliza, to compensate for William Ætheling's teenage death, the vacuum morphed into a chasm, into which the subjects on both sides of the Channel fell headlong. It was to stop this from happening that he had so passionately and consistently championed his daughter Matilda as his successor. The alternative had always been clear to him: anarchy, in both his lands.

FIFTEEN

Stephen

I pledge myself to keep peace, and do justice to all, and to preserve them to my utmost ability.

From the coronation oath of King Stephen, December 1135

Stephen of Blois had been on the *White Ship* when a bout of diarrhoea struck him. It had been severe enough to persuade him to disembark rather than set sail while feeling wretched and suffer embarrassment on a vessel crowded with other distinguished passengers. Stephen had decided to wait in Barfleur; he could sail for England when he had recovered. While his stomach upset upended his travel plans, it saved the life of the king's nephew.

Stephen was the third son of Adela, Countess of Blois, King Henry's favourite sister: they were the siblings closest in age to one another, Adela being the second youngest and Henry the youngest of the Conqueror and Matilda of Flanders's children. Since at the time of her birth she was referred to in poems as the daughter of a king, it seems probable that Adela was born after her father's coronation in 1066 – several years later than was long thought.

Adela was cultured and literate, being able to read and write in several languages. Most likely the Conqueror's youngest daughter received a formal education, either from a tutor or at a convent. When older, she became a noted patron of writers, and had poems dedicated to her and written about her. Baudri of Bourgueil, a celebrated contemporary writer, saluted Adela for possessing 'a lively talent for writing poems'.

She was further recognised by contemporaries for her spirituality, with Archbishop Anselm applauding her for supporting papal reforms and for her help in steering Henry I towards compromise over the investiture contest. During one of the archbishop's periods of exile, Adela welcomed Anselm into her home, as an honoured guest.

Meanwhile her correspondence with Bishop Ivo of Chartres (Chartres being the principal city of the Blois-Chartres dynasty) demonstrates a probing but effective working relationship with the Church in her husband's lands. In 1098 she joined with Bishop Ivo to condemn the monastery of St Fara of Marmoutier, in north-eastern France, which was rumoured to be 'not . . . a place of nuns, but a brothel, of devilish women prostituting their bodies to the shameful uses of men of all kinds'.[1]

Adela would also prove herself a formidable politician. In 1100 she supported Henry's acquisition of the English crown before Curthose could act. She helped to negotiate William Ætheling's homage to Louis VI in 1119, to spare her brother Henry from the humiliation of having to bow to a fellow king – especially one he had soundly defeated in battle.

As a girl Adela was intended in marriage for the count of Amiens, but he had chosen to take orders as a monk rather than a wife. In 1085 William the Conqueror married his teenaged daughter to the forty-year-old Stephen-Henry, Count of Blois. He saw the value of a son-in-law who could serve as a well-placed counterweight to troublesome Anjou.

Contemporaries hailed Stephen-Henry as 'a man of great eloquence and knowledge'.[2] He became a leader of the First Crusade, in 1096, the expense of his expedition underwritten by Adela's personal wealth. But Stephen-Henry would have an uneven time of things in the Holy Land.

In early June 1098, after a gruelling seven-and-a-half-month siege, the Crusaders took the city of Antioch, although the citadel still held out against them. Falling ill soon after the triumph, Stephen-Henry went to recuperate nearby. His convalescence was interrupted by news that the Turks were approaching Antioch in huge numbers, to recapture the city and relieve the garrison. Stephen-Henry climbed a mountain, 'from where', wrote Orderic Vitalis, 'he saw the Turkish tents spread out over several miles, countless as the sands of the sea'.[3] The sight completely unnerved him and his companions. They fled for their lives.

As they made off, they came across a strong Crusader force that was heading to reinforce Antioch. Stephen-Henry persuaded its leaders that they must retreat. If they did not, he warned, they would only add to the number of the dead in the imminent slaughter. Yet, despite being deprived of these reinforcements, the Christians in Antioch stood fast and pulled off the famous victory against the odds that would so enhance Robert Curthose's military reputation. On returning home later that year, Stephen-Henry found himself in disgrace because of his cowardice.

Although fifty-six years old, Stephen-Henry returned to the Crusade in 1101, in response to Pope Urban's demand that all who had taken the cross of Christ but had failed to complete the Crusade should either set out again or suffer excommunication. He wanted to salvage his military reputation, too.

In May 1102 he was riding in a squadron of two hundred knights, twenty-five miles north-west of Jerusalem, when faulty reconnaissance led them to mistake the enemy's main army for a minor expeditionary force. By the time the Crusaders realised the enormity of their error it was too late to get away. Their opponents outnumbered them twenty to one.

In the ensuing engagement, the Second Battle of Ramla, Stephen-Henry was one of the few Christian knights to escape the battlefield carnage. He made it to a defensive tower, but this proved merely a staging post on the way to his doom. Enemy engineers burrowed beneath the tower's foundations, while fires were lit to smoke out the Crusaders. Stephen-Henry took part in what all its participants knew would be a suicidal charge. However, his spirited end, preferring an honourable death on the open battlefield to being killed like a cornered rat, redeemed his name as a fighting man.

On embarking on the First Crusade Stephen-Henry had entrusted the executive power of Blois-Chartres to his wife. In one of his letters home he had encouraged Adela to 'keep well, govern your land excellently, and deal with your sons . . . honourably'.[4] During his three years away, Adela discharged her duties with ability, intelligence and a gift for leadership. When Stephen-Henry had returned in disgrace, she carried on in her role and urged her husband to return to the Holy Land as soon as he could, to redeem himself. Contemporaries noted how Stephen-Henry tended to do his wife's bidding, Orderic Vitalis putting his obedience down to the irresistible effect of Adela's 'conjugal caresses'.[5]

As a widowed matriarch Adela continued to wield power in the best interests of her lands, and her children: she had at least five sons and one daughter, as well as several stepchildren. She sidelined her eldest son, who was known as 'William the Simple', believing him incapable of effective rule. While William was allowed to carry the title of count of Chartres, the family's true power base was Blois. Adela saw that this county went instead to her second son, Theobald, who was a boy of great promise.

As Theobald was twelve at the time of his father's death, Adela stayed in power as regent. Documents show that mother and son frequently travelled together to administer their lands. Adela remained a forceful voice in the family until she chose to retire to a nunnery, in 1120. Even after that Adela promoted her children's interests vigorously. She would live until 1137 and would see several of them achieve great importance; none more so than Stephen.

Stephen had grown up in the Anglo-Norman court of King Henry, where he was favoured by his uncle. Henry increased his nephew's prestige by giving him estates in England, which included the feudal baronies of Eye, in north Suffolk, and Lancaster, confiscated from Robert de Bellême's brother, Roger the Poitevin.

The king also built up Stephen's status across the Channel, in 1113 making him count of Mortain in place of his disgraced predecessor. Stephen now possessed status and wealth independent of his elder brother, Theobald. But Mortain came at a cost. It was a frontier land in the south-west of the duchy of Normandy, bordering with enemy France. An insatiable appetite for fighting was a key part of the count of Mortain's duties. This, Stephen certainly possessed. By the time he had boarded the *White Ship* in Barfleur, in his late twenties, he had established a reputation for bravery in battle in Normandy and Flanders, and was noted in particular for 'leading a very large force of Normans' in an attack on Évreux, south of Rouen, in July 1119.[6] He had left the town ablaze.

Stephen was also recognised for a rare approachability in one of such an elevated lineage. 'When he was count,' William of Malmesbury wrote, 'he had by his good nature and the way he jested and ate in the company even of the humblest, earned an affection that can hardly be imagined.'[7] The anonymous author of *Gesta Stephani* agreed that Stephen 'was in fact a thing acknowledged to be very uncommon among the rich of the present day, rich and at the same time unassuming, generous, and courteous'.[8] His popularity extended to his fellow aristocrats, too.

After the wrecking of the *White Ship*, the appalling losses among his leading men left King Henry scrambling to fill positions of power and responsibility in England and Normandy. He entrusted Stephen with some of the estates of Eudo Dapifer, a Norman lord who had died earlier in 1120. Eudo had served in senior positions to the Conqueror, Rufus and Henry and, like many leading men, he had a direct connection to the dead of the *White Ship*: his daughter had been the wife, and was now the widow, of Otuel FitzEarl, the drowned royal tutor.

Stephen's standing received its greatest boost in 1125 when he married Mathilde, the heiress to Count Eustace III of Boulogne. Her mother had been sister to Henry's queen, Matilda of Scotland, making Mathilde the first cousin of William Ætheling and of his sister Matilda. Count Eustace died in the same year that Mathilde and Stephen wed, leaving the twenty-two-year-old Mathilde as countess of Boulogne in her own right, with Stephen by her side.

Along with a strong fleet, and a lucid understanding of the complicated diplomatic relations between the patchwork of counts and dukes whose lands surrounded France, Mathilde brought with her fabulous power and wealth. These centred on her family's ancestral Flemish lands, which formed a crossroads on the trading routes of the Channel and the North Sea. Flemish trade with England had Wissant at its heart: Calais had yet to challenge Wissant in importance and would only do so later in the twelfth century, after Wissant's harbour silted up.

Mathilde also conveyed to Stephen substantial properties in south-eastern and eastern England, acquired by the wealthy county of Flanders.

Equally importantly, Mathilde brought herself: able, accomplished, organised and decisive, she would bear five children, as well as the burden of a husband who, although brave and charming, had ambitions that exceeded his middling abilities. The author of *Gesta Stephani* called Mathilde of Boulogne 'subtle and steadfast'.[9] Stephen would rely heavily on both these qualities in the challenging years to come.

Although Stephen had been second in line, behind David of Scotland, when Henry called on his lay leaders to guarantee his daughter Matilda's succession to his throne, Stephen showed, in time, that he had no intention of honouring his oath. On hearing of Henry's death, in December 1135, he immediately sailed from Wissant to Dover, and went directly from Dover to London to persuade the leading citizens there to choose him as their king. He had a claim, being both a grandson of the Conqueror and a son of Adela – the only child other than Henry to be born 'in the purple'.

Stephen understood that the English needed reassurance, after the death of the king whose reign had lasted longer than those of Harold, the Conqueror and Rufus combined. He swore to continue the same strong style of rule that his dead uncle had adopted. He was not offering any outlandish promises, just more of the same. London was, according to a contemporary writer, 'filled with excitement and [the citizens] came to meet him with acclamation, and whereas it had been sadly mourning the grievous death of its protector Henry, it revelled in exultant joy as though it had recovered him in Stephen'.[10]

While what Stephen promised was appealing, his bid for the crown was sealed by the support of two bishops. First, Roger of Salisbury wasted no time in casting aside the oaths he had overseen and given, committing the succession to Matilda. He transferred the administrative power of Henry's rule to support the new claimant, and with it went command of the royal treasury. Stephen was quick to reconfirm Roger in the unique importance he had enjoyed in the previous reign, joking that he would give the bishop half of England if he asked for it. A small step towards this concession involved promoting the bishop's son, Roger le Poer, to the role of chancellor.

Nearly as important was Stephen's younger brother, Henry of Blois-Chartres. He was Adela and Stephen-Henry's youngest son, conceived during the time between his father returning home in disgrace from the First Crusade and setting off again with redemption in mind.

When Henry reached the age of two, Adela had promised him to the service of God and later sent him to the founding monastery of Cluny, where he spent his boyhood before moving to England. Through the influence of his uncle, King Henry, he became abbot of Glastonbury in 1126, and bishop of Winchester – the richest see in England – three years later. *Gesta Stephani* said that Henry of Winchester 'was reckoned to surpass all the great men of England in judgement and wisdom and to be their superior in virtue and wealth'.[11]

In 1135 Bishop Henry welcomed Stephen into Winchester, 'the second place in the kingdom',[12] and home of the treasury. He helped Stephen transmit a series of promises to leading prelates and barons that were designed to secure their support for his rule. Stephen swore to allow the Church to elect its own bishops, while dangling the possibility that he might even abolish the geld, the hated royal land tax. At the same time he reassured the people that if they chose him as their king, they would continue to enjoy the freedoms and laws imposed so effectively by his late uncle.

Still, there was a problem. William de Corbeil, who had been

Archbishop of Canterbury since 1123, refused to contemplate a coronation until the oaths that Stephen and his leading supporters had given to support Matilda's succession were addressed. Stephen's backers claimed the late king had bullied them into taking a vow that they could not reasonably be expected to keep. The breaking of an oath secured through fear could therefore, they alleged, not be counted as perjury. Some of Stephen's men even pretended that Henry had freed all from the oath, as he lay 'in his death agony'.[13] This was untrue: indeed, Henry had spent the lucid parts of his dying days fixated on the desire for his daughter to inherit the throne.

But the distortions were accepted, given the need quickly to fill the vacancy on the throne, and because Stephen – of royal blood, a fine soldier, extremely popular and (crucially) male – had much to commend him as an incumbent. Three weeks after Henry's death Stephen was crowned by Archbishop William with two other prelates in attendance. Few noblemen were present, such was the rush to anoint the new king before Matilda could make her move. Many of those absent were happy to wait in their castles to see how things would develop.

Stephen's coronation charter was thin and vague, in contrast to the meaty document that Henry had circulated round the kingdom thirty-five years earlier. The new king offered continuity rather than a new agenda, but it was enough at the time. Stephen further advertised his deep connection with his predecessor when, on 5 January 1136, he acted as one of the pallbearers at Henry's funeral at Reading Abbey. But the man helping to carry the coffin had reneged on the one promise that had mattered above all others to his dead uncle.

It would return to haunt him.

It seems astonishing now, given how unanimous and easily won the support had been for Henry's intentions for Matilda in 1127 and 1131, that her claims could be so quickly and completely sidelined. Besides, Matilda had clear qualities. William of Malmesbury believed the queen 'displayed her father's courage and her mother's piety; holiness in her found its equal in energy, and it would be hard to say which was more admirable'.

However, whatever Henry's hopes and plans, the concept of a woman ruling a country was anathema to many in mid-twelfth-century England and Normandy. Even Henry had touched on the problem, when commending Matilda to his great men in 1127: he made a distinction between William Ætheling, his dead son who would have naturally inherited the crown from him if the *White Ship* had not sunk, and Matilda, his daughter, 'through whom alone there lay the lawful succession'.[14] To Henry, his son had been his undisputed heir, while his daughter (because of her gender) was only capable of being his successor.

Indeed, the English title of 'queen' came from the Saxon word '*cwén*', which meant a consort of a king, rather than an independent ruler in her own right as a king in a woman's body. Matilda's grandmother, Matilda of Flanders, had wielded power on the Conqueror's behalf, and her own mother Matilda had done so in her father's absence from England; but neither of them had been anything other than a regent, doing the true ruler's bidding when he was away from home. Equally when Matilda had found for the abbey over the church in Italy, she had been sitting in judgement only because her husband Henry V was on pressing imperial business in Germany.

And a lot of that husbandly absence had been while leading armies into battle. This was a prime duty of medieval kingship. William the Conqueror and Henry's seals each showed them seated on their thrones on one side, fonts of wise and fair rule, but on the other side portrayed them as armed commanders on horseback, ready to fight their enemies. To the twelfth-century Anglo-Norman aristocrat, a woman could not lead them and their men into battle.

Baudri of Bourgueil, who dedicated a poem to Adela of Blois, in the early twelfth century, compared her favourably to her father William the Conqueror – but with a proviso:

Equally worthy herself, the daughter follows her father,
With the exception that she cannot bear warrior's arms.
Surely she would bear arms if custom did not forbid it;
But such delicate limbs should not be burdened with steel.[15]

Orderic Vitalis reflected the prevailing prejudice when he wrote that 'women are unwarlike by nature'.[16] The battlefield was a place of brutal carnage and of knightly chivalry, both of which were seen to have a peculiarly masculine bent. Kings fought alongside their men and risked being cut down in battle. Queens did neither.

Matilda's cause was further undermined by her husband's nationality. The Normans had long faced rivalry from the surrounding states, Orderic Vitalis writing that: 'The greedy animals who ring them round are the French, the Bretons, the Flemings and the Angevins . . . who are jealous of the prosperity of Normandy.'[17] Being Angevin, Geoffrey was viewed with deep suspicion by many leading Normans, as well as by other traditional enemies of Anjou, such as Theobald of Blois-Chartres and his brother, Stephen.

The *Anglo-Saxon Chronicle* stated that Matilda and Geoffrey's marriage had 'displeased all the French and the English'. To most of Henry's leading subjects, Geoffrey of Anjou was an enemy outsider who had achieved through marriage a level of strategic gain that they would have resisted to the end on a battlefield.

And there were those who believed that the house of Anjou descended from a diabolical source. Supposedly an Angevin count had long before returned from a visit to a far-off land with a beautiful wife who was a suspiciously reluctant churchgoer. When she did attend, she always left before the consecration. One day her husband had four of his knights tread on the fold of her cloak so she could not slip away mid-service. Forced to witness the priest holding aloft the host she was said to have screamed, slipped her cloak and flown away with two children in her wake. This was how she revealed herself to be Melusine, the Devil's daughter.

This Satanic figure was alleged to be Geoffrey's ancestor. It surely explained the family's temper, which was infamous for its heat. The great French reforming abbot Bernard of Clairvaux, a contemporary of Geoffrey of Anjou's, said of the count's family: 'From the Devil they came, and to the Devil they will return.'[18]

Stephen's supporters would choose to refer to Matilda as 'the countess of Anjou', to emphasise her connection to a husband who was not only foreign, but also a danger to the good people of England and Normandy.

In addition there was the issue of what role Geoffrey of Anjou was to have. While King Henry had urged his daughter on his prelates and magnates, he had not defined how Geoffrey would fit into the new scenario: by the time of King Henry's death, Geoffrey was the father of his grandson, Henry, who was Matilda's heir; but what was Geoffrey's function, while his wife was alive and his son was growing up? Was he to rule England and Normandy on Matilda's behalf, with his wife and their son's best interests at heart? Or was he expected merely to be a consort, lending Angevin military power to Matilda so she could establish herself as queen and duchess, while taking no active part in her rule? It was an awkward loose end that Henry had left behind, especially when some noted how reluctant the late king had been even to invite Geoffrey to attend his court.

Stephen had seized the throne despite his elder brother, Theobald, apparently having the stronger claim, if Matilda's rights were to be ignored. Indeed, it was on this assumption that Theobald had already been proclaimed duke of Normandy by the most powerful figures there, when they met in consultations in Caen and eastern Normandy soon after Henry's death.

Theobald certainly seemed to be a sound choice, being a forty-five-year-old man of experience and accomplishment, with a distinguished reputation in warfare and politics. But the leading Anglo-Normans were clear that they did not want a separate ruler on either side of the Channel: a return to the divisive days of Curthose, Rufus and Henry had to be avoided. So Theobald was quietly replaced as duke of Normandy by Stephen, who later gave his brother a pension of two thousand marks per year as compensation for not challenging his coup, and supported his becoming count of Champagne and of Brie in 1125.

The only problem now seemed to be the Scots. Having co-existed happily with England during Henry's reign, everything now changed. King David of Scotland had witnessed the casting aside of his pledge with incredulity and outrage. He was 'greatly vexed that Stephen had come to take the tiller of the kingdom of the English', instead of allowing his niece to do so, and he felt justified in invading England on her behalf.[19]

David also had his own motives for attacking: a religious man, he hoped to advance as far south as York, to claim the city for Scotland and to secure its archbishopric for his people, for the Scots had no such office of their own. An able soldier (he had learned much from his time in Henry's court, including military skills), he captured Newcastle and Carlisle, and received oaths of support for Matilda from several lords in the north of England.

In early 1136 Stephen moved to meet the Scottish threat, taking with him a strong mercenary force from Flanders to support his English and Norman troops. By then King David had had time to see how the majority of England's powerful men were supporting Stephen's kingship, and were clearly prepared to forget their solemn oaths to King Henry. Realising that now was not the time to fight the crown's usurper, David 'wisely pondered the ultimate result and waited quietly for some time to see to what end the enterprise would come'.[20]

Stephen was relieved to find David open to a swift conclusion of their hostilities. In return for peace, he allowed the Scot to hold on to some of his gains in northern England. Among these were silver mines at Alston in Cumbria, in recognition that much of the area around Carlisle was effectively under Scottish control anyway. The deposits at Alston enabled David to be the first Scottish king to mint his own coins; crudely forged, sterling silver pennies.

David had gained enough for now, and he was prepared to see how things progressed for the new, English, monarch. Stephen had impressed many by quelling the Scottish threat, and they felt reassured in their choice of king. They were soon comforted further by the arrival of a letter from Pope Innocent II supporting Stephen's coronation and excusing those who had failed to uphold their oaths to King Henry on Matilda's behalf.

Stephen was a softly spoken man, accused by contemporaries of possessing 'such a kindly and gentle disposition that he commonly forgot a king's exalted rank'.[21] He did, though, have a pronounced weakness for the pomp of kingship: he loved the ostentation of it all, preening himself in the reflection of his new-found power and position.

Shortly after settling the north with David of Scotland,

Stephen displayed his wealth and generosity at the Easter court held at Westminster, making it in the estimation of Henry of Huntingdon: 'more splendid for its throng and size, for gold, silver, jewels, robes, and every kind of sumptuousness, than any that had ever been held in England'.[22] David was there in biddable attendance, as was his son Henry, who had previously paid homage to Stephen in York, and who now joined Stephen's court. It seemed that all would quietly forget Matilda and her claims, and Stephen would set about building on the strong monarchical foundations laid with such care by his late uncle.

The settlement was short-lived. They were few, but the absentees from the dazzling Easter court were notable. Many of those men who had 'been raised from the dust' by the late king remained steadfast in their loyalty to him and his wishes – 'and though the [new] king promised that he too would confer upon them the same favour of friendship and the same lofty position that King Henry had,' Stephen's main contemporary propagandist wrote, 'they long hung back around their castles and refused to obey the king's letters, both on account of the loyalty and the oath that they had owed to their foster-sister, King Henry's daughter, and because the noblest men of the kingdom grudged their distinction and their splendour, inasmuch as they were of the lowest origin and [yet] exceeded in wealth and surpassed in power those far better born than themselves'.[23]

Among the few notables who were absent from the sumptuous and triumphant Easter court was Baldwin de Redvers, whose father Richard had supported Henry in his youth, through the testing period from 1090 when William Rufus and Robert Curthose turned on their brother for their mutual territorial benefit, and again when Curthose contested Henry for the English throne. Richard de Redvers had been rewarded for his loyalty with estates in the south of the kingdom: Devon, Dorset and the Isle of Wight. After Richard de Redvers's death in 1107, his son Baldwin had become an equally stalwart servant of Henry's. Now he was openly observing the oath he had made to his late master, committing to Matilda's succession. He made it known that he was prepared to fight for his beliefs, and stocked Exeter Castle with men, weaponry and supplies.

Stephen led his forces to bring de Redvers to heel, settling into a siege during that stiflingly hot summer. After three months the castle's well ran dry. Baldwin's wife, Adelize, her hair worn loose, led a barefoot delegation of the besieged, to ask Stephen to allow them water. They made a pitiful sight, a chronicler noting their 'sagging and wasted skin, the look of torpor on their faces, drained of the normal supply of blood, and their lips drawn back from gaping mouths'.[24]

The king's bishop brother, Henry of Winchester, advised that this was no time for clemency, since it would only encourage further rebellion elsewhere. But Robert, Earl of Gloucester, who had arrived at the Easter court late, and with grave reservations about the new royal regime, persuaded Stephen to act with mercy. Henry of Winchester would see Robert of Gloucester's intercession as a deliberate subversion of the new king.

When Exeter Castle fell Stephen decided that all the defendants should keep their lives and liberty. Having presented himself as the natural heir to Henry because he was the most likely to continue the impressive record of peace in England, perhaps the new king felt this could best be achieved through leniency? Maybe he was, as John of Worcester would claim, at heart 'a pious and peaceable man'?

But many of his other followers thought the new king's failure to set an example by punishing the leaders of the rebel garrison a great mistake. It was so early in the reign, and he needed to lay down his mark as a man not to be meddled with. This compassion could be seen as a worrying sign of weakness. De

Redvers had clearly been guilty of treason, but he was being allowed to keep his life, and even his eyes.

De Redvers was sent into exile, with his wife and children, but he did not go far. He established himself at Carisbrooke Castle, on the Isle of Wight, from where he operated as a pirate harassing Stephen's ships. When, in time, he was forced from this family stronghold, he joined Matilda in Anjou, ready and eager to fight for her once more.

Stephen squandered more respect through an ineffective campaigning season in Normandy in 1137. A meeting in May of that year with Louis the Fat – now enormously large; so much so that for a decade he had been unable to mount a horse – managed to lay the basis for friendlier relations than Henry had enjoyed with his greatest adversary. This was because Louis did not fear the new English king, for he knew Stephen did not have full control of the Anglo-Norman realm that had caused the French so much pain in the past. Those wars, of 1104–13, then of 1116 until before the *White Ship* set off on its final voyage in 1120, had been brutal, and ruinously expensive. Louis was happy to accept the homage of Stephen's eldest son, Eustace, as the future duke of Normandy.

Whatever diplomatic advances Stephen may have made with France were wiped out a few weeks later, when Louis fell gravely ill. He took a week to die of dysentery. As death approached, he insisted on being dressed as a monk, and on being laid out on a carpet that was covered in ashes symbolic of his repentance. From his position on the ground he gave advice on kingship to his eldest surviving son, Louis the Young.

But the greatest final gift from father to son was not the wise words, but rather a wealthy wife. The teenaged heir, born at the time of the *White Ship*'s sinking, married Eleanor of Aquitaine, heiress to an enormous tract of France, that same year. Louis the Fat's ultimate act of diplomacy had been to engineer this match. In this way he ensured his successor would have huge resources to call upon, in future struggles with England, Normandy and their allies.

With his friend on the French throne dead, Stephen faced deepening problems on the Continent, as the Angevins began adding to his woes. Geoffrey of Anjou had moved quickly after his father-in-law's death to arm the castles that Henry had given as Matilda's dowry, and this gave him footholds at key points along the south border of Normandy.

In the winter of 1136 Geoffrey began leading his men from these into the disputed dukedom, as he championed his wife's claims. Orderic Vitalis recorded that in a single two-week raid, Geoffrey's men 'made themselves hated forever by their brutality'.[25] They raped and slaughtered, and set churches, houses and farms ablaze.

Stephen tried to counter, ordering an attack on the border castle of Argentan, which Matilda had received in her dowry, and which she and Geoffrey of Anjou used as the headquarters of their Norman operations. But the king soon ran into the same self-interest of great men that had derailed the aggressive intentions of Henry and his oldest brother Curthose in 1101. As with the Treaty of Alton, hatched to stall a battle that could only be bloody and costly, the nobles on both sides now worked behind the scenes to block Stephen's impetus. He was finding out the limits of his royal authority early on in his reign.

Tensions between Stephen's Norman soldiers and his Flemish mercenaries, commanded by William of Ypres, further undermined the king's cause. William was a descendant of a former count of Flanders. He had twice tried to become the count himself, but his noble blood was fatally tainted by illegitimacy. This and the humble rank of his mother – a wool carder – proved barricades to his ambition.

Louis the Fat had ended the second of William of Ypres's

failed tilts at becoming count of Flanders, when he insisted on William Clito's election. This snub had provoked William of Ypres to put together a force of three hundred men, paid for by King Henry, to fight against Clito, and so starting William's rise as one of the earliest, most powerful and most feared mercenary captains in medieval Europe.

After Clito's death in July 1128 Thierry of Alsace had become count of Flanders and, when William of Ypres tried to take the county from him, Thierry sent him into exile. As a result William made his living by fighting for money, but he was fiercely loyal to King Stephen. Through that Flanders blood link, William of Ypres was – albeit via the dotted lines of illegitimacy – the king's second cousin. He was also related to Stephen's wife, Mathilde of Boulogne, and it was she who had secured his and his soldiers' services for her husband's cause.

When Henry died, some had urged Robert of Gloucester – who had been at Barfleur on the fateful day that the *White Ship* was lost – to seize the throne. Robert was not only the king's eldest son, he was one of his most impressive generals: contemporary chroniclers often noted how Henry turned to him for military advice.

Other allies of Robert's advised, reluctantly, that his illegitimate birth ruled him out of contention. A century earlier, in the 1030s, the Burgundian chronicler Ralph Glaber had written disapprovingly about how the Normans would recognise bastard sons as their heirs: 'This had been the custom of this people ever since they first appeared in Gaul.'[26] Meanwhile there was a rare occasion in Europe that might possibly have encouraged him to come forward: two decades earlier King Alfonso VI of Castile had chosen his natural son Sancho as his heir, instead of Urraca, a daughter from his marriage. But Sancho had died before this could come about.

However, Normandy and England had both experienced significant ecclesiastical reform. Thanks to the authority gained by the Church over such matters in subsequent decades, the days when the likes of Robert's grandfather William the Bastard could ascend a throne were over. People remembered too how difficult the early years of William's rule had been, thanks to his illegitimacy. Besides England, by custom, accepted only the legitimately born on its throne.

This remained true, despite even his enemies admitting that Robert of Gloucester was 'a man of proved talent and admirable wisdom'.[27] As he fully understood: 'If he were to resist, it would bring no advantage to his sister or nephews, and would certainly do enormous harm to himself.'[28] When Stephen seized the throne, Robert of Gloucester found himself in an invidious position. For the decade before Henry I's death, he had been vocal in support of his father's clear intent to leave Matilda as his successor. He had always been loyal to his father, and it was his insistence on accompanying Henry's body on its slow journey back through Normandy, to England, that had helped allow Stephen to scoop up the crown on his dash from Wissant to London.

Gloucester displayed rare foresight when, in the period of uncertainty following his father's death, he said he would not attempt to become king, while advising that the crown truly belonged to the empress's elder son, Henry: it should be kept safe for the boy, until he was old enough to rule. When Stephen rejected this plan, Robert laid aside his commitment to his father's wish and his half-sister's claim, and swore fealty to the new king with one clear condition: 'As long as you shall maintain me as senator, I will support you as emperor.'[29] At other times, including on his seal, Robert of Gloucester would refer to himself as a 'consul' – he clearly liked to see himself in a classical light, supreme in his sphere of influence in judicial and military matters like a leading figure in Ancient Rome.

Robert of Gloucester had become used to the eminence he had achieved under his late father, with the gifts of an earldom, a wealthy heiress, and castles in key points of England and Normandy. Now that his father was dead, failing to swear loyalty to the new king could have left him and his acquisitions vulnerable. If he was to betray Matilda through inactivity, his price was being made clear. Woe betide Stephen if he failed to respect his powerful, gifted cousin.

On learning of her father's death, Matilda had moved quickly to seize the frontier castles that had been promised to Geoffrey of Anjou as her dowry. As well as Argentan, these included Exmes and Domfront – a fortress that had always been uniquely close to Henry's heart, as its lordship had underpinned his rise from obscurity to greatness (and he had housed various mistresses there).

Retaining these strongholds was essential to Matilda's cause, but at this crucial time she failed to do more to bolster her support, leading William of Malmesbury to say this was 'for certain reasons'.[30] We know that her husband Geoffrey was forced to deal with rebels in Anjou just then. In his absence, perhaps Matilda was being careful with a new pregnancy, given how the last one had almost cost her her life? In late July 1136, nearly eight months after her father's death, she gave birth to her third son, William, in Argentan.

The examples of her uncle and her father should have been uppermost in her mind: Rufus and Henry had rushed to take the throne before anyone else could. All the most important men had vowed to uphold her right to succeed her father, and she cannot have expected so many to fail to see through what they had sworn publicly.

There had been succession crises in 1087 and 1100 that had forced the nobility to take sides supporting different children of William the Conqueror. A generation on, they were being asked to choose between one of the Conqueror's granddaughters and one of his grandsons.

SIXTEEN

Unravelling

When all should be at peace through fear of the king, who should be as a roaring lion, there is in many places . . . depopulation and devastation.

John of Worcester

Stephen found that some of the most powerful men in Britain, who had bowed to the inevitability of his rule in its earliest days, were now prepared to declare their support for Matilda, publicly recognising her as King Henry's rightful heir. Some of these had found their voice after being alienated by the new king: when, for instance, Stephen confiscated Eustace FitzJohn's Bamburgh Castle, he pushed FitzJohn into Matilda's arms. Meanwhile, after the exile of Matilda's supporter Robert of Bampton, in 1136, Stephen seized the estates of several of Robert's relatives. They fled to Scotland asking King David to come to their assistance.

Likewise, those reforming Church leaders who had believed Stephen's coronation pledges were quickly disillusioned. When he needed their support he had promised to allow them free

and independent elections, so they could regulate their religious appointments without meddling from the crown. But
Stephen soon interfered, on behalf of his family. In 1138 he
had his natural son Gervase created abbot of Westminster.
Not long afterwards he helped one of his nephews, Hugh (an
illegitimate son of Count Theobald of Blois-Chartres), to
become abbot of St Benet of Holme, in Suffolk. Stephen saw
too that his sister Agnes's son, another Hugh, was promoted:
he would, in time, receive the important bishopric of Durham.
It was all disturbingly reminiscent of the bad old days of
William Rufus, when the Church's key offices were seen as
royal playthings.

In the meantime, Mathilde of Boulogne was proving to be a
great asset to her husband Stephen's cause. In 1138 she was on
the ground in England to help to organise the siege of Dover,
while sending to her county of Boulogne to throw a naval
blockade around the key Channel port. This pincer movement
on Matilda's garrison commander, Walchelin Maminot, persuaded
him to surrender to Mathilde. From this point on Maminot
would serve Stephen.

Next Matilda wrote to her uncle, King David of Scotland,
seeking his help. He had felt uncomfortable agreeing to Stephen's
seizing of the English throne, and in 1136 is recorded by the
chronicler Richard of Hexham as securing oaths of loyalty to
Matilda from leading noblemen in the north of England. Having
done little since in support of his dispossessed niece, he now
compensated for his years of inaction.

David had claims to Cumbria and Northumbria, which had
once been joined with Scottish Lothian. He saw an opportunity
to take advantage of the growing conflict in England to reclaim
them for Scotland. With Yorkshire in his sights as well, David
sent a decree throughout his kingdom 'and summoned all to
arms and, giving them free licence, he commanded them to

commit against the English, without pity, the most savage and cruel deeds they could invent'.[1]

Richard of Hexham, an Augustinian canon writing in the north of England soon after the conflict, recorded how the invaders obeyed their king with bloodthirsty enthusiasm: 'And then that execrable army, more atrocious than the whole race of pagans, neither fearing God nor regarding man, spread desolation over the whole province, and murdered everywhere persons of both sexes, of every age and rank, and overthrew, plundered, and burned towns, churches, and houses. For the sick on their couches, women pregnant and in childbed, infants in the womb, innocents at the breast, or on the mother's knee, with the mothers themselves, decrepit old men and worn-out old women, and persons debilitated from whatever cause, wherever they met with them, they put to the edge of the sword, and transfixed with their spears; and by how much more horrible a death they could dispatch them, so much the more did they rejoice.'[2] Even allowing for the age-old prejudice of Englishmen against the Scots, often present in records of Anglo-Scottish warfare, it is clear that David had unleashed a torrent of violence on the north of England in support of his niece.

The south-western Scots, allied to King David, were led by Fergus of Galloway. Having married one of Henry's illegitimate daughters, Fergus was one of Matilda's brothers-in-law. His people were particularly feared. Referred to by their ancient name of the Picts, or as 'the Galwegians', they were accused of being at the forefront of the invaders' atrocities. These included allegations that before downing their drinks they spiced them with the blood of slaughtered children.

It took Stephen's presence at the head of a powerful army, 'with a great number of earls and barons', to push the Scots back north, in early February 1138. The English then laid waste to the land they captured, stopping their plundering only when the booty ran out, and Lent – that forty-day period of prayer, alms giving and fasting – was upon them.

Along with these barbarous threats from the north came trouble from the west. Like David of Scotland, Robert of Gloucester suddenly acted on his oaths to see that Matilda would become ruler of England on their father's death. After Stephen usurped her, Robert had reached a pragmatic accommodation with his newly crowned first cousin. This, despite being viewed by Henry as the senior of the two during his final years: in 1130 it seems that Henry had demoted Stephen. Until that point, when Stephen and Robert of Gloucester witnessed royal acts, Stephen's signature would come first. From 1130, Robert of Gloucester's name took precedence.

Robert now claimed, astonishingly, that Stephen had planned to have him murdered in an ambush in Normandy the previous year. In June 1138 Robert sent an envoy to the king, bearing a letter that declared his determination to see his half-sister Matilda on the throne, as their father had always intended and repeatedly arranged.

Robert expressed annoyance and frustration too that Stephen had failed to seek his advice. Henry had always consulted his great men, whether clerics or barons, even if he chose not to act on what they had to say. It was a polite recognition of status and a tactful thanks for support. Robert of Gloucester felt that someone of his eminence should have been one of the crown's '*consiliarii*' – counsellors – and Stephen's failure to treat him as such was a grave insult. He had said at the start of Stephen's reign that the king must look to him for advice, and Stephen had failed to do so.

This proved a decisive moment, for Robert of Gloucester was a gifted and charismatic general, as well as exceedingly rich. He quickly became 'the chief of the king's enemies, and the readiest to undertake any great enterprise'.[3] With her half-brother's support Matilda felt able to push forward her claims in Normandy. Rather than merely remain secure in her dowry forts of Argentan, Exmes and Domfront, through Robert's backing she now had the men and the power to make military inroads into the dukedom.

Stephen soon learned the difficulty of fighting on both sides of the Channel. He was able to land in Normandy only after more than a year of establishing himself as king of England, and his nine months in the duchy were a disaster. As he headed to attack Matilda in her stronghold at Argentan, his Flemish mercenaries fell out spectacularly with his Norman followers. Widespread desertion rendered Stephen's army unfit to fight.

The king returned to England, leaving his Norman military interests under the command of Waleran de Meulan, the elder of the Beaumont twins knighted by Henry I in 1120, the year of the *White Ship*. On the old king's death Waleran had promised to support Matilda, but he had instead reverted to his customary opportunism and self-interest, attaching himself to Stephen.

Robert of Gloucester's support for Matilda had an even greater impact in England than in Normandy. The earl controlled swathes of the west, south-west and south-east of the kingdom, with the Exchequer accounts for 1129–30 showing he owned property in twenty-three shires in southern England alone. The city of Bristol was effectively his capital. He had replaced the wood and earthworks of its castle with stone, brought over at his direction from Caen. Further interconnected defences made Bristol, in the view of the author of *Gesta Stephani*, 'the most strongly fortified city in England'.[4]

Stephen's followers began to hear bloodcurdling tales involving Robert of Gloucester's forces. They believed claims that wealthy supporters of the king were being hauled into the centre of Bristol, blindfolded and gagged, with horses' bits jammed into their mouths. They were then left to starve, it was said, or else were tortured till they handed over all that they possessed. John of Worcester, sympathetic to the king, wrote of how the city was the place 'where, at that time there had emerged, as though from Hell, cruelties worthy of the times of Nero'.[5]

It quickly became clear that there was nothing the king could do about Bristol as the enemy headquarters: when he laid siege to it, Stephen discovered it was too well defended and too richly supplied to fall. He chose instead to lay waste to the lands and villages roundabout that belonged to Robert of Gloucester, before leading his forces to Dorset, then Somerset. He next advanced a hundred miles north-east to Dudley Castle, then swung west to attack Shrewsbury Castle.

The castle's owner, William FitzAlan, fled with his family before the king arrived. FitzAlan had made his garrison swear to hold Shrewsbury come what may, but Stephen's men filled the moats and, under a pungent smokescreen, rolled forward a siege engine. They broke open the main gate and the castle fell. In a sign that the civil war had got bloodier, and the king more ruthless, Stephen saw to it that 'five men of rank were hanged' as a deterrent to those who dared to fight against the crown, while the entire garrison of eighty-eight men was either put to the sword in battle or executed on surrender.[6]

Meanwhile northern England had endured months of terrifying forays by David of Scotland's forces. The people of Yorkshire had not been spared their excesses: 'When they [the Scots] had arrived there, and had gained the victory, on account of the sins of the people, they destroyed by fire and sword the main part of the possessions of a splendid monastery situated in Southerness, and in the district called Craven. Then, sparing no rank, no age, no sex, no condition, they first massacred, in the most barbarous manner possible, children and kindred in the sight of their relatives, masters in sight of their servants, and servants in the sight of their masters, and husbands before the eyes of their wives; and then (horrible to relate) they carried off, like so much booty, the noble matrons and chaste virgins, together with other women. These naked, fettered, herded together; by whips and thongs they drove before them, goading them with their spears and other weapons.'[7]

These outrages were brought to a head at the Battle of the Standard, in Yorkshire, on 22 August 1138. English resistance to the Scots was directed by Thurstan, Archbishop of York, who had long before served as one of King Henry's chaplains. Too frail to take up arms himself, Thurstan used fiery oratory to inspire the northern English lords, knights and churchmen.

The local militias had been summoned too. Their leaders erected a ship's mast at their centre, on a moor near Northallerton. They flew Christian banners from it, as a symbol of their resistance to the Scots and as a rallying point on a day that started in thick fog. The English knights dismounted, some mixing in the front line with their archers, the rest standing with the barons around the mast, ready to fight the invaders who they regarded as barbarians.

The first attack came from the dreaded Galwegians, who had caused such panic with their cruelty. They bravely ran forward without armour or shields and launched their spears. Eyewitnesses commented on their courageous deaths, inflicted by the relentless English bowmen, who loosed so many arrows into the skies that their volleys 'buzzed like bees and flew like rain'. The Galwegians were so completely riddled with projectiles that, Aelred, later the abbot of Rievaulx, said, they looked 'like porcupines'; but they continued to wield their swords, fighting on while mad with pain, until collapsing in death.

The Battle of the Standard turned into a bloodbath for the Scots as they fled the field in defeat. 'But wherever they were discovered, they were put to death like sheep for the slaughter,'

Richard of Hexham recorded with satisfaction, 'and thus, by the righteous judgment of God, those who had cruelly massacred multitudes, and left them unburied, and giving them neither their country's nor a foreign rite of burial, left as prey to the dogs, the birds, and the wild beasts, were either dismembered and torn to pieces, or decayed and putrefied in the open air.'[8] King David and his heir managed to escape this massacre, but only just, while only nineteen of their two hundred armoured knights got away without losing their lives or their weapons and horses.

However, Stephen's inadequacies as a leader were revealed once more, in the Peace of Carlisle of April 1139. While his perceptive and impressive wife, Mathilde of Boulogne, took a leading role in negotiating with the Scots, by the time that Stephen agreed final terms he had made such liberal concessions to his enemy that it was hard to know who had won the recent great battle.

David was handed Carlisle and much of Cumberland. His son Henry received the earldom of Northumbria and the hand in marriage of Ada, the daughter of the immensely powerful William II de Warenne, Earl of Surrey. Stephen even allowed northern English lords to choose if they wanted to offer their loyalty to the Scottish king, 'and this many of them did'.[9] David's courtiers felt that, somehow, and against all odds, their king had emerged the winner from a campaign in which he had been trounced on the battlefield.

Such apparent weakness gave Stephen's enemies hope, while driving some of his allies to despair. But he was under so much pressure from so many quarters – political, military and financial – that strong and coherent policies eluded him.

Propaganda circulated on both sides, further fuelling the bitterness and the desire for retribution. Stephen's backers invented bogeymen, who could be held up as examples of the barbarity of those who dared to stand against their king. Accordingly Geoffrey Talbot, a landowner from Kent who had supported Stephen until turned by his friendship with Robert of Gloucester, was alleged to have returned from exile in order 'to breathe out everywhere the poison of his furious hatred and to do every cruel deed that a frenzied and unbalanced mind is wont to imagine'.[10] This included the sacrilege of transforming Hereford's new cathedral into a fort from which to attack Stephen's castle in the same city, but it also involved gruesome atrocities against captives.

In this climate of mortal fear law and order utterly disintegrated. The days of the Conqueror's strong rule – when, it had been claimed, a girl laden with gold could cross the land unmolested – were long gone. The ghastliness of civil war, when your enemy looked and spoke just as you did, when there was no beginning or end to the campaigning season, and when danger might lurk in every shadow, had seen to that. 'So it was that none trod the king's highway untroubled as before,' recorded Henry of Huntingdon. 'Nor did man trust himself to man with the old confidence, but wherever one caught sight of another on the road his whole body straightaway trembled and anxiously he shrank from view, either in neighbouring wood[land] or in some by-road until at last his courage came again and he pursued the journey before him in greater safety and with a stouter heart.'[11]

The pressures of such a bitter conflict played on Stephen's already rickety judgement. He was driven on by a lack of funds, and by division among his supporters. He was increasingly seen to be under the influence of the Beaumont twins, Waleran de Meulan and Robert of Leicester. They had meddled in ecclesiastical affairs before, in December 1138 securing the archbishopric of Canterbury for Theobald, Abbot of Bec, when Henry, Bishop of Winchester had felt sure the role would be his. This had encouraged them to set their sights on the most powerful churchman in the land.

Despite being the instigator and the overseer of those oaths taken in Henry's presence to proclaim Matilda his successor, Roger of Salisbury had been one of the first to shun them. The bishop claimed he had only been party to the ceremonies on condition that he and the senior nobility would be consulted as to who Henry would choose as his new son-in-law. Roger stated that Geoffrey of Anjou's selection as Matilda's husband, without his input or approval, had dissolved his oath. This, despite the pledge in Northampton Castle of September 1131 taking place after Matilda and Geoffrey had been married for more than three years.

Just as he had been during Henry's reign, Roger of Salisbury was reckoned to be second only to the king in the kingdom. But Stephen began to doubt Salisbury's loyalty just as he was encouraged by Waleran de Meulan and Robert of Leicester to look jealously at the bishop's enormous power and wealth.

Roger controlled the administration and the treasury of England. His son, Roger le Poer, was chancellor, while two of his nephews, Alexander and Nigel, were respectively bishop of Lincoln and bishop of Ely. Despite their offices, these were not men of humble and pious devotion. They preferred to exert their influence on the battlefield, and add to the splendour and sturdiness of their castles, and they were blatant *bons viveurs*. They antagonised those envious of all they had accumulated by appearing at Stephen's court attended by throngs of resplendent knights.

Roger of Salisbury's wealth was even more eye-catching, with his network of patronage adding to the income from his estates. This had allowed him to spend liberally on that most satisfying of hobbies of Henry's 'new men', as they asserted their freshly acquired status – constructing and fortifying magnificent castles. Roger had built four in his diocese, including one at Devizes, on the site of an earlier one that had burned down.

Henry of Huntingdon believed the new version to be unrivalled in Europe. It was common in Henry's reign for the wooden constructions of the Conqueror and William Rufus's time to be replaced by stone castles. Roger had upgraded the rebuilt Devizes in this way, using the most sumptuous stone designs, in accordance with his sophisticated architectural tastes.

Stephen summoned Roger of Salisbury and his nephews to attend his court at Oxford, in June 1139. Roger was a reluctant guest, saying as he set out: 'I shall be of as much good at this council as a young colt in battle.'[12] It soon became clear that the bishops had stumbled into a trap: the de Beaumont twins' men succeeded in provoking a quarrel over the seemingly trivial question of which force would get use of the superior lodgings. The violent reaction from the bishops' retinue left a young nobleman dead.

Affronted by such aggression in his royal presence, Stephen demanded the three bishops hand over their castles. When they objected the king ordered the arrest of Roger of Salisbury, his son Roger le Poer and Alexander of Lincoln. Nigel of Ely fled for safety in the family's principal stronghold, Devizes Castle, which he found occupied by Roger's mistress, Matilda de Ramsbury.

The king marched to Devizes, with his disgraced prisoners in tow. He kept them in a wretched condition, feeding both bishops inadequately, placing Alexander of Lincoln in 'a mean hut' while penning Roger of Salisbury in 'the crib of a cowshed'. Roger le Poer, despite having served as the king's chancellor for the previous four years, was hanged by chains in front of the castle, with a noose cast loosely around his neck. Stephen informed the bishop of Ely that his cousin would be executed if Devizes was not surrendered to him.

When Nigel refused to hand over the castle, Roger of Salisbury was allowed to meet with him. Roger castigated his nephew for bringing such grief to his home, when Nigel had castles of his own in which he could have sought refuge. Despite Roger of Salisbury's spirited intervention, Nigel still would not yield. The sources vary as to whether Roger left the castle, vowing to fast until his nephew changed his mind, or whether Stephen simply ordered him to be starved for having failed to end Nigel's resistance.

After a three-day deadlock Matilda de Ramsbury took matters into her own hands. Appalled that the noose around her son's neck might be tightened to end his life, she secretly handed over the keys to the keep. While she saved her son's life, he was committed to jail and released only after swearing to live out his days overseas.

Roger of Salisbury's time in the sun was over. During the summer of 1139 he handed possession to the king of his castles at Malmesbury, Salisbury and Sherborne, as well as much of his worldly wealth. This was a timely infusion of resources, because Stephen 'had drained his own treasuries to exhaustion',[13] but the rough treatment of the three bishops repulsed many – the clergy in particular. The Bible was clear on the point: 'Do not touch My anointed ones, and do My prophets no harm.'[14] More recently, Pope Urban II had, in the same 1095 Council at Clermont at which he had called for the First Crusade, insisted: 'Anyone who lays hands on a bishop shall be outlawed.'[15]

King Stephen's youngest brother, Henry of Winchester, reacted decisively to the violation of the bishops. He was still aggrieved at having been passed over as archbishop of Canterbury the year before, but ample compensation arrived when the pope appointed him his legate, in March 1139. The promotion gave him supreme ecclesiastical authority in England, surpassing that of either archbishop.

On 29 August that year Henry of Winchester insisted his brother must answer for his treatment of the three bishops, which he framed as crimes against the Church's freedoms. The tribunal sitting in judgement failed to reach a verdict, although it was later agreed that Roger of Salisbury and his nephews could keep those castles that went with their bishoprics, but nothing else. Stephen was forced to do penance, yet for many of the clergy, and for others who believed the king's actions unforgivable, there could be no washing away of his sin.

Roger of Salisbury was said to have been broken by his disastrous fall, after nearly half a century of royal service. He died in Salisbury a few months later, some believed after having lapsed into insanity. He had spent much on his cathedral there, and bequeathed forty thousand marks of silver and gold to its further maintenance and glory. But Stephen swooped on this wealth for his own coffers, adding to the outrage of his ever-growing band of critics.

One of the first laymen to transfer allegiance to Matilda because of the ill treatment of the three bishops was William de Mohun, owner of the imposing Dunster Castle in Somerset. He was quickly joined by others, prompting the anonymous contemporary author of *Gesta Stephani* to note how Henry's 'kingdom of peace and tranquillity, joy and triumph' was turned to 'strife and rebellion, to weeping and lamentation'.[16]

This was the medieval nightmare that Henry I had striven to avoid: a land with a disputed crown, torn apart by factions. The discord of Stephen's reign would be called 'the anarchy' in the nineteenth century. It was the most devastating consequence of the *White Ship*'s sinking, and Henry's inability in his final fifteen years to father another legitimate male heir to the throne.

The agonies of the anarchy were so severe that contemporaries felt they must be suffering divine retribution for their sins:

> So, because the English people, softened by luxury and ease, weakened by wantonness and drunkenness, puffed up with pride and insolence, had many times provoked God to anger, and because their rulers, in the same degraded and monstrous ways of living, but with yet more utter abandonment, wallowed without discrimination and without repentance in every kind of sexual intercourse, every kind of unnecessary debauch in eating and drinking, everything in fact that is regarded as fullest of vice and most harmful to the soul, and vexed God thereby and made him exceeding wroth with them, it was no wonder if England was tormented by so much internecine strife, such confusion of wars, so many crimes on every side.[17]

The gluttony and cruelty of William the Conqueror, the indolence and homosexual shenanigans of William Rufus, the womanising of Henry, all were to blame, as were the moral failings of their subjects. God's patience had been tested until it broke. How else to explain the utter disintegration of the kingdom?

Stephen's position grew increasingly complicated in the autumn of 1139. Baldwin de Redvers returned from exile and settled into Corfe, 'the most secure of all the English castles'.[18] The king himself went to command the siege there, but was forced to move on when he heard that Matilda and Robert of Gloucester were planning to land together in England. Matilda appeared finally ready to claim what her father had bequeathed her.

At Easter that year, when Pope Innocent II had summoned many hundreds of his leading churchmen to the Second Lateran Council, Matilda had sent advocates to plead for papal condemnation of Stephen's breaking of his vows to her father, and of his theft of her throne. Her case was laid out by Bishop Ulger of Angers in a clear and linear argument.

Stephen's counter-voice was Arnulf of Sées, who saw little to be gained in tackling his opponent's argument. As it stood, it was irrefutable. Instead, he had dragged the argument back to 1100, to the legitimacy of Henry's marriage to the Scottish princess Matilda. Arnulf insisted that Matilda, Countess of Anjou, could have no legitimate claim to the English throne because she herself was illegitimate, being the daughter of a nun: Stephen was prepared to have his uncle's marriage denigrated, such was his determination to brush Matilda's claims aside. The pope failed to find decisively for either side, preferring to adjourn the case than to adjudicate. By doing so, Innocent (by default) left Stephen in place as the anointed and acknowledged king.

Now that King David had agreed peace terms with Stephen, and she had not been given papal authority to unseat the man who had taken the throne in her place, Matilda felt she had no option but to come to England to fight for her rights in person.

Stephen ordered his forces at all the harbours along the English south coast to stand ready to repel the invaders, while he rushed to attack Marlborough. But Matilda and Robert of Gloucester went instead to Arundel Castle, which Henry had left to his widow Adeliza.

She lived there with her second husband, William d'Aubigny, who had been a senior officer in Henry's household. From Buckenham, near Norwich, d'Aubigny was a nephew of William Bigod, who had died on the *White Ship*. On marrying the widowed queen, who was six years older than him, d'Aubigny had been made earl of Arundel – an elevation in status that he celebrated by rebuilding his north Norfolk stronghold, Castle Rising, in stone.

The chronicler Robert de Torigni says that William d'Aubigny invited Matilda and Robert of Gloucester to Arundel, but this seems most unlikely because d'Aubigny was a strong supporter of Stephen. It must have been Adeliza who suggested the bold move. She would have been extremely conscious of her late husband's wishes for Matilda to succeed him, and stepmother and stepdaughter had been close when both were teenagers in attendance at the imperial court at Aachen, two decades earlier: Matilda's first action as the fiancée of the Roman Emperor had been to stand up for Adeliza's father, Godfrey, Count of Louvain. Godfrey was in disgrace, having been a supporter of the former emperor, during warfare between father and son. Matilda had helped secure his forgiveness.

Matilda, Robert of Gloucester, 140 knights and 3,000 infantry landed at Arundel on 30 September 1139. While Matilda stayed at the castle with the main force, Robert of Gloucester and his handpicked entourage rode on to distant Bristol, travelling at night to avoid detection by the king's men. Now the already bitter civil war would escalate towards its gruesome summit.

SEVENTEEN

Anarchy

Behave in such a way that the bad shall fear you, and the good love you.

Archbishop Anselm's advice to kings

The arrival of Matilda in England gave her backers renewed hope and energy, just as doubts about Stephen were intensifying in his ranks. The *Gesta Stephani*, while sympathetic to him, conceded that at the time that Matilda landed to fight for her inheritance: 'Those who obeyed the king were brought low as though cowering beneath a dreadful thunderclap.'[1]

It was important for Stephen to defeat Matilda before her support could take root and thrive. His chance came when Adeliza had a change of heart about providing Matilda with a safe haven at Arundel. Perhaps awed by the anointed king's presence before her, with a large army, Adeliza told her step-daughter that she would have to leave the security of the castle. It seemed to be a godsend for Stephen.

But things took a surprising turn in the king's camp. Henry of Winchester intervened, warning that striking against the daughter of the late king would prove dangerously unpopular. It would be far cleverer, the bishop proposed, to grant Matilda safe passage to Bristol, where she would be reunited with Robert of Gloucester. In this way, he advised, Stephen's army could remain intact, concentrating on both enemy leaders in one place. This must be preferable to being pulled in two directions.

When Stephen agreed to this puzzling advice, Matilda 'went uninjured through the midst of her enemies',[2] and was escorted to Bristol by Henry of Winchester and Waleran de Meulan. The king's failure to take the would-be queen captive, when she was entirely at his mercy, was greeted with incredulity by his increasingly exasperated followers. It also emboldened those who had, all along, secretly supported Matilda's succession to the throne. Their plan had been to wait and see, and now they felt inspired to act.

One of the first to step forward on the empress's behalf was Miles FitzWalter who, being the third consecutive generation of his family to be made sheriff of that city, was known as Miles of Gloucester. Miles's importance under Henry I had extended beyond this inherited position: he had also served the late king as constable, the senior military position in the royal household. Miles's prime duty had been keeping the peace along a large section of the Anglo-Welsh border. He was an experienced and accomplished military man.

The chronicler John of Worcester marked the pairing of Robert, Earl of Gloucester, and Miles of Gloucester at the head of Matilda's forces as the moment England's destiny was consigned to misery: 'This was the beginning of despair, the most grievous, no, the ultimate, discord, bringing about the destruction of the kingdom.'[3] When Miles heard that Matilda had arrived in Bristol, he went to her to swear his allegiance and to recognise her as his rightful sovereign. He then welcomed her to Gloucester. A contemporary chronicler noted that Miles 'was so unquestioning in his loyalty to King Henry's children as not only to have helped them, but likewise to have received the countess of Anjou herself with her men and always behaved to [Matilda] like a father, in deed and counsel'.[4] He was just the sort of dependable, powerful and intelligent champion the empress needed if she was to have a chance of toppling Stephen from the throne.

Miles faced action soon enough, assisting others who had dared to declare for Matilda, such as Brian FitzCount, a natural son of Duke Alan IV of Brittany. FitzCount was another of the late king's most loyal devotees: Henry had overseen his upbringing, selecting him to be part of a band of young men who he had added to William Ætheling's entourage. Henry had hoped these would form a nucleus of trusted, lifelong, companions to his son who would in time help him navigate the duties of the crown. Brian would recognise his debt to the late king in a letter of around 1143 in which he described himself as one 'whom good king Henry had brought up, and to whom he gave arms and an honour'.[5]

Henry had rewarded FitzCount for loyal household service with the lordship of Abergavenny, in Wales. He had also given him an eligible wife to increase his standing and power. Matilda of Wallingford was much older than her teenaged groom, but extremely wealthy, and the town of Wallingford contained (along with Windsor and Oxford) one of the three great strategic castles of the Thames Valley. Its dungeons were considered among the most secure in the land: Henry I had sent Waleran de Meulan from Rouen to Wallingford for safekeeping, after his capture at Bourgthéroulde. FitzCount oversaw Wallingford Castle's improvement from wooden fortress to stone citadel.

Wallingford became one of the most obstinate centres of resistance to King Stephen's rule in the entire civil war. Early in the contest for the crown FitzCount stocked it with enough supplies to withstand a siege lasting several years. In 1139 Stephen arrived to test Wallingford's defences and FitzCount's resolve, but he soon despaired of breaking either.

Realising that the best he could manage was to neutralise the stronghold, Stephen built two counter-castles nearby, one of them on consecrated, Church, ground. He hoped these twin garrisons would keep FitzCount's troops hemmed in behind their fine defensive walls, instead of roaming free on Matilda's behalf.

In 1140 Brian FitzCount's men struck out from Wallingford Castle. Stephen's two counter-castles were so utterly defeated that chroniclers noted: 'Clearly such a disastrous calamity befell the king and his men in that place for the reason that from a church there, that is to say a house of religion and prayer, he allowed a castle to be made and a home of blood and war to be raised up.'[6] To build a fortress on holy ground was the worst sort of sacrilege.

At this point Stephen became concerned that his capital was exposed to Matilda's forces. He decided to retreat towards London to lend it more protection but, as he did so, Miles of Gloucester took the opportunity to attack Worcester. Waleran de Meulan, who had been created earl of Worcester by Stephen, arrived in the city of his title to find it devastated. In retaliation he captured Tewkesbury, one of Robert of Gloucester's favourite retreats, and in turn set it ablaze.

While the union of Matilda with Robert of Gloucester tightened its grip on the west and south-west of England, the empress's cause attracted supporters in many other parts. Stephen spent 1140 responding to one emergency after another, crisscrossing the kingdom as his support began to show cracks across a broad front.

Stephen had enjoyed much backing on becoming king, but the arrival of Matilda had shown how shallow much of his support had been. One of those to desert the king at this point was Richer de L'Aigle, whose two brothers had perished on the *White Ship*; one of them after seeing through most of that freezing night lying next to Berold the butcher on the broken mast.

Richer had recruited troops for Stephen in 1139 before defecting to Matilda's side in England and Geoffrey of Anjou's in Normandy. He would return to Stephen's standard later in the conflict, but de L'Aigle never enjoyed the king's trust: Stephen confiscated the Pevensey estates that Richer had stolen from his two brothers.

Like her father, Matilda appreciated and understood the value of loyalty. Now she was in England in person, she rewarded her leading followers. Her half-brother Reginald, one of Henry's many illegitimate children,* was created earl of Cornwall in 1140, when Robert of Gloucester presided over his half-brother's investiture. This was a revival of the earldom that had been forfeited by William de Mortain when he fled to Normandy to serve Robert Curthose.

In a civil war where loyalties twisted and turned, Reginald never let Matilda down. Likewise Baldwin de Redvers would be 'the only major baron who never at any time recognised Stephen as king',[7] and in 1141 the empress rewarded him with the earldom of Devon.

When Matilda encountered disloyalty, she handled it with a swiftness and severity that her father would have understood and applauded. As the turmoil increased in England, Robert FitzHubert from Flanders deserted Robert of Gloucester's army and, using leather scaling ladders, led his men into Devizes

---

* Reginald's mother was Sibyl Corbert, who is also credited with giving birth to three other of Henry's children, including Sibylla of Scotland.

Castle. He declared that he would keep it for himself. But FitzHubert was captured, and placed in chains. Death came to him only after he was, in the words of *Gesta Stephani*, 'worn out by divers tortures'.[8]

Meanwhile Stephen became increasingly bitter about the growing number of objectors to his rule: 'When they have chosen me king, why do they abandon me?' William of Malmesbury quoted him as asking. Sensing that the civil war was at a pivotal and dangerous point, Stephen's wife Mathilde of Boulogne worked with Henry of Winchester to see if peace with the empress could be achieved. It could not.

But the following year was to prove infinitely more debilitating for the king. At the end of 1140 Stephen had largely acknowledged the right of Ranulf de Gernon, Earl of Chester* to take possession of Lincoln Castle. But, when Ranulf married Robert of Gloucester's daughter, the king quickly changed his mind and returned to Lincoln to besiege it.

Ranulf's mother, Lucy of Bolingbroke, was heiress to large estates in Lincolnshire, and probably a descendant of the Saxon earls of Mercia, too. She was also mother of that William de Roumare who had, on seeing the worrying drunkenness of the crew of the *White Ship*, wisely disembarked before it set sail. De Roumare had since succeeded his father as lord of Bolingbroke.

Reflecting the confusing division among the leading families caught up in the civil war, de Roumare, so loyal to Stephen that he would later be created earl of Lincoln by the king, had married Hawise, a sister of Baldwin de Redvers, one of Matilda's chief supporters. This meant de Roumare was therefore the enemy of his brother-in-law (de Redvers) and of his half-brother (Ranulf

---

* His father, Ranulf le Meschin, Earl of Chester, had succeeded to the title on the drowning of his first cousin, Richard of Chester, after the loss of the *White Ship*.

de Gernon). Such intermingling of bloodlines and loyalties was common at this time.

In early 1141, with Lincoln threatened by the king, Robert of Gloucester came to the rescue from the west with an army comprised of what one chronicler called 'a dreadful and unendurable number of Welsh'.[9]

Before battle was joined, on 2 February 1141, Robert gave a rousing speech to encourage his comrades on to great feats that day: 'It is not unbecoming that you seek the honour of the first blow,' he supposedly said, 'whether from the nobility or the virtue in which you excel. But if you argue the point, I, the son of a most noble king, and grandson of the greatest of kings, cannot be surpassed in nobility.'[10]

The examples of the Conqueror and of Henry helped to inspire Gloucester's forces. When Matilda's supporters gained the upper hand in the battle, Stephen's cavalry fled for their lives. Judging the day lost, William of Ypres led his mercenaries away to safety. This left the king exposed at the head of his beleaguered infantry, but Stephen fought on, with defeat certain, wielding his great sword until it shattered. He reached for his 'double-headed Norse axe',[11] swinging it fiercely until he was struck on the head with a rock. As he lay there dazed, he was overwhelmed, disarmed and taken into captivity. The king was soon heard to acknowledge, 'in a humbled voice of complaint', that his battlefield defeat was the inevitable penalty for his rough treatment of the three bishops.[12]

Robert of Gloucester took the captive king from Lincoln to the empress in Gloucester, before escorting him to his headquarters at Bristol. There Stephen was imprisoned in a great tower, where he was expected to remain 'until the last breath of life'.[13]

After the king gave his word that he would not try to escape he was allowed some freedom from the confines of his cell.

However, he was discovered in places where he should not have been, noted William of Malmesbury, 'especially at night, outside his appointed place of custody, after deceiving or winning over his guards'.[14] Stephen's suspicious behaviour led to concerns that he was planning to abscond. Robert of Gloucester kept his uniquely important prisoner in chains after that.

With Stephen committed to the same eternal incarceration that her uncle Robert Curthose had endured, Matilda at last seemed to be in a position to occupy the throne as her father had planned. Henry of Winchester met her and, reassured that he would be consulted on all major issues, including the choice of bishops and abbots, he declared that his brother Stephen was no longer ruler. He welcomed Matilda 'in cordial fashion' into Winchester, handed over to her the castle, the crown and what was left in the exhausted treasury, and addressed the citizens in the marketplace. William of Malmesbury wrote that the bishop reminded his audience of 'the vitality, the zeal and the magnificence' of Henry I, and the author of *Gesta Stephani* recorded him as commending Matilda to them as 'their lady and queen'.[15]

Bishop Henry believed in a vengeful, Old Testament, God who used his strength to uphold the peace and punish wrong-doers: his psalter was decorated with an image of the damned being crammed into the teeth of hell, to endure eternal suffering alongside Judas Iscariot. He felt sure that a king was supposed to act on earth as God's punisher-in-chief, in order to protect the people. But, he conceded, his brother had failed in this crucial duty. As William of Malmesbury registered: 'No justice was enforced upon transgressors, and peace was at once brought entirely to an end, almost in that very year; bishops were arrested and compelled to surrender their property; abbacies were sold and churches despoiled of their treasure; the advice of the wicked was hearkened to, that of the good either not put into effect or altogether disregarded.'[16] Far from perpetuating the firm rule of

Henry I, as he had promised to do when seizing the crown, Stephen was guilty of having let his kingdom plunge into leaderless disarray. The bishop concluded that his brother had surely earned his fall and imprisonment, and now the empress could replace him.

In the build-up to her coronation a Church council bestowed on Matilda the title of 'lady of England and Normandy'. This gave her a form of royal authority, and she felt able to impose herself as the ruler-in-waiting. Some seem to have been surprised that Matilda was planning to rule in her own right; they had expected her to do so on behalf of her eldest son Henry until he was of an age to reign by himself.

The forcefulness of her tone from this point on clearly startled those who had assumed that Matilda would be subservient to her male advisers, a consort to their actual rule. 'On being raised with such splendour and distinction to this pre-eminent position,' the author of *Gesta Stephani* complained, she 'began to be arbitrary, or rather headstrong, in all that she did'.[17]

It is impossible to imagine such criticism being raised against a male ruler of the time: Matilda's grandfather and father had done much as they wished, after all, and their strong and independent drive had underpinned their successes. Loyalties were complicated by Stephen's refusal to formally surrender the crown. For some, the oaths given him at his coronation still stood as sacred bonds.

Perhaps many of Matilda's problems arose from her apprenticeship in monarchy, which had taken place in the uncompromising environment of the Roman Empire, with her husband often away fighting the papacy or German rebels, leaving her in charge of administering his business. This she had done with full imperial authority, refusing to allow a voice to those whom she judged. Such a firm hand from a female ruler was unknown in England. The recent regencies of Matilda of

Flanders and of Matilda of Scotland had operated in conjunction with powerful male advisers who had been appointed, respectively, by the Conqueror and by Henry I.

Henry of Huntingdon reckoned that, at this point, the county of Kent (so close to Flanders) was the only part of England still loyal to Stephen. But, now her crown was within touching distance, several contemporary chroniclers chose to see Matilda's chances being scuppered by an off-putting manner, a foul temper, and a blend of gracelessness and petulance. Such traits had, to varying degrees, been abundantly evident in the three previous kings – the Conqueror, Rufus and Henry – and had been accepted or tolerated. However, in a twelfth-century female ruler, they were deemed unacceptable.

Wealthy Londoners summoned to an audience with Matilda were astonished when she called for large sums from them. They had supposed that Stephen's defeat and imprisonment would lead to the restoration of peace and the return to the good order of King Henry's day – not to continued claims for money.

They explained how ruinous the years of civil war had been for them, particularly when meeting Stephen's constant financial demands. They asked Matilda to be understanding, and patient: they would give her what she wanted, but they needed time for their finances to recuperate from a protracted pummelling.

Gesta Stephani recorded Matilda erupting with anger at the Londoners' refusal to pay, and at the reminder of their former support for Stephen: 'She, with a grim look, her forehead wrinkled into a frown, every trace of a woman's gentleness removed from her face, blazed into unbearable fury, saying that many times the people of London had made very large contributions to the king . . . [to her detriment], and therefore it was not just to spare them' now.[18]

Matilda was similarly uncompromising when Mathilde of Boulogne sought her husband's release from his 'filthy dungeon'.[19]

Mathilde swore to live in perpetual exile with Stephen if he was set free. Alternatively, she promised to persuade him to swap his crown for a monk's habit, in a final repudiation of his earthly ambitions. Matilda rejected these proposals out of hand, just as her father had dismissed all attempts to release his brother, Robert Curthose. Henry's decision had generally been viewed as sensible, whereas Matilda's was interpreted as mean-spirited, and wrong.

Henry of Winchester approached Matilda, suggesting that Stephen's eldest son Eustace (the bishop's nephew) should not suffer for his father's mistakes. The bishop wanted Eustace to hold on to the county of Mortain, and to the dowry possessions of Mathilde of Boulogne. But Matilda was not prepared to store up problems for the future by giving power to her enemy's family. Her father's greatest mistake had been to leave the three-year-old William Clito free to reappear as the greatest threat that his rule and line would have to encounter. Matilda was not going to repeat the error.

Matilda acted equally uncompromisingly with her chief allies. The three most important of these – David of Scotland, Robert of Gloucester and Henry of Winchester – formed a triumvirate that frequently attended her. They expected respect, gratitude and influence in return for their backing. But, *Gesta Stephani* recorded, when they 'came before her with bended knee to make some request, she did not rise respectfully, as she should have, when they bowed before her, or agree to what they asked'.[20]

Matilda perhaps felt the need to emulate the force with which her first husband and her father had held sway. When they had shown ruthlessness and determination, they had been viewed as powerful and assertive. Such qualities, especially necessary during a civil war, were judged quite differently when they emanated from a woman, however well-born. Henry of Winchester was more understandably shocked when Matilda overrode his choice of candidate for the bishopric of Durham. Given the promises made to him as queenmaker, he had assumed that he would be in charge of the governance of England. Now it was clear that he was not even to control Church appointments.

While Matilda alienated her allies, and crushed enemies who could have been won over to her cause, Mathilde of Boulogne impressed contemporaries as 'a woman of subtlety and a man's resolution'.[21] She unified her husband's supporters and undertook to fight on his behalf, both on the battlefield and in diplomacy.

She realised that her husband's cause needed a counterweight to Geoffrey of Anjou's power. In 1139 she had started to plan marriage between her eldest son, Eustace, and Louis the Fat's daughter, Constance. The following year Mathilde took Eustace to France, where the betrothal was confirmed. The newly married Eustace and Constance then crossed to England, having brought French influence and interest into Stephen and Matilda's civil war.

Mathilde ordered William of Ypres to take his mercenaries to the south side of the Thames from London with the command to 'ravage property'. The Flemish troops went hard at this, causing consternation in the capital and fomenting further unrest among those already disillusioned by the prospective queen. Why put up with all this suffering, on behalf of a woman who was 'always breathing a spirit of unbending haughtiness'?[22] Mathilde's secret dialogue with influential Londoners offered an answer to that question.

With Matilda's coronation beckoning, Henry of Winchester and many other great churchmen and lords quit the capital. On 24 June 1141, just three months after her victory at Lincoln, and with the imminent prospect of Matilda entering their city, Londoners erupted in rebellion. They poured out of the capital and swarmed into Westminster Palace, where Matilda was about to sit down for a feast. The angry mob overturned the tables laden with food and pillaged the empress's quarters. She just managed to get away, joining Robert of Gloucester on horseback and heading for Oxford. A chronicler noted with surprise how 'she escaped without scathe from the midst of the Londoners when they were assailing her'.[23]

Mathilde of Boulogne now entered London, begging for and buying allies, who she urged to help her free Stephen from his foul prison. Unhappy with Matilda, Henry of Winchester met Mathilde at Guildford, south-west of London, and agreed to return to his brother's cause.

Denied her coronation, Matilda was determined to lose no impetus. She led her army to Winchester in an attempt to capture the bishop before he could further damage her support. But, as she entered the city through one gate, Bishop Henry fled through another on 'a swift horse'.[24]

The civil war was running at such a speed that Matilda was caught on the hop. Having plundered the bishop's palace and castle, her army was encircled at Winchester by a powerful army loyal to Stephen. It was directed by Mathilde of Boulogne and contained William of Ypres's mercenaries, as well as a strong contingent of Londoners. They closed down all routes out of the city, yet Matilda 'stole away alone, in wonderous fashion, from the Rout of Winchester', as it became known.[25] It was such an inexplicable escape the king's men wrongly concluded that the empress must have been smuggled out in a coffin.

A spirited rearguard action, commanded by her half-brother, bought Matilda time to get away. But Robert of Gloucester was pursued for ten miles to the north-west, until he was overpowered at Stockbridge by William of Ypres. The earl was sent as prisoner to Mathilde of Boulogne's stronghold, Rochester Castle.

Miles of Gloucester, the sheriff who was another of Matilda's foremost champions, returned with the devastating news of

Robert's capture. Miles had escaped the disaster, jettisoning his armour en route, and somehow found his way to Matilda, 'exhausted, tired, and half-naked'.[26]

Matilda fled towards Devizes, riding hard for forty miles. Then, curled up in pain after such exertion, she was carried on a stretcher slung between a pair of horses for the onward retreat to Gloucester. Although she apparently looked close to death, a hostile chronicler conceded that she retained a 'mind steeled and unbroken in adversity'.[27]

England resembled a chessboard, with a queen in retreat and the opposing king held in a corner. But the capture of Matilda's principal knight, Robert of Gloucester, had evened up the game. In late 1141, after declining offers to defect, Robert gained his freedom, bought with Stephen's release.

A Church council convened in December, this time asserting Stephen's right to the throne and excommunicating all his enemies except for Matilda. Over Christmas, at Canterbury Cathedral, Stephen and Mathilde of Boulogne were crowned once again. Stephen rewarded William of Ypres for his military feats – the Rout of Winchester and two lesser victories – by giving him Kent to control.

The king celebrated his liberty with a campaign in the north of England, in early 1142, but he fell gravely ill between April and June, and was tended to in his castle at Northampton. Matilda, also battling ill health, set about shoring up her defences across England.

The renewal of civil war was disastrous for England, 'the result being', *Gesta Stephani* recalled, 'a most grievous oppression of the people, a general depopulation of the kingdom, and the sprouting everywhere of seeds of war and strife'.[28] With open battle seen as risky and costly, much of the action in 1142 involved siege warfare.

Stephen made good headway, capturing Robert of Gloucester's castle at Wareham. In late September the king approached Oxford, which was serving as Matilda's temporary capital, taking strongholds loyal to her at Cirencester, Bampton and Radcot as he advanced. His successes left Matilda holed up in Oxford Castle.

Her grandfather, William, had stormed Oxford during the Conquest. He had then ordered his new governor to improve the castle's defences. Deep trenches diverted the River Isis, and towers and walls were constructed on man-made mounds. Thanks to these improvements, Oxford Castle became a commanding bastion for whoever controlled it. But Matilda's position was perilous, with Robert of Gloucester deployed in Normandy assisting Geoffrey of Anjou. Stephen laid close siege to the castle, unable to cross the moats but posting guards at every exit from the town. By early December, with snow on the ground, the empress had dwindling supplies, and morale among her forces was ebbing away. It looked certain that she would be in Stephen's hands by Christmas.

Yet Matilda never lacked for courage, and she thrived under adversity. After three months and three days, she decided to make a break for it. According to Wace: 'She escaped . . . unbeknown to anyone, apart from those who took her away, for she needed an escort; as she left, she did not even say farewell to her closest friends.'[29] The escort of her three most loyal knights lowered Matilda down the castle wall one night while she was wrapped in a white bedsheet – perfect camouflage in the winter landscape.

Matilda and her handpicked companions crossed the River Isis on foot, thankfully finding its waters frozen beneath the snow. They successfully navigated the dangers that lay on the thirteen miles between Oxford and Brian FitzCount's Wallingford Castle, where safety lay.

It was an escape so daring that it drew the admiration of Matilda's enemies. God's hand was spotted in the detail of it all: 'What was the evident sign of a miracle, she crossed dry-footed, without wetting her clothes at all, the very waters that had risen above the heads of the king and his men when they were going to storm the town, and through the king's pickets, which everywhere were breaking the silence of the night with the blaring of trumpeters or the cries of men shouting loudly, without anyone at all knowing.'[30]

Matilda's flight from certain capture proved crucial. Even though her garrison in Oxford Castle surrendered the following day, she could continue her fight for the crown. The stiff price paid for Robert of Gloucester's release was swiftly redeemed. He returned from Normandy with reinforcements and, more importantly, with Geoffrey of Anjou and Matilda's eldest, nine-year-old son. The boy would frequently be referred to by contemporaries as Henry 'Fitz Empress', rather than by his Angevin title, since it was his mother's claims to the Anglo-Norman lands that defined him.

The war turned yet again. On 1 July 1143, as Stephen prepared to assault Salisbury from Wilton Abbey, Robert of Gloucester launched a surprise sunset attack on the king's position. Stephen was nearly captured once more, while Robert's forces gorged on prisoners and plunder.

Gloucester built on this success, taking several more castles and replacing their garrisons with troops loyal to Matilda, and to her son. Eight years after her father's death, Matilda was fighting for her eldest son, Henry, to succeed to the throne, rather than seeking it for herself.

The atrocities continued, as did the disloyalties. Philip FitzRobert, one of Robert of Gloucester's sons, and Matilda's nephew, controlled Cricklade Castle, in Wiltshire. It was considered impregnable, being 'inaccessible because of the barrier of water and marsh on every side'.[31] But, after suspiciously feeble resistance to Stephen's siege in 1145, Philip meekly surrendered, and the following year, he paid homage to King Stephen. In return for this betrayal Philip received castles, estates and lavish gifts. He turned on his family's supporters with trademark cruelty, 'and everywhere breathing threats and strife against the king's opponents', *Gesta Stephani* noted, 'he raged in all directions with fire and sword, violence and plunder; and far and wide reducing to bare fields and a dreadful desert the lands and possessions not only of those barons who opposed the king, but even those of his own father, he showed himself cruel and unendurable everywhere'.[32]

Matilda and Robert of Gloucester experienced further betrayal when, in late 1145, Ranulf de Gernon – earl of Chester and Robert of Gloucester's son-in-law – also made peace with Stephen. Ranulf helped the king attack Bedford Castle and Wallingford. Stephen chose to host his Christmas court of 1146 at Lincoln Castle – Ranulf's stronghold where, five years earlier, the king had all but lost the war and the crown.

Other of Matilda's key supporters had already fallen away as the civil war ground, bloodily, on. Miles of Gloucester, who had shown such unswerving loyalty to her since her arrival in southern England in 1138, had been rewarded for his service with the earldom of Hereford in 1141. However, he had died in a hunting accident on Christmas Eve, 1143.

The mighty Robert of Gloucester died in Bristol Castle, where he had once kept King Stephen prisoner, on 31 October 1147. He was succeeded by his eldest son, William, who offered little of the vigour or generalship that had been Robert's hallmarks.

William of Gloucester was, in the estimation of the *Gesta Stephani*, 'effeminate and more devoted to bedchambers than to war'.[33]

Deprived of her most able and powerful supporters, Matilda crossed to Normandy in the spring of 1148, as exhausted by the civil war as the kingdom that she now departed. A year later Geoffrey of Anjou made a grant to the priory of Notre-Dame-du-Pré, near Rouen, to provide for Matilda's life there. She also spent a lot of time in Quevilly, a royal manor house built nearby by Henry I.

Given that her life's work had been carried out in furtherance of her father's aims, it was fitting that Matilda retreated to a place with close connections to him. Gilbert Foliot, Abbot of Gloucester from 1139, wrote admiringly of Matilda's consistent and selfless daughterly submission: 'In accordance with her father's wishes,' he noted, 'she crossed the sea, passed over mountains, penetrated into unknown regions, married there at her father's command, and remained there carrying out the duties of imperial rule virtuously and piously until, after her husband's death, not through any desperate need or feminine levity but in response to a summons from her father, she returned to him. And though she had attained such high rank that, it is reported, she had the title and status of Queen of the Romans, she was in no way puffed up with pride, but meekly submitted in all things to her father's will.'[34]

Although Matilda had found somewhere suitable to live, she remained actively involved in her son's life. She supported and advised Henry as Adela of Blois had counselled Stephen, and she remained determined to have her voice heard when necessary. Matilda would act as regent in Normandy when her son was absent, displaying the clarity of mind and of purpose that she had shown when standing in for her first husband, Henry V, a generation earlier. As ever, she took her status seriously, being referred to as 'Empress', and completing her documents with a great seal that, when translated from the Latin, read: 'Matilda, by the grace of God, Queen of the Romans'.

While Matilda had failed to win the throne of England that her father had left to her as his only surviving legitimate child, her eldest son, Henry, now took up the fight on his own behalf.

EIGHTEEN

Order

The mercy of God brought to the broken realm of England a dawn of peace at the end of a night of misery.

Henry of Huntingdon

By the time Matilda sailed away the civil war had sunk into stalemate. The king controlled much of the country but could make no meaningful inroads into the enemy-held south-west and west. The empress's supporters, likewise, could not hope to conquer the king's cause, which was funded by London and Flanders, and supported by large swathes of England. Many leading men looked increasingly to their own interests rather than risking all in a conflict that promised no outright victory.

Typical of this selfishness was Hugh Bigod – younger brother of William Bigod, the royal steward who had perished on the *White Ship*. Hugh had succeeded the childless William not only in his court position, but also as a major landowner in East Anglia. Inheritances from an aunt had given him further power in pockets of England and in Normandy.

Hugh had served Henry I for the remainder of his reign and,

judging by the number of occasions on which he witnessed the king's charters, he was frequently to hand. But after Henry's death, Bigod let his master down terribly. He was among those to claim dishonestly, in 1135, that the dying monarch had recanted and decided that he wanted his nephew Stephen to succeed him rather than Matilda. This, despite Bigod not having been at the king's deathbed.

Bigod had therefore started as a supporter of Stephen, but deserted him in 1136, after reports circulated that the king was mortally ill. Bigod quickly seized Norwich for himself. When Stephen recovered, and advanced into Norfolk to force him to surrender, the opportunistic Bigod returned to the king's standard, only to desert again at the Battle of Lincoln, in 1141, leaving Stephen to be captured. Next Bigod declared for Matilda who, wary of his fickleness, made him earl of Norfolk. But the promotion was not enough to secure the loyalty of Bigod, who would continue largely to satisfy his own needs throughout the civil war.

It was a time of every person looking after himself. This even applied to men of God, one chronicler noting how most bishops, 'girt with swords and wearing magnificent suits of armour, rode on horseback with the haughtiest destroyers of the country and took their share of the spoil; knights captured through the fortune of war, or any rich men they met, they handed over to bonds and torments'.[1]

England had fallen spectacularly from the strictly administered harmony of Henry to the bloody purgatory of Stephen: what had been 'a kingdom of joy and quiet, tranquillity and peace' had, in the view of *Gesta Stephani*, been abandoned to 'sadness and strife, slaughter and devastation'.[2] To add to the terror, unpaid mercenaries from both sides roamed the land, raping and pillaging as they went.

Chroniclers reported that many Englishmen decided to seek

a safer existence overseas. Others, choosing to remain, built their houses in defensive blocs, often around churches. Famines fell hard, one after the other, as fields went untended. The half-starved turned to eating bitter herbs and roots, and even their horses and dogs.

It was a similar tale of disorder in Normandy, where Stephen never managed to make headway. After Henry's death, Empress Matilda and Geoffrey of Anjou had moved quickly, to reinforce their castles and to build alliances. Stephen had planned to cross to Normandy in 1136, but a false report that Roger of Salisbury had died persuaded him to turn back. By the time he had established that the bishop was alive, and fit to administer England in his absence, Stephen decided it was too late in the year to cross the Channel safely. It proved a costly delay.

By 1137 Stephen's Normans had been defeated by their hated Angevin neighbours, and the muscle available to him from William of Ypres's mercenaries – so badly needed there – instead had to be deployed on English soil. Stephen's single success in Normandy that year was persuading Louis the Fat to recognise his eldest son, Eustace, as the rightful duke of Normandy, even though he lacked the power to go with the title.

The absence of a firm hand in the duchy meant that Normandy, in the words of Orderic Vitalis, 'suffered continually from terrible disasters and daily feared still worse, for she saw to her sorrow that the whole province was without an effective ruler'.[3] It was even more dangerous than in the chaotic days of Robert Curthose.

On behalf of his wife and sons, Geoffrey of Anjou led the fighting in Normandy with drive and energy, riding into battle with a '*Planta Genista*' – the Latin name for a type of yellow-blooming flower – as his talisman. This was, it is said, the root of his nickname of 'Plantagenet'.

Geoffrey was helped greatly by news of Stephen's capture at

the Battle of Lincoln, in 1141. Appearing soon afterwards Geoffrey urged the Norman aristocracy to accept him as their duke. Over the next two years he won significant territorial gains in the duchy to further his claim, and even overran Mortain, the county granted to Stephen by Henry I in 1113. In the summer of 1144, to general acceptance, including recognition by Louis VII of France, Geoffrey was ceremoniously created duke of Normandy. He presented himself not as its conqueror, but as its guardian until his son Henry was old enough to succeed to the dukedom in his own right.

Having lost Normandy, Stephen also faced increasing hostility from the papacy. There was to be no assistance in this relationship from his brother, Henry, Bishop of Winchester, for he had lost his position as legate after four and a half years, in September 1143, on the death of Pope Innocent II. Stephen continued clumsily to push for his relatives to receive important positions in the English Church: in 1148, two of the three candidates that he presented for the bishopric of Lincoln were his nephews, while the third was his illegitimate son, Gervase. None of the trio was blessed with more than borderline competence.

Pope Eugenius III was incredulous, then furious, at Stephen's unashamed nepotism. He prepared to excommunicate the king, but this calamity was averted after an unsanctioned intervention by Theobald, Archbishop of Canterbury. However, the bad feeling between the pope and the king rumbled on for the next four years. When Stephen asked Archbishop Theobald to crown his son Eustace, to secure the succession, Eugenius forbade the ceremony, even though Mathilde of Boulogne had lent her persuasive voice to the plan.

Like Matilda, Stephen suffered the loss of his right-hand men as the civil war rumbled on. In the late 1140s he was deprived of the services of William of Ypres, one of his most loyal and able generals, after the mercenary captain lost his sight, and therefore his ability to fight.

With Stephen weakened on several fronts, Geoffrey pushed forward the youth who represented the hope of both his parents to take the reins of England, Normandy and Anjou. Henry FitzEmpress was encouraged by his supporters to, in the words of a contemporary, 'get the emblems of a knight's rank from his father, or else from the King of Scots, his intimate and special friend, and then with renewed vigour rise up against the king and gain with resolution and spirit what was rightfully his'.[4]

As Henry contemplated these prizes, his aunt Matilda of Anjou achieved elevation of her own. The widow of William Ætheling, who had been intended to rule England and Normandy, had spent the previous two decades as a nun in Fontevrault. The abbey had been established in 1100 with the regulation that its abbess be somebody who had broad experience of the world outside. In 1149 Matilda accepted this leading role at Fontevrault, and stayed in office for the remaining five years of her life.

Henry of Anjou returned to England in the spring of that year. King David knighted him in Carlisle, and in return Henry promised that, if he ever became king, he would cede Northumbria to the Scots. But Henry found it hard to make an impact at this time. The viciousness of the fighting did not relent, with Stephen's forces 'taking everything that they found'[5] in the counties that had been Robert of Gloucester's strongholds.

Having achieved little Henry left for Normandy in January 1150, to regroup and gather Norman and Angevin reinforcements. While he was there Geoffrey of Anjou brought to an end his six years of firm rule in Normandy, and abdicated in favour of his eldest son, as he had always insisted he would. Geoffrey handed over the dukedom in good order. Indeed, he had salvaged it from chaos.

The sixteen-year-old Henry's reception was enthusiastic in the extreme and, at a time of fraught and disputed successions, the Normans greeted him as 'their lord and lawful heir': 'He was most amply honoured by everyone in the whole duchy . . . and presented most lavishly with gifts.'[6] The greatest of these was strategic, for Geoffrey had given his son a powerful base from which to plan and launch the conquest of England.

Henry had grown into a handsome man (like his father, Geoffrey) of red hair, fine proportions, and (like his grandfather, Henry) medium height. His appearance would remain impressive, and his vicious temper noted, throughout manhood: 'His eyes are round, and white and plain, while he is of calm spirit,' the courtier Peter of Blois wrote to the Archbishop of Palermo, in 1177, 'but in anger and disorder of heart they shine like fire and flash in fury.' The Angevin pepperiness would spill over in later years: once, on hearing praise for the rival king of Scots, Henry tore his bed's blanket in two, and started chewing hard on the contents of his mattress.

After Louis VII accepted his homage, in August 1151, Henry prepared to invade England, but his father was struck down by a fever while returning from a council of war. Geoffrey of Anjou died soon afterwards, aged thirty-eight, having never set foot in England, the prize he had fought for on his wife and son's behalf since Henry I's death a decade and a half earlier.

A few years later a contemporary would reckon Geoffrey to have shown himself to be, in his short life, 'a very noble knight, well-educated and a good warrior'.[7] He had also been a statesman and diplomat, who had worked tirelessly to further his family's dynastic potential. Henry was now duke of Normandy, count of Anjou, and count of Maine.

More was to come. Eleanor of Aquitaine's marriage to Louis VII was annulled in the spring of 1152. A few weeks later she married Henry in Poitiers, 'putting into his hands all the very wealthy county of Aquitaine'.[8]

In an echo of the era when Louis the Fat backed William Clito against Henry I and William Ætheling, Louis VII now sponsored King Stephen's son, Eustace (who was Louis VII's brother-in-law) as the man to run against a dangerously powerful enemy. Those who wanted to see Henry of Anjou lose some of his immense power joined the alliance against him. The French attacked Normandy. It seemed certain that Henry would be crushed, but he saw off the assault to be recognised as the only plausible candidate as a unifying king of England.

In April 1152 Mathilde of Boulogne fell ill, and she died in early May. She had helped Stephen to remain on the throne through all the turbulence of the anarchy. Meanwhile Stephen kept doing what he was best at, fighting in England. By the end of the year he was on the point of finally cracking the superior defences of Wallingford Castle. News of this provoked Henry into crossing the Channel again, despite the season. He was 'driven on by a storm', Henry of Huntingdon noted. 'That he should have embarked on a stormy sea in the very middle of winter, his supporters considered to be heroic, while others thought it rash.'

Henry landed in England on 6 January 1153 with 140 knights and 3,000 infantry – precisely the same size and composition of army as had supported his mother's arrival at Arundel Castle, a decade and a half earlier. But this landing had a startlingly different effect to that of its predecessor.

Henry appeared with a blistering energy and ruthlessness that shocked even a nation as used to excess as England had become. He led his men to Malmesbury in February, his troops pillaging as they went and even putting to the sword those seeking sanctuary in the town's church.

Such a sin demanded divine retribution, and one chronicler noted how a body of Henry's more notorious soldiers headed to the coast, to return to the Continent: 'But when their ships were already at sea, with sails spread and a favouring wind, a mighty storm suddenly broke on them and they were wrecked, and as God, in wondrous fashion, sought vengeance on the profaners, in a moment, to the number of five hundred, they perished in the waves.'[9]

Henry progressed from Devizes to Bristol, while Stephen learned that many of his leading supporters were secretly negotiating to switch allegiance to his enemy. The young duke was received with rapture in his uncle Robert of Gloucester's twin power bases, Bristol and Gloucester. Henry of Huntingdon depicted war-weary England rising to welcome its new-found saviour with grateful relief: 'Duke Henry, greatest descendant of King Henry the Great, I am falling into ruin. I, noble England, am falling, though not yet in complete ruin . . . Rightfully I belong to you. As you have the power, raise me from my fall.'[10]

When Henry arrived at Wallingford in early August, both sides prepared to engage in a major battle outside the town. But after contemplating the imminent bloodshed barons in each army demanded peace rather than fighting. Henry FitzEmpress and King Stephen agreed the Treaty of Wallingford, ending seventeen-year-old Eustace of Blois's hopes of succeeding his father.

Eustace had been relying on Stephen to secure his royal inheritance by force of arms. He was so furious at this disappointing outcome that, in mid-August 1153, he went to Bury St Edmunds where he had a fierce row with the monks in the abbey. He refused to accept their hospitality and seized some of their treasures. Eustace died immediately afterwards, one report saying he choked to death on his food, while others have him meekly surrendering to a minor illness.

Henry of Winchester felt convinced that the time had come

for peace: 'Seeing everything destroyed by robbery, fire, and slaughter,' Henry of Huntingdon wrote, the bishop 'was moved to repentance, and worked towards the ending of such evils through concord between the princes'.[11] Winchester was joined in this mission by Theobald, Archbishop of Canterbury.

Three months later they concluded the final settlement in a grand ceremony at Winchester Cathedral. Stephen and Henry had met to work out the details in a private interview. The two men sealed the longed-for peace accord with a kiss, and Stephen took Henry to London where the young duke was received with joy by an exhausted but hopeful people. Stephen declared: 'Know that I, King Stephen, establish Henry, Duke of Normandy, after me as my successor in the kingdom and as my heir by hereditary right, and in so doing I give to him and his heirs the kingdom of England.'[12]

Stephen was later persuaded to fight again, one last time, but Henry of Winchester convinced him to stand down and reconfirm Henry as his heir, in return for peaceful enjoyment of his kingdom for the remainder of his life.

'So it was arranged and firmly settled,' *Gesta Stephani* recorded, 'that arms should be finally laid down and peace restored everywhere in the kingdom, the new castles demolished, the disinherited restored to their own, and laws and enactments made binding on all according to the ancient fashion.'[13] Henry withdrew to Normandy in early April 1154, taking his hated mercenaries with him.

Stephen, enthralled as ever by the trappings of kingship, indulged in a laboured progress, 'encircling the bounds of England with regal pomp, and showing himself off as if he were a new king'.[14] But it was the empty posturing of a battered, elderly, peacock.

Within a few months Stephen 'caught a slight fever',[15] and this time there was to be no escape from death. On 25 October

1154, nearly thirty-four years after his violently upset stomach spared him from being claimed by the icy waters off Barfleur, Stephen died. He breathed his last at Dover, the port where he had arrived so soon after Henry's death to seize the English throne. Stephen was buried at Faversham Abbey, next to his wife, Mathilde of Boulogne, and his son, Eustace.

Wace wrote the simplest of epithets on the king's failure as a ruler: 'Stephen never had peace and never deserved to have any, for he accepted bad advice and bad advice harmed him.' There were many examples that could be attached to this verdict, principally his agreeing to the idea that Matilda be allowed to travel under escort from Arundel to Bristol, rather than taking her as his prisoner before attracting broader support.

Henry heard the news but was unable to cross to England until mid-December because of strong winds and rough seas. He arrived with his wife and brothers eventually, bringing a strong army and a bevy of leading advisers, nobles and churchmen. After regrouping in the New Forest, the victorious duke of Normandy moved to London for his coronation, which took place on 19 December 1154. 'He was,' *Gesta Stephani* conceded, 'crowned for sovereignty with all honour and the applause of all.'[16]

In many ways Henry II was a worthy descendant of his grandfather. He had the same physical energy and was noted by his courtiers for never sitting down, except at mealtimes or on a horse. And he was constantly on the move around his realms, checking on those he had left in charge on his behalf. He presented as a model medieval monarch, Peter of Blois recording: 'No one is more honest in speech than our king, more polite in eating, more moderate in drinking; no one is more magnificent in gift-giving, no one more munificent in alms-giving; and therefore his name is like poured oil, and the entire church of saints describes the alms of such a one . . .

Always in his hands are bow, sword, spear and arrow, unless he be in council or in books. As often as he is able to rest from cares and anxieties, he occupies himself by reading alone, or in a crowd of clerics he labours to untangle some knots of enquiry.'

Henry II, like William the Conqueror and Henry I, fully appreciated the throne because he had won it, rather than simply inheriting it. Like his namesake grandfather, the younger Henry had spent his early years watching relatives fight for the crown. While his mother had failed to overcome her cousin Stephen, she and his father had contested the king hard enough to pave the way for their eldest son to win the crown in the end.

Henry II would father eight children, five of whom became kings or queens. This was the start of a cascading of Henry I's blood into the centuries to come. He had prophesied, in 1133, that his grandson would 'inherit all', but he had been thinking of the Anglo-Norman realm that he had made his, with Anjou and Maine as strategic additions.

Yet Henry II was an Angevin prince first and foremost, whose prime success on behalf of his people was the union of Anjou and Normandy. That is what his other grandfather, Fulk V, had sought each time, when proffering his children – first Matilda, then Sibylla and finally Geoffrey – in marriage to the most likely successor to the Norman duchy.

Henry II's Plantagenet bloodline would, after the reigns of his sons Richard the Lionheart and King John, split off into different tributaries. But the broader house of Plantagenet would occupy the throne of England from Henry II's succession in 1154 until Richard III's slaying by the Tudors in 1485. Yet the catastrophe of November 1120 deprived Henry I of seeing his dynasty progress in the male line, causing him perpetual torment in his final years and changing the identity of the British royal line for ever. The shipwreck impacted spectacularly on the next generation, resulting in the bloodiest anarchy that England has ever suffered.

'No Ship that ever sailed brought England such Disaster,' wrote William of Malmesbury soon after the *White Ship* went down. That remains the case, nine hundred years on.

Notes

CHAPTER ONE – CONQUEST

1. Henry of Huntingdon, *The History of the English People 1000–1154 (HEP)*, p. 31.
2. Suger, *The Deeds of Louis the Fat*, p. 70.
3. Orderic Vitalis, *The Ecclesiastical History (EH)*, V, p. 103.
4. Henry of Huntingdon, *HEP*, p. 31.

CHAPTER TWO – YOUNGEST SON

1. Robert Wace, *Roman de Rou*, Part Two, p. 196.
2. Orderic Vitalis, *EH*, V, p. 115.
3. Ibid., p. 97.
4. Ibid., p. 103.
5. Ibid., p. 97.
6. Ibid., p. 55.
7. Orderic Vitalis, quoted in Crouch, *The Image of Aristocracy*, p. 137.
8. Orderic Vitalis, *EH*, V, p. 115.
9. Ibid., IV, p. 94.
10. Ibid., p. 96.
11. Wace, *Roman de Rou*, Part Two, p. 196.
12. Ibid., p. 220.
13. Orderic Vitalis, *EH*, IV, pp. 225–7.

14. William of Malmesbury, *Chronicle of the Kings of England (Chronicle)*, p. 469.
15. Orderic Vitalis, *EH*, IV, p. 250.
16. Wace, *Roman de Rou*, Part Two, p. 198.
17. *The Chronicle of John of Worcester*, p. 59.
18. William of Malmesbury, *Chronicle*, pp. 364–5.
19. Wace, *Roman de Rou*, Part Two, p. 197.
20. William of Malmesbury, *Chronicle*, p. 365.
21. Henry of Huntingdon, *HEP*, p. 33.
22. Orderic Vitalis, *EH*, IV, p. 254.

CHAPTER THREE – OUT OF THE SHADOWS

1. Orderic Vitalis, *EH*, V, p. 137.
2. Ibid., p. 139.
3. Ibid., p. 149.
4. Ibid., p. 227.
5. Henry of Huntingdon, *HEP*, p. 105.
6. Wace, *Roman de Rou*, Part Two, p. 203.
7. *Chronicle of John of Worcester*, p. 71.
8. Henry of Huntingdon, *HEP*, p. 38.
9. Orderic Vitalis, *EH*, V, p. 25.
10. Christopher Tyerman (ed.), *Chronicles of the First Crusade*, p. 10.
11. Ibid.
12. Orderic Vitalis, *EH*, V, p. 27.
13. *Chronicle of John of Worcester*, p. 85.
14. Orderic Vitalis, *EH*, V, p. 217.
15. *Vita S. Anselmi* 'Life of St Anselm' (*c.*1124), pp. 43–4.
16. Henry of Huntingdon, *HEP*, p. 49.
17. Ibid.
18. Orderic Vitalis, *EH*, V, pp. 201–3.
19. Ibid., p. 203.
20. *Chronicle of John of Worcester*, p. 65.
21. Henry of Huntingdon, *HEP*, p. 37.
22. *Vita S. Anselmi* 'Life of St Anselm' (*c.*1124), p. 52.
23. Henry of Huntingdon, *HEP*, p. 47.
24. William of Malmesbury, *Chronicle*.

CHAPTER FOUR – OPPORTUNITY

1. *The Anglo-Saxon Chronicle, a Revised Translation*, p. 165.
2. Henry of Huntingdon, *HEP*, p. 32.
3. Orderic Vitalis, *EH*, V, p. 283.
4. Ibid., pp. 287–9.
5. William of Malmesbury, *Chronicle*, p. 344.
6. Orderic Vitalis, *EH*, V, p. 289.
7. Wace, *Roman de Rou*, Part Two, p. 205.
8. Henry of Huntingdon, *HEP*, p. 48.
9. Wace, *Roman de Rou*, Part Two, p. 205.
10. Orderic Vitalis, *EH*, V, p. 293.
11. Henry of Huntingdon, *HEP*, p. 49.
12. Wace, *Roman de Rou*, Part Two, p. 205.
13. Suger, *The Deeds of Louis the Fat*, p. 70.
14. Quoted in Crouch, *The English Aristocracy, 1070–1272*, p. 220.
15. Henry of Huntingdon, *HEP*, p. 32.
16. Ibid., p. 48.
17. Ibid., pp. 47–8.
18. Orderic Vitalis, *EH*, V, p. 23.
19. Anselm of Canterbury, *Opera Omnia*, ep. 215.
20. *Chronicle of John of Worcester*, p. 67.
21. Quoted in Marjorie Chibnall, *The Empress Matilda*, p. 7.

CHAPTER FIVE – CONSOLIDATION

1. Henry of Huntingdon, *HEP*, p. 41.
2. Wace, *Roman de Rou*, Part Two, p. 200.
3. Henry of Huntingdon, *HEP*, p. 49.
4. Wace, *Roman de Rou*, Part Two, p. 207.
5. Orderic Vitalis, *EH*, VI, p. 217.
6. William of Malmesbury, *Chronicle*, p. 471.
7. Henry of Huntingdon, *HEP*, p. 49.
8. *Vita S. Anselmi* 'Life of St Anselm' (*c.*1124), p. 127.
9. Wace, *Roman de Rou*, Part Two, p. 208.
10. C. Warren Hollister, 'The Anglo-Norman Civil War: 1101', *English Historical Review*, Vol. 88, No. 347 (April 1973), p. 332.
11. *Vita S. Anselmi* 'Life of St Anselm' (*c.*1124), p. 131.

12. Orderic Vitalis, *EH*, V, p. 225.

13. Ibid., VI, p. 30.

14. Ibid., V, p. 283.

15. Ibid., V, pp. 163–4.

16. Ibid., V, p. 283.

CHAPTER SIX – THE HEIR

1. William of Malmesbury, *Chronicle*, p. 455.

2. Collectan [*sic*], Vol. I, p. 55; quoted in British History Online, Stratford-le-Bow.

3. Quoted in Edmund King, *Henry I*, p. 32.

4. William of Malmesbury, *Chronicle*, p. 456.

5. Ibid., p. 454.

6. Wace, *Roman de Rou*, Part Two, pp. 205–6.

7. *Cassell's Illustrated History of England*, Vol. 1, p. 161.

8. Wace, *Roman de Rou*, Part Two, p. 213.

9. Henry of Huntingdon, *HEP*, p. 50.

10. Ibid.

11. Wace, *Roman de Rou*, Part Two, p. 213.

12. Ibid., p. 214.

13. Orderic Vitalis, *EH*, VI, p. 64.

14. Ibid., pp. 64–6.

15. Wace, *Roman de Rou*, Part Two, p. 217.

16. Henry of Huntingdon, *HEP*, pp. 50–1.

17. Ibid., p. 51.

18. Ibid., p. 50.

19. *Anglo-Saxon Chronicle*, 1106.

20. Wace, *Roman de Rou*, Part Two, p. 219.

21. Henry of Huntingdon, *HEP*, p. 51.

22. Ibid., p. 235.

23. Wace, *Roman de Rou*, Part Two, p. 219.

24. Orderic Vitalis, *EH*, VI, p. 88.

25. Ibid., IV, pp. 114–15.

26. Henry of Huntingdon, *HEP*, p. 51.

CHAPTER SEVEN – KINGSHIP

1. Henry of Huntingdon, *HEP*, p. 51.
2. Ibid., pp. 51–2.
3. Wace, *Roman de Rou*, Part Two, p. 197.
4. Richard FitzNeal, *The Dialogue concerning the Exchequer*, p. 15.
5. Quoted in Crouch, *The Birth of Nobility*, pp. 42–3.
6. Henry of Huntingdon, *HEP*, p. 58.
7. Wace, *Roman de Rou*, Part One, p. 6
8. *Gesta Stephani*, pp. 4–5.
9. Crouch, *The Birth of Nobility*, p. 42.
10. William of Malmesbury, *Chronicle*, p. 447.
11. Walter Map, quoted in Edmund King, *Henry I*, p. 45.
12. William of Malmesbury, quoted in King, p. 45.
13. A.R. Myers (ed.), *The Household of Edward IV*, p. 126.
14. *Gesta Stephani*, p. 27.
15. Orderic Vitalis, *EH*, VI, p. 17.
16. Crouch, *The Image of Aristocracy*, p. 60.
17. Orderic Vitalis, *EH*, VI, p. 217.
18. Ibid., p. 305.
19. Ibid., p. 17.
20. Ibid., V, p. 203.
21. *Gesta Stephani*, p. 23.
22. R.W. Southern, *Medieval Humanism*, pp. 220–1.

CHAPTER EIGHT – LOUIS THE FAT

1. Orderic Vitalis, *EH*, V, p. 215.
2. Henry of Huntingdon, *HEP*, p. 52.
3. Orderic Vitalis, *EH*, V, p. 189.
4. Ibid., VI, p. 178.
5. Henry of Huntingdon, *HEP*, p. 52.
6. Ibid., p. 54.
7. Quoted in King, p. 42.
8. 'William of Poitiers' in David C. Douglas and George W. Greenaway (eds), *English Historical Documents 1042–1189*, p. 227.
9. Wace, *Roman de Rou*, Part Two, p. 206.
10. Orderic Vitalis, *EH*, VI, pp. 210–12.

11. Suger, *The Deeds of Louis the Fat*, p. 116.
12. Ibid.
13. Ibid.
14. Suger, p. 117.
15. Henry of Huntingdon, *HEP*, p. 55.
16. Ibid.
17. Suger, p. 117.

CHAPTER NINE – CONTEMPLATING REWARDS

1. Orderic Vitalis, *EH*, VI, p. 295.
2. William of Malmesbury, *Chronicle*, p. 447.
3. Ibid., p. 455.
4. Henry of Huntingdon, *HEP*, p. 101.
5. William of Malmesbury, *Chronicle*, p. 455.
6. Henry of Huntingdon, *HEP*, p. 101.
7. Orderic Vitalis, *EH*, V, p. 99.
8. Ibid., VI, p. 18.
9. Wace, *Roman de Rou*, Part Two, p. 206.

CHAPTER TEN – THE SEA

1. Wace, *Le Roman de Brut,* II, pp. 190–238.
2. *Chronicle of John of Worcester*, p. 61.
3. Anon., *Les voyages merveilleux de saint Brandan à la recherche du Paradis terrestre*, p. 896.
4. Anon. (possibly Denis Pyramus), *Partenopeus de Blois*, line 1620.
5. Benoît de Sainte-Maure, *Le roman de Troie*, 27, 3563.
6. Anon., *Les miracles de Notre Dame*, chapter XXXII, p. 905.
7. Anon., *Li Romans de Bauduin de Sebourc.*
8. Sainte-Maure, *Le roman de Troie*, 27, 480.
9. Adenet le Roi, *Berte aus grans piés*, 737.
10. Orderic Vitalis, *EH*, V, pp. 255–7.
11. Wace, *Roman de Rou*, Part Two, p. 202.
12. Ibid.
13. Orderic Vitalis, *EH*, VI, p. 297.

CHAPTER ELEVEN – BOUND FOR ENGLAND

1. William of Malmesbury, *Chronicle*, p. 455.
2. *Chronicle of John of Worcester*, p. 147.
3. Orderic Vitalis, *EH*, VI, p. 297.
4. Ibid.
5. Ibid., p. 301.
6. Ibid., p. 297.
7. Ibid., pp. 306–7.
8. Wace, *Roman de Rou*, Part Two, p. 206.
9. William of Malmesbury, *Chronicle*, p. 455.
10. Wace, *Roman de Rou*, Part Two, p. 206.
11. Orderic Vitalis, *EH*, V, p. 200.
12. William of Malmesbury, *Chronicle*, p. 456.
13. Orderic Vitalis, *EH*, VI, p. 299.
14. Wace, *Roman de Rou*, Part Two, p. 206.
15. *Chronicle of John of Worcester*, p. 147.
16. Orderic Vitalis, *EH*, VI, p. 301.
17. Henry of Huntingdon, *HEP*, p. 56.
18. Henry of Huntingdon, letter to Walter.

CHAPTER TWELVE – REACTION TO TRAGEDY

1. Wace, *Roman de Rou*, Part Two, p. 206.
2. Orderic Vitalis, *EH*, VI, p. 297.
3. Ibid., p. 301.
4. Ibid., p. 303.
5. Suger, *The Deeds of Louis the Fat*, p. 69.
6. Ibid.
7. Wace, *Roman de Rou*, Part Two, p. 206.
8. Orderic Vitalis, *EH*, VI, p. 307.
9. Ibid., p. 303.
10. Henry of Huntingdon, *HEP*, p. 101.
11. Wace, *Roman de Rou*, Part Two, p. 207.
12. Ibid.
13. Henry of Huntingdon, *HEP*, p. 56.
14. Orderic Vitalis, *EH*, VI, p. 59.
15. Wace, *Roman de Rou*, Part Two, p. 207.

16. Ibid.

17. From *Brut y Tywysogion, or The Chronicle of the Princes*.

18. Henry of Huntingdon, *HEP*, p. 102.

19. Orderic Vitalis, *EH*, VI, p. 350.

20. Ibid., p. 355.

CHAPTER THIRTEEN – THE EMPRESS

1. Quoted in King, pp. 6–7.

2. Henry of Huntingdon, *HEP*, p. 52.

3. Ibid.

4. Reg. RAN, 2, no. 919 – quoted in the *DNB* of Matilda.

5. Quoted in Castor's *She-Wolves*.

6. Orderic Vitalis, *EH*, V, p. 201.

7. Ibid.

8. *Anglo-Saxon Chronicle*, ed. D. Whitelock, s.a. 1127.

9. *Gesta Stephani*, p. 5.

10. Quoted in King, p. 74.

11. *Gesta Stephani*, p. 139.

12. Suger, *The Deeds of Louis the Fat*, p. 138.

13. Henry of Huntingdon, *HEP*, p. 476.

14. Suger, p. 141.

15. Henry of Huntingdon, *HEP*, p. 61.

16. Ibid.

17. Wace, *Roman de Rou*, Part Two, p. 207; Henry of Huntingdon, *HEP*, p. 61.

18. William of Tyre, *The Conquest of Jerusalem and the Third Crusade*, p. 121.

19. Henry of Huntingdon, *HEP*, p. 61.

20. Suger, p. 150.

21. Quoted in King, p. 87.

22. Orderic Vitalis, *EH*, V, p. 201.

23. Henry of Huntingdon, *HEP*, p. 63.

CHAPTER FOURTEEN – A SURFEIT OF LAMPREYS?

1. Henry of Huntingdon, *HEP*, p. 64.
2. William of Malmesbury, quoted in Castor, *She-Wolves*.
3. Quoted in King, p. 65.
4. William of Malmesbury, *Chronicle*, p. 447.
5. Ibid.
6. Quoted in King, p. 82.
7. Walter Map, quoted in King, p. 61.
8. *Chronicle of John of Worcester*, p. 255.
9. Suger, *The Deeds of Louis the Fat*, p. 70.
10. Orderic Vitalis, from Castor, *She-Wolves*.

CHAPTER FIFTEEN – STEPHEN

1. Kimberly LoPrete, *Adela of Blois*, p. 546, fn. 62.
2. Orderic Vitalis, *EH*, V, p. 107.
3. Ibid.
4. R.H.C. Davis, *King Stephen*, 3rd edition, p. 3.
5. Orderic Vitalis, *EH*, V, p. 20.
6. Ibid., VI, pp. 228–9.
7. William of Malmesbury, *Historia Novella*, p. 19.
8. *Gesta Stephani*, p. 6.
9. Ibid., pp. 122–3.
10. Ibid., p. 7.
11. Ibid., p. 119.
12. Ibid., p. 9.
13. Ibid., p. 13.
14. Quoted in King, p. 87.
15. Otter, Monika, 'Bourgueil, Baudri of, "To Countess Adela"', *Journal of Medieval Latin*, Vol. 11 (2001), Ll. 33–6.
16. Orderic Vitalis, *EH*, V, p. 179.
17. Ibid., p. 107.
18. Gerald of Wales, *The Journey Through Wales/The Description of Wales*, p. 309.
19. *Gesta Stephani*, p. 53.
20. Ibid., p. 53.
21. *Gesta Stephani*, quoted in Castor, *She-Wolves*.

22. Henry of Huntingdon, *HEP*, p. 68.
23. *Gesta Stephani*, p. 23.
24. *Gesta Stephani*, from Castor, *She-Wolves*.
25. Orderic Vitalis.
26. Radulfus Glaber, *Historiarum Libri Quinque*, pp. 204–5.
27. *Gesta Stephani*, p. 13.
28. William of Malmesbury, from Castor, *She-Wolves*.
29. Matthew Paris of St Albans, *Chronica Majora*, ii, p. 164.
30. Quoted in Castor, *She-Wolves*.

CHAPTER SIXTEEN – UNRAVELLING

1. *Gesta Stephani*, p. 55.
2. Richard of Hexham, from *The Church Historians of England*.
3. *Gesta Stephani*, p. 211.
4. Ibid., p. 56.
5. *Chronicle of John of Worcester*, pp. 249–51.
6. Ibid., p. 51.
7. Richard of Hexham, from *The Church Historians of England*.
8. Ibid.
9. Ibid., pp. 177–8.
10. *Gesta Stephani*, p. 59.
11. Ibid.
12. William of Malmesbury, *Historia Novella*, p. 548.
13. *Gesta Stephani*, p. 81.
14. Psalm 105: 15.
15. Orderic Vitalis, *EH*, V, p. 13.
16. *Gesta Stephani*, p. 81.
17. Ibid., pp. 86–7.
18. Ibid., p. 85.

CHAPTER SEVENTEEN – ANARCHY

1. *Gesta Stephani*, p. 87.
2. Ibid., p. 145.
3. *Chronicle of John of Worcester*, p. 253.
4. *Gesta Stephani*, pp. 96–7.

5. Quoted in H.W.C. Davis, 'Henry of Blois and Brian fitzCount', *English Historical Review*, 25 (1910), p. 303.
6. *Gesta Stephani*, p. 95.
7. Ibid., p. 31.
8. Ibid., p. 107.
9. *Gesta Stephani*, p. 111.
10. Henry of Huntingdon, *HEP*, p. 76.
11. *Dictionary of National Biography*, 'King Stephen'.
12. *Gesta Stephani*, p. 113.
13. Ibid., p. 115.
14. William of Malmesbury, *Historia Novella*, p. 50.
15. *Gesta Stephani*, p. 119.
16. William of Malmesbury, *Historia Novella*, p. 53.
17. *Gesta Stephani*, p. 121.
18. Ibid., p. 123.
19. Ibid.
20. Ibid., p. 121.
21. Ibid., p. 123.
22. Ibid., p. 139.
23. Ibid., p. 145.
24. Ibid., p. 127.
25. Ibid., p. 145.
26. *Chronicle of John of Worcester*, p. 303.
27. *Gesta Stephani*, p. 135.
28. Ibid., p. 139.
29. Wace, *Roman de Rou*, Part One, p. 5.
30. *Gesta Stephani*, p. 143.
31. Ibid., p. 113.
32. Ibid., p. 187.
33. Ibid., p. 211.
34. Quoted in Castor, *She-Wolves*, p. 101.

CHAPTER EIGHTEEN – ORDER

1. *Gesta Stephani*, p. 157.
2. Ibid., p. 171.
3. Orderic Vitalis, *EH*, VI, pp. 546–7.

4. *Gesta Stephani*, p. 215.
5. Ibid., p. 220.
6. Ibid., p. 225.
7. Wace, *Roman de Rou*, Part Two, p. 207.
8. *Gesta Stephani*, p. 227.
9. Ibid., p. 233.
10. Henry of Huntingdon, quoted in King, p. 88.
11. Henry of Huntingdon, *HEP*, p. 93.
12. Quoted in King, p. 89.
13. *Gesta Stephani*, p. 241.
14. William of Newburgh, *Historia rerum Anglicarum*, p. 94.
15. *Gesta Stephani*, p. 241.
16. Ibid.

Acknowledgements

I owe profound thanks to Arabella Pike, my editor at William Collins. When I had researched this tale and had taken a first stab at having it make sense on the page, I found myself in a muddle. Arabella spotted the problems that I had foisted on my book's structure and quickly identified a much more sensible running order. She has spared the reader from much confusion.

Others at William Collins to have been of great assistance are Helen Ellis, Iain Hunt and Jo Thompson.

I am also very grateful to my literary agent, Georgina Capel, who has been a constant source of encouragement (and humour) throughout.

Further thanks are due to Dr Sam Willis, for his generous ideas as to where best to research nautical matters nine hundred years ago, and for his thoughts on colours in Viking culture.

Dr Catherine Handley kindly read through the final manuscript, to check it for basic mistakes I might have made over names and dates. If any errors remain, they are my responsibility.

Laura Bailey, PhD history student at King's College, Cambridge, kindly helped me to interpret many phrases of Old French that my A level French was, to be fair, never going to crack.

Sarah Summers learned new secretarial skills to help me present the manuscript and images to my publisher in an intelligible manner.

This book only happened because I was asked to give a speech at Leeds Castle a few years ago, on the queens of England. I threw in Matilda – designated queen by her father, but never destined to rule – as an alternative to the obvious subjects. Thanks to the audience that night for making me realise that the tragedy of the *White Ship* was a tale worth revisiting.

And, if I may, I would like to thank Henry I, for being the pillar on whom I could lay this tale. To think that such a brilliantly effective and strategic king – one of the great monarchs of British history – most likely rests for eternity under a (very fine) school building in Reading, rather than in the monumental pomp that he planned, is – to me – as sad as it is wrong.

Bibliography

Printed Primary Sources

Aelred of Rievaulx, *The Historical Works*, trans. Jane Patricia Freeland, ed. Marsha L. Dutton, Cistercian Fathers Series 56 (Kalamazoo: Cistercian Publications, 2005)

The Anglo-Saxon Chronicle, a Revised Translation, ed. D. Whitelock et al. (New Jersey: Rutgers University Press, 1961)

Anon., *Gesta Stephani*, ed. and trans. K.R. Potter (Oxford: Clarendon Press, 1976)

Anon., *The Warenne Hyde Chronicle*, ed. Elisabeth Van Houts and Rosalind Love (Oxford University Press, 2013)

Anselm of Canterbury, *Opera Omnia*, ed. F.S. Schmitt, Vol. 5 (of 6) (Edinburgh, 1946–61)

Brut y Tywysogion, or The Chronicle of the Princes (National Library of Wales)

Durham, Symeon of, *Symeonis Dunelmensis Opera Et Collectanea* (London: Forgotten Books, 2018)

FitzNeal, Richard, *The Dialogue concerning the Exchequer*, ed. and trans. Emilie Amt and S.D. Church (Oxford University Press, 2007)

Fulcher of Chartres' account of Urban's speech, 'Urban II: Speech at Council of Clermont, 1095'

Glaber, Radulfus, *Historiarum Libri Quinque*, ed. J. France, 92nd edition (Oxford: Clarendon Press, 1993)

Hexham, Richard of, from Joseph Stevenson, trans., *The Church Historians of England*, Vol. 4, Part 1 (London, 1853–8)

Huntingdon, Henry of, *The History of the English People 1000– 1154*, trans. Diana Greenway (Oxford University Press, 1996)

Malmesbury, William of, *Chronicle of the Kings of England*, trans. J.A. Giles (London: Henry G. Bohn, 1897)

Malmesbury, William of, *The Deeds of the Bishops of England*, trans. David Preest (Woodbridge: Boydell Press, 2002)

Malmesbury, William of, *Historia Novella*, ed. and trans. K.R. Potter (London: T. Nelson, 1955)

Map, Walter, *De Nugis Curialium*, ed. and trans. C.N.L. Brooke (Oxford Medieval Texts, 1983)

Monmouth, Geoffrey of, *The History of the Kings of Britain*, trans. Lewis Thorpe (London: Penguin, 1966)

Newburgh, William of, *Historia rerum Anglicarum*, ed. R. Howlett (Rolls Series, 1884)

Paris, Matthew, of St Albans, *Chronica Majora*, ed. Henry Richards Luard (Cambridge University Press, 2013)

Suger, *The Deeds of Louis the Fat*, trans. Richard Cusimano and John Moorhead (Washington, DC: Catholic University of America Press, 1992)

Tyre, William of, *The Conquest of Jerusalem and the Third Crusade*, Sources in Translation (Crusade Texts in Translation, new edition, 1998)

Vita S. Anselmi 'Life of St Anselm' (*c.*1124), ed. and trans. R.W. Southern, *The Life of St Anselm, Archbishop of Canterbury* (New York: T. Nelson, 1962; 2nd edition, Oxford University Press, 1972)

Vitalis, Orderic, *The Ecclesiastical History of Orderic Vitalis*, Vol. IV (Books VII and VIII), ed. and trans. Marjorie Chibnall (Oxford: Clarendon Press, 1973)

Vitalis, Orderic, *The Ecclesiastical History of Orderic Vitalis*, Vol. V (Books IX and X), ed. and trans. Marjorie Chibnall (Oxford: Clarendon Press, 1975)

Vitalis, Orderic, *The Ecclesiastical History of Orderic Vitalis*, Vol. VI (Books XI, XII and XIII), ed. and trans. Marjorie Chibnall (Oxford: Clarendon Press, 1978)

Wace, Robert, *Le Roman de Rou*, trans. Glyn S. Burgess (Woodbridge: Boydell Press, 2004)

Wace, Robert, *Le Roman de Brut*, ed. Arthur Wayne Glowka, Medieval and Renaissance Texts and Studies, Volume 279 (2005)

Wales, Gerald of, *The Journey Through Wales/The Description of Wales*, ed. Betty Radice et al. (London: Penguin Classics, 1978)

Worcester, John of, *The Chronicle of John of Worcester: Volume III: The Annals from 1067 to 1140 with the Gloucester Interpolations and the Continuation to 1141*, ed. and trans. P. McGurk (Oxford Medieval Texts, 1998)

Published Sources

Anon., *Les miracles de Notre Dame* (thirteenth century), G. Paris and U. Robert, 8 volumes, Paris, 1876–93

Anon., *Les voyages merveilleux de saint Brandan à la recherche du Paradis terrestre*, with introduction by Francisque Michel (Paris, 1878)

Anon., *Li Romans de Bauduin de Sebourc* (fourteenth century), ed. M.L. Boca (Valenciennes, 1845)

Anon. (possibly Denis Pyramus), *Partenopeus de Blois*, ed. J. Gildea (Villanova, Pennsylvania, 1967)

Archer, Rowena E. and Simon Walker (eds), *Rulers and Ruled in Late Medieval England: Essays Presented to Gerald Harriss* (London and Rio Grande: Hambledon Press, 1995)

Banbury, John, Robert Edwards and Elizabeth Poskitt (eds),

Woodstock and the Royal Park (Oxford: Chris Andrews Publications, 2010)

Barlow, Frank, *William Rufus* (University of California Press, 1983)

Barrell, A.D.M., *Medieval Scotland* (Cambridge University Press, 2000)

Baxter, Ron, *Blood and Bones: The Veneration of Relics at Reading Abbey*, readingmuseum.org.uk, December 2017

Benton, John F., *Culture and Personality in Medieval France* (London: Hambledon Press, 1991)

Bloch, Marc, *Feudal Society* (London: Routledge & Kegan Paul, 1961)

Borman, Tracy, *Matilda: Queen of the Conqueror* (London: Jonathan Cape, 2011)

Bracken, Damian, 'Ua Briain, Muirchertach [Murtagh O'Brien] (*c.*1050–1119)', *Oxford Dictionary of National Biography*, 2004

Bridgeford, Andrew, *1066: The Hidden History of the Bayeux Tapestry* (London: Harper Perennial, 2004)

Bruges, Gilbert of, *The Murder, Betrayal and Slaughter of the Glorious Charles, Count of Flanders*, trans. Jeff Rider (New Haven and London: Yale University Press, 2013)

Cassell, *Cassell's Illustrated History of England*, Vol. 1 (London: Cassell Petter & Galpin, 1865)

Castor, Helen, *She-Wolves: The Women Who Ruled England Before Elizabeth* (London: Faber, 2010)

Chandler, Victoria, 'The Last of the Montgomerys: Roger the Poitevin and Arnulf', *Historical Research*, Vol. 62, Issue 147 (February 1989)

Chibnall, Marjorie, *The World of Orderic Vitalis: Norman Monks and Norman Knights* (Woodbridge: Boydell Press, 1984)

Chibnall, Marjorie, *The Empress Matilda* (Cambridge, Mass.: Blackwell, 1992)

Chibnall, Marjorie, 'Matilda of Boulogne', *Oxford Dictionary of National Biography*, 2004

Christelow, Stephanie Mooers, 'Anglo-Norman Administrations and Their Historians', *History Compass*, Vol. 9, Issue 7 (2011)

Churchill, Sir Winston S., *The Island Race* (New York: Dodd, Mead & Co., 1964)

Clanchy, M.T., *England and Its Rulers, 1066–1272* (London: Fontana, 1983)

Crouch, David, *The Image of Aristocracy* (London and New York: Routledge, 1992)

Crouch, David, *The Birth of Nobility* (London: Routledge, 2005)

Crouch, David, 'Robert, first Earl of Gloucester', *Oxford Dictionary of National Biography*, 2006

Crouch, David, *The English Aristocracy, 1070–1272* (New Haven and London: Yale University Press, 2011)

Davis, H.W.C., 'Henry of Blois and Brian fitzCount', *English Historical Review*, Vol. 25 (1910)

Davis, R.H.C., *King Stephen*, 3rd edition (University of California Press, 1967)

Ditchburn, David, 'Union before Union: The Failure of "Britain" in the Middle Ages', from Andrew Mackillop and Micheál Ó Siochrú (eds) *Forging the State* (Dundee University Press, 2009)

Doherty, H.F., 'Henry I's New Men', *Oxford Dictionary of National Biography*, 2009

Eales, Richard, 'William of Ypres', *Oxford Dictionary of National Biography*, 2004

Fleming, Peter, *Family and Household in Medieval England* (New York: Palgrave, 2001)

Foundation for Medieval Genealogy, fmg.ac – England, kings, 1066–1603

Garnett, George, 'Robert Curthose: The Duke Who Lost His Trousers', *Anglo-Norman Studies*, Vol. 35 (2013)

Gillingham, John, *William II* (London: Allen Lane, 2015)

Green, John Richard, *History of the English People* (London: Macmillan, 1881)

Green, Judith A., *The Government of England under Henry I* (Cambridge University Press, 1986)

Green, Judith A., 'David I and Henry I', *Scottish Historical Review*, Vol. 75, No. 199 (1996)

Green, Judith A., *Henry I: King of England and Duke of Normandy* (Cambridge University Press, 2006)

Green, Judith A., 'King Henry I and Northern England', *Transactions of the Royal Historical Society*, Sixth Series, Vol. 17 (2007)

Green, Judith A., 'Geoffrey Ridel', *Oxford Dictionary of National Biography*, 2008

Green, Judith A., 'Robert Curthose Reassessed', *Anglo-Norman Studies*, Vol. 35 (2013)

Greenway, D.E. (ed.), *Charters of the Honour of Mowbray, 1107–1191* (Oxford University Press, 1972)

Hanley, Catherine, *Matilda: Empress, Queen, Warrior* (New Haven and London: Yale University Press, 2019)

Harper-Bill, Christopher and Elisabeth Van Houts (eds), *A Companion to the Anglo-Norman World* (Woodbridge: Boydell Press, 2002)

Haskins, Charles Homer, *Norman Institutions* (Clark, New Jersey: The Lawbook Exchange Ltd, 2007)

Haywood, John, *North Men: The Viking Saga 793–1241* (London: Head of Zeus, 2015)

Hollister, C. Warren, 'The Misfortunes of the Mandevilles', *History*, Vol. 58, Issue 192 (1973)

Hollister, C. Warren, 'The Anglo-Norman Civil War: 1101', *English Historical Review*, Vol. 88, No. 347 (April 1973)

Hollister, C. Warren, 'Royal Acts of Mutilation: The Case Against Henry I', *Albion: A Quarterly Journal Concerned with British Studies*, Vol. 10, No. 4 (Winter 1978)

Hollister, C. Warren, *Monarchy, Magnates and Institutions in the Anglo-Norman World* (London and Ronceverte: Hambledon Press, 1986)

Hollister, C. Warren, *Henry I* (New Haven and London: Yale University Press, 2003)

Holt, James Clarke, *Colonial England, 1066–1215* (London: Hambledon Press, 1997)

Hudson, J. (ed. and trans.), *Historia Ecclesie Abbendonensis*, 2 Vols, 2002–7

Huneycutt, Lois L., 'Adela, Countess of Blois', *Oxford Dictionary of National Biography*, 2004

Hunt, William, 'Robert of Bellême', *Oxford Dictionary of National Biography*, Vol. 4, 1885–1900

Johns, Susan M., *Noblewomen, Aristocracy and Power in the Twelfth-Century Anglo-Norman Realm* (Manchester University Press, 2003)

Jones, Dan, *The Plantagenets* (London: HarperPress, 2013)

Jones, Peter J.A., *Laughter & Power in the Twelfth Century* (Oxford University Press, 2019)

King, Edmund, *Henry I* (London: Allen Lane, 2018)

Kingsford, Charles Lethbridge, 'Roger of Salisbury', *Oxford Dictionary of National Biography*, Vol. 49, 1885–1900

Lack, Katherine, 'Robert Curthose: Ineffectual Duke or Victim of Spin?', *Haskins Society Journal*, Vol. 20 (2008)

Le Roi, Adenet, *Berte aus, grans piés*, A. Henry (Brussels and Paris, 1963)

Lewis, C.P., 'Hugh d'Avranches, 1st Earl of Chester', *Oxford Dictionary of National Biography*

Leyser, Henrietta, *Medieval Women* (London: Weidenfeld & Nicolson, 1995)

LoPrete, Kimberly, 'The Anglo-Norman Card of Adela of Blois', *Albion*, Vol. 22, Issue 4 (1990)

LoPrete, Kimberly, *Adela of Blois, Countess and Lord (c.1067–1137)* (Dublin: Four Courts Press, 2007)

Madigan, Kevin, *Medieval Christianity* (New Haven and London: Yale University Press, 2016)

Mason, J.F.A., 'William Aetheling', *Oxford Dictionary of National Biography*, 2004

Mitchison, R., *A History of Scotland*, 2nd edition (London and New York: Methuen, 1988)

Morris, Marc, *William I* (London: Allen Lane, 2016)

Musset, Lucien, *The Bayeux Tapestry*, trans. Richard Rex (Woodbridge: Boydell Press, 2002)

Myers, A.R. (ed.), *The Household of Edward IV: The Black Book and the Ordinance of 1478* (Manchester University Press, 1959)

Newman, Charlotte A., *The Anglo-Norman Nobility in the Reign of Henry I: The Second Generation* (Philadelphia: University of Pennsylvania Press, 1988)

Norgate, Kate, 'Robert, Duke of Normandy', *Oxford Dictionary of National Biography*, Vol. 48, 1885–1900

O'Connor-James, Harriet, *The Impact of the White Ship Disaster of 1120*, Medievalists.net

Otter, Monika, 'Bourgueil, Baudri of, "To Countess Adela"', *Journal of Medieval Latin*, Vol. 11 (2001)

Patterson, Robert B., *The Earl, the Kings, and the Chronicler* (Oxford University Press, 2019)

Rodger, N.A.M., *The Safeguard of the Sea* (London: Penguin, 2004)

Rose, Susan, *England's Medieval Navy* (Barnsley: Seaforth Publishing, 2013)

Sainte-Maure, Benoît de, *Le roman de Troie*, ed. L. Constance (Paris: La Société des Anciennes Textes Françaises, 1904–12)

Shopkow, Leah, *History and Community* (Washington, DC: Catholic University of America Press, 1997)

Smith, Katherine Allen, *War and the Making of Medieval Monastic Culture* (Woodbridge: Boydell & Bower, 2013)

Southern, R.W., *Medieval Humanism* (Oxford University Press, 1970)

Strickland, Matthew, *Anglo-Norman Warfare: Studies in Late*

Anglo-Saxon and Anglo-Norman Military Organization and Warfare (Woodbridge: Boydell Press, 1993)

Swanton, Michael (trans. and ed.), *The Anglo-Saxon Chronicles* (London: Phoenix, 1996)

Tabuteau, Emily Zack, 'The Family of Moulins-la-Marche in the Eleventh Century', *Medieval Prosopography*, Vol. 13, No. 1 (Spring 1992)

Thatcher, Oliver J. and Edgar Holmes McNeal (eds), *A Source Book for Medieval History* (New York: Scribners, 1905)

Thomas, C.H., 'William Fitzosbern (died 1071)', *Dictionary of Welsh Biography*, https://biography.wales/article/s-FITZ-WIL-1071

Thompson, Kathleen, 'The Lords of Laigle: Ambition and Insecurity on the Borders of Normandy', in Christopher Harper-Bill (ed.), *Anglo-Norman Studies*, XVIII (Woodbridge, 1996)

Thompson, Kathleen, 'Affairs of State: The Illegitimate Children of Henry I', *Journal of Medieval History*, Vol. 29 (2003)

Tyerman, Christopher (ed.), *Chronicles of the First Crusade* (London: Penguin, 2012)

Van Duzer, Chet, *Sea Monsters on Medieval and Renaissance Maps* (British Library, 2013)

Van Houts, Elisabeth, *The Normans in Europe* (Manchester University Press, 2000)

Varagine, Jacobus de, *The Golden Legend* (London: Penguin, 1998)

Villain-Gandossi, Christiane, 'La mer et la navigation maritime du XII au XIV siècle', *Revue d'histoire économique et sociale*, Vol. 47, No. 2 (1969)

Walker, Barbara MacDonald, 'King Henry I's "Old Men"', *Journal of British Studies*, Vol. 8, No. 1 (Cambridge University Press, 1968)

Warren, W.L., *King John* (London: Eyre Methuen, 1978)

Watkins, Carl, *Stephen* (London: Allen Lane, 2015)

'William of Poitiers' in David C. Douglas and George W. Greenaway (eds), *English Historical Documents 1042–1189* (London, 1959)

Winters, Jane, *Forest Law*, Early English Laws – https://early-englishlaws.ac.uk/reference/essays/forest-law/

Index